Josephine B. Pasquarello

Love & Loyalty

An Immigrant Italian Mom Raising Her
Family of Twelve in the Shadow of a Mafia Crime

by

Josephine B. Pasquarello

josephine b pasquarello @ gmail.com

D1522091

DORRANCE
PUBLISHING CO
EST. 1920
PITTSBURGH, PENNSYLVANIA 15238

The contents of this work, including, but not limited to, the accuracy of events, people, and places depicted; opinions expressed; permission to use previously published materials included; and any advice given or actions advocated are solely the responsibility of the author, who assumes all liability for said work and indemnifies the publisher against any claims stemming from publication of the work.

Dorrance Publishing Co
585 Alpha Drive
Suite 103
Pittsburgh, PA 15238
Visit our website at *www.dorrancebookstore.com*

ISBN: 978-1-4809-3988-2
eISBN: 978-1-4809-3965-3

Dedication

Dedicated to my mother who was a survivor. Who taught me and my eleven siblings to never fold.

Acknowledgments

I would like to thank my husband, Robert, for his understanding of how important this book was to me. My Aunt Myra for giving me information on my family history. My cousin, Ralph, for opening the door to enlightenment.

Table of Contents

Preface

I would like those who read this book to get to know and hopefully relate to my parents, my sisters and brothers, and me. I want to convey how all of our lives were intertwined with one dark never-ending secret, how we all carried an overwhelming weight for the benefit of our family, and how my mother never wavered in her love of and loyalty to my father, and the children they had together.

My parents had twelve children together, and if Dad had lived longer they would have liked to have one or two more. Twelve wasn't enough for them—the more the merrier, they felt. Besides, we were Italian Catholics, and back in the day—the 1940s and '50s—the Church would instruct its parishioners to have many children, so that there would be many Catholics to strengthen the congregation. My parents were happy to oblige the Church. Every Sunday was their time for happiness, and maybe Mom would get pregnant and add to their brood.? I would have loved to have had a younger brother. But, because of Dad's death, that was not to be.

Through all the years we children were growing up in South Philadelphia, no one ever spoke openly about our father's death. To this day, we still don't. This guardedness has now trickled down to the next two generations. There was always the fear of learning the truth about what happened, and even after we learned it, the fear of it continued. I guess you could say this book is about the destructive power of secrets and the heavy toll they can take on a family. But it's also about, more positively, the amazing strength and devotion of my mother, Romania Pasquarello. Having lost her husband, she managed to raise twelve children on her own. With little help, she figured it all out—how to keep feeding us three healthy meals a day, to have coal in the heater, hot running water, and a clean house. She definitely was a "mama bear" when it came to protecting her cubs, and she did a damn good job at it.

My mom passed away at the age of 66. She was too young to leave us, but she had grown old and tired before her time due to nonstop work. Besides, she was ready to go and reunite, finally, with her husband. After Mom's death, our previously united family started to disintegrate. In the hardest of times we had circled our wagons in order to survive as a family unit, but now, we were falling apart.

In writing my family's story, I have reconstructed many situations and conversations. Of course I can't remember every long-ago conversation word-for-word, but I have tried to be as truthful as I can to the spirit of what happened and to my recollections of each scene, both, the happy and the sad.

Josephine B. Pasquarello
Kennett Square, Pennsylvania
April 29, 2016

My Father's Nightmare

It was the fall of 1954, and Mike was having a nervous breakdown. The doctors said he was depressed, and he was hearing voices in his head. God only knows what the voices were telling him to do. He spent a couple of weeks at Pennsylvania Hospital in the psychiatric ward. He had the weight of his family on his soul. There wasn't anything he wouldn't do for them. He wanted to keep his wife and the children happy, but he realized this was out of his control.

Like it or not, Mike would be leaving his loved ones soon, and he knew it. How did it feel to know he would be dead soon? He didn't know the day, but he knew it would be soon. After all, he stood in the way of the Philly mob and the police. He had no control over his destiny—he'd be leaving his loved ones forever. His thoughts were always about their wellbeing—never his own. He'd have to stay strong for them till the end. But how?

There were other awful, unanswerable questions: Why should he take the fall for someone in the mob? And how could a man like Mike leave his family to fend for themselves? What man wants to check out on the only thing on earth that matters to him? That thing was his family—his wife and twelve children—and who would take care of them? How could Ro manage all the children on her own? The questions were unbearable, but they kept racing through his head. He had to figure them all out before he died. Death was knocking at his door, and he felt like a man walking the earth all by himself.

1

His thoughts always returned to his wife, Romania: How could he help her before he was gone forever? Love her more than he already did? But what good would that do anyway?

He wasn't the man he thought he was. How could he have gotten himself involved in someone else's problem? For that, he was leaving the 13 loves of his life! He had to get the courage up to tell Ro. But this was not an easy thing for a man to do, especially an Italian man.

How does he tell his wife she will soon be on her own? That she will have to take care of their children, the business, and the house, all by herself? How will she manage all this weight on her shoulders? He would ask her to keep the family together—all the children in one house with her there to protect them from the outside world. He would say to Ro, *You are strong enough to handle this. If I felt you couldn't do this then I wouldn't ask it of you.*

Mike goes ahead and says these things. How does Ro comprehend all this information? Does she faint from all that he is saying to her? Or is she wondering if this is a joke?

How could something like this happen to us and our family? she is asking. *Why should we pay the price for someone else?* She's getting hysterical. He must calm her down.

He tells his wife there is no way out. *I must take whatever is coming my way. I need your help more than ever, Ro—you must take over for me with the family. We can't allow them to ruin our children.*

They lie in bed holding on to each other, talking and crying all night. They talk about how it was supposed to be for them as a family. Now, everything would be different. He's trying his best to be strong for her.

He tries to convince Ro that everything will work out, although maybe not the way they thought their lives together would be. But this is the best he can do for them. This is what they must live with from this moment on.

He is stroking her hair and telling her they must both get some sleep. *The kids will be up soon and we have to be ready for the day, and for the days to come. We must live… and I can do it only with you by my side.*

As she lies there trying to close her eyes she wonders what she will do without him. There will never be better days, she thinks, no matter what he says to me. But she will not say any of her dark thoughts to him. She doesn't want to make him feel any worse than he already does.

She moves closer to him. He holds her tightly with her head on his chest and she cries softly in his arms. She doesn't want to cause him any more pain. She will carry his burden for him, because … how does a woman deny her husband's last wish? His dying wish.

Mike is speaking softly to Ro so as not to wake the children. He is telling her that she is the only love of his life. He is whispering in her ear… *I never loved any woman until I met you… I always wanted a large family. Never did I think I would find a woman to give me so many children. You gave me what I needed in this world—even when people thought we were both crazy. That's what I will take in my soul when I leave this earth… You are the woman who gave me an extraordinary life… Thank you for being a good Italian wife… No man could have received anything more than the love you have given me.*

• • •

As he drifted in and out of sleep, Mike suddenly awakened and realized he was having a nightmare. But then he realized something worse: The awful dream was based on reality. How could he ever tell Ro his fate and hers? He didn't have the courage to tell her. Not yet anyway, but that would come soon enough, and with heartbreaking consequences.

The Day Dad Didn't Come Home

Wednesday, May 11, 1955, was the day my family went into a tailspin, a rapid, out-of-control descent with a devastating emotional impact that would be felt for many years to come. Our lives as we knew them would be forever changed.

It began that day when I was six, and my dad didn't come home for dinner. We all missed him. Dad, who always sat at the head of our table, had a presence that made us feel secure and loved. When he was there, I knew I was safe; he wouldn't allow anyone to harm us.

Mom was puzzled about his not being home, but focused on getting dinner on the table for us. At that moment, her task was to act as if everything was normal. But she knew something was wrong. Dad didn't come home that night.

The next day, my mom walked over to my dad's produce store at 1829 North Seventh Street in South Philadelphia, just a couple of blocks from our house on Sixth Street. The door was locked, so she knocked. Why was the door locked in the middle of the day? And where was Dad? Wasn't he in there working? After some time of Mom knocking and yelling "Brownie!"—my father's nickname—Dad finally appeared, walking from the back of the store toward the front door.

But he wouldn't let Mom in, and, acting strange, he pleaded with her, "Go home, Ro. I won't let you come in and see me like this. Please, Ro, go home and take care of our kids."

"There's no way I will leave you here," Mom responded. "Let me in. Why do you have your gun in your hand? What is happening, Brownie? Tell me. I want to help you." Then— "Oh, my God! You're covered in blood! What's going on?"

Mom realized that Dad was in big trouble. Since she couldn't get him to let her into the store, she went next door to ask the meat cutter to call the cops. "Please hurry—my Brownie is hurt!" she told him.

When the two cops arrived, my mom begged Dad to let them in, but he held his ground, telling her that no one was entering. The cops, who knew my dad well, said, "Come on, Mike, you know us. We just want to help you. You're hurt. Tell us what happened in there."

"I will shoot anyone who tries to come in here, so stay away from me and bring Ro home to our kids. Get her away from the store and from me."

A half hour later, my mom made a request of the police officers: "Go down to the upholstery store at the end of the block. It's where Nick is—my husband's youngest brother. Ask Nick to come over to help get my husband out of the store. Please!" She told the police that if they went in there with their guns, Dad might hurt them. "Or you might hurt him. But you can't—he's already been hurt enough! He needs medical help now!" She screamed, "Please help my husband!"

So the police brought Uncle Nick to the store. "What's going on with Mike?" he asked my mother. "What happened in there?"

My mom said, "Nick, I don't know exactly what's going on, but Mike needs help and won't let anybody in. You have to help your brother. Do whatever you have to do get him out of there. The cops want to break down the door. If they do that, I'm afraid Mike will shoot at them and they'll kill him on the spot. Talk to your brother. Tell him that we all need him and he has to come out. We need to get him to a hospital. He's been in there since yesterday morning. I don't know how long he's been hurt, but he's got blood all over him and all over the front of the store. He can't bleed much longer like that, Please talk him out of there, for my kids' sake. They need him even more than I do."

By now, my mom was crying hysterically and running around in circles out of frustration. Dad not only wouldn't come out, he wouldn't even look at her, retreating to the back of the store. Dad yelled to the cops, "Don't come in, or I'll kill you. I just want to be by myself. Leave me alone!" To let them know he was serious, he shot a bullet into the ceiling. Basically, my dad was saying just leave me here to die.

Uncle Nick held Mom's shoulders as he told her he was going to get his brother out of there—he just needed a minute to think of what to say. Then, he walked over to the door and put his hand on the doorknob. It opened. My uncle was startled to find the door unlocked because no one had seen Dad unlock it. With that, Uncle Nick called in to my dad: "Mike, it's Nick, your brother. Don't shoot me. I am here to help you and get you to a hospital. We need a doctor to look at you and maybe get some stitches on that wound. We all love you, Mike. Ro needs to talk with you now."

My dad walked into the front of the store looking somewhat deranged and confused. He was about to pass out from blood loss. Nick and the cops grabbed him and laid him down on the floor. Mom kissed and hugged Dad, telling him, "Everything is going to be fine, but we must get to the hospital now."

An ambulance waiting outside transported my dad. The driver rushed through the tiny streets of South Philly on the way to Philadelphia General Hospital. Mom thought they would crash before they got there. At the hospital, two doctors were waiting, and a room in the emergency area was ready for Dad.

Uncle Nick and Mom were asked to sit in the waiting room and told that the doctors would inform them of the situation as soon as they had more information. When the examination was over, the doctors told Mom and Uncle Nick that it did not look good for my dad, that he had not only stabbed himself but had eaten rat poison. There was no hope of recovery from that. They would try to keep him as comfortable as possible, but they could not save his life. In a few days, the poison would consume him, and there wasn't anything or anyone that could change the outcome.

Mom could not believe what she had just heard and fell to the floor. Her husband was going to die in the next few days, and they couldn't help him. There wasn't anything they could do but wait for the end.

How was my mom going to live her life without the man she loved? How could she take on all the responsibility for the lives of 12 children?

As Uncle Nick helped Mom get up from the floor, he encouraged her to be strong. "You must go on for the kids," he said. But for now, all she could feel was her emptiness. She knew that for the sake of the children she must move forward, but first she had to deal with her own shock and pain.

Mom and Nick went to Dad's hospital room. Dad was sedated to help him sleep, as he had been up for two days without eating or drinking anything and was very weak. Mom would stay at the hospital waiting for Dad to wake up— she needed to talk with him as soon as possible.

Mom had many, many questions for Dad, but for now she must wait. During that wait, she had so many thoughts and feelings. She wanted Dad to wake up so she could hear his voice again. She was thinking that never to hear his voice would forever silence her own heart, mind, and soul. She became teary thinking that she couldn't go on without him by her side. Not to feel his presence around her—how could she stand that? But she couldn't think of herself. She would concentrate only on his needs. There must be something she could do to save his life.

Mom asked Uncle Nick to go back to his shop. "As soon as I know anything, I'll tell you," she said, crying and holding on to Nick, who himself was not steady on his feet. He looked pale and saddened and told Mom he would help her in any way possible. Again she said, "Go back to work. Let me stay with Mike, so when he wakes up, I'll be here. He needs me now more than ever, as much as I need him."

Uncle Nick kissed my Dad on his forehead and said, "I always loved you as a dad. Now is the time to thank you for raising me and our family. We all love you. I will be back after work tonight."

He walked over to Mom and kissed her on her forehead. Then out the room he went.

Mom knew she had to pull herself together. She sat on the chair and began talking to Dad in Italian. This was unusual because Dad always told Mom that her dialect was slang and that his was the proper Italian learned in school. He said we kids should learn our language in school and not in the house from her. As it turned out, we never learned Italian from her or in school. What a shame, because, to me, the Italian language is so beautiful.

Mom was telling Dad that she didn't know what had happened in his store. She said that, whatever it was, she forgave him. "We will walk through this together every inch of the way. I will always be there for you and our family. Just say what you want me to do. I won't ask anything of you, Brownie. You are and always will be my true love on this earth. If I have to carry this as my cross in life, then so be it. It's done. Now rest, and when you are able to talk to me, we will put our plan together for the sake of our children."

Ordinarily, when my dad slept, he didn't move around at all. But in that hospital bed, he couldn't lay still. Mom tried to comfort him by rubbing his arms and legs. He would fall back into a deep sleep for about 15 minutes, then stir again. This went on for about five hours.

Then Dad woke out of his sleep and tried to get out of bed, but the pain in his chest stopped him. He had had a lot of stitches from the stab wound and had to lie back down.

My mom told him to be still and called for the nurse. The nurse wanted to give Dad more painkillers, but Mom said, "Don't take any more, Brownie. I need you awake and alert." Dad told the nurse he didn't need any more pills.

Mom got up and told the nurse to please leave them alone. She closed the door, looked at Dad, and lost control of herself. She froze. For a minute, she found herself unable to move a muscle, even her tongue. But knowing she needed to pull herself together in order to speak to Dad, to be strong even if she wasn't, Mom put her pain aside. She cleared her throat and her mind for a few seconds, moved toward Dad, and said, "What are we going to do? You must give me direction on how to handle this nightmare. This is much bigger than the two of us. But with our love, we will conquer this."

Dad asked Mom what the doctors thought of his condition. "Will I live or die?" That's when Mom had to gather the strength to tell Dad about his impending death from the rat poison. He accepted the fact that he would die soon and said to Mom, "I am truly sorry for all that I have put you through."

There was so much on his mind; all his questions and concerns spilled out. "How can I leave you and the children? My father died when I was 16, and I know firsthand what it feels like not to have a dad. How could I have done this to my kids? Why am I leaving my family when I know the pain from my own loss? How will the children ever forgive me? I am a bad father. I should have known better than this. I was selfish and thinking only of my needs, not yours or the children's. How will you ever forgive me? You are and always have been my true love. I was nothing before I met you. You fulfilled me as a man. I always wanted to protect you and our family. Look at how I have failed … I will go to my grave with uncertainty. Maybe it's best that I die;

maybe all of you will be better off without me? Please tell the children I will take each and every one in my heart—they are everything to me. They will be with me for eternity. Of that I am certain."

Mom tried to calm him down so that they could put their story together. She told him, "You are the best anyone—woman, man, or child—could have as a husband, brother, or father. You are a good person with a huge heart and much kindness. No one will ever speak a bad word about you to our children. I will make sure of that. But Brownie, we need to talk about last night. I must know what happened. Even if it will hurt you again and hurt me, I must know. I am prepared."

Dad started to cry as he asked Mom to sit on the bed next to him. "I need you close to me," he said. Mom got in the hospital bed with Dad and held him close to her as he began his horror story.

Guarded Secrets

Dad began, "Last night, Salvatore and two of his soldiers came to the store. I was in the back going through the inventory when I heard Sal calling my name. I knew it wasn't going to be good. I walked to the front of the store, and Sal said, 'Mike, have you made up your mind?' I told him, 'I can't take the rap for your guy. He's going to have to do the time, not me. I have all these kids and a wife. Who will take care of them?' Sal was getting really upset. His face was turning red, he was waving his arms in the air, and he was talking really fast. I said, 'Sal, let's go upstairs, sit at the table, and talk this through. After all, Salvatore, you are my goombah, my friend and protector.'

"As the two of us went upstairs, Sal called down to his guys, 'Make sure the front door is locked and that all the lights are off.' It was totally dark now upstairs and downstairs as Sal and I talked about the matter of John killing Tony at the card game in my store. 'You know, Mike,' Sal said, 'if you didn't have the card game here, this never would have happened.' But I told him, 'It didn't matter where the card game was. John was itching to shoot someone anywhere.'"

Then Sal told Dad, "Well, if Tony wasn't a fuckin' cheat at the card game, John never would've had to kill him." Dad made Sal aware that this was not the first time Tony had got caught cheating. The first time a couple of the guys had thrown him out the second-story window. It took Tony six months to recover from that, and he walked with a limp from then on. But the guys would still let him in their games because Tony was a loser at cards and they could easily take his money.

"How could we know it would end like this?" Dad asked. "It was your guys who wanted him in the game, not me. Tony is dead because John had a fast trigger. John is your soldier, Sal, and you must decide how he pays for this. But I can't help you. Your guy must pay the price. Maybe he'll learn from his mistake." Then he went on, "You want me to take the rap and the cops want me to tell them who killed Tony. You don't know the pressure I've been under."

Sal stood up and said to Dad, "Mike, you will pay the price. If you don't go to prison for John, we will take you out of the game completely now and forever. Do you understand me? We have been friends for over 30 years, but this doesn't have a thing to do with friendship. This is business and only business. Our business is to take care of everyone in our circle, and that's what I'm doing. You will sacrifice yourself and your family for our family... Who is bigger and stronger? Do you understand? Capisce? ... So, what will it be? I know you, Mike, and you think you have more time than you do. I want the answer now, and if I don't like the answer, then it will be up to my two guys to settle this now and forever. Do you get it?"

Dad told Sal that he got it, but that he wouldn't go to prison for his stupid guy, or for that matter any other guy who was going to act like a fool. With that, Sal called his soldiers upstairs and told them to make Dad eat rat poison. That's when all hell broke loose. They were trying to hold Dad down, but he fought back, throwing anything and everything he could at them. At one point, he was throwing chairs, and even picked up the table, bringing it down over Carmen. That's when Carmen cried and told Sal to shoot Dad. But Sal couldn't do it; he and Dad had been through too much together. That's why Sal had brought his guys with him.

Sal had been like family. When his son-in-law beat the hell out of his daughter, Maria, it was Dad who broke the son-in-law's leg, so that the cops wouldn't go looking for Sal. The son-in-law never touched Maria again. That's the love the two men had had for each other then. But now all that was over. They were finished as family and friends. It was hard for Dad to believe that Sal no longer cared about our family. "Maybe he never did?" Dad told Mom, "and I didn't see it. But now I do. It's my life, and I will fight until the end to preserve it—and let no one stand in my way." Dad told Mom that all through his ordeal, he kept thinking of her and the kids.

He continued with his story: "I was trying to get downstairs but Mario was chasing me. He jumped from behind and knocked me to the floor. He punched the back of my head and started kicking my back and side ribs. That's when I fell down the stairs to the first floor. Carmen sat on my chest and Sal told them to pour it down my throat. I couldn't breathe, and this white powder was flying all over me. I couldn't see anything anymore because it was in my eyes. They picked me up by my shirt and put me in a chair. I didn't know how I was going to get out of this.

"Carmen was saying, 'Let me stab this son of a bitch in his heart.' Everything was starting to spin. I got dizzy and passed out. When I came to, they had me tied to a chair with my head back and were pouring more powder down my throat. I was spitting it out of my mouth, but they kept pouring it in. I don't know how it happened, but I got loose. The rope around my wrist gave way, and I ran toward the front door. Mario caught me, and we started fighting with our fists. I was landing shots to his face, one right after another, and then I felt this awful pain in my chest. I looked down, and saw I had a large knife sticking out of my chest. Carmen had stabbed me. That's when I thought it was over for me.

"Sal walked over and said, 'It's over, Mike. Just lay down and die. This will all stop once you're dead. It will all be put to rest.' Carmen grabbed the knife and pulled it out of my chest. I fell to the floor and pretended to be dead. Mario came out and kicked me. He said, 'Sal, he's gone. It's finally over.' Then the three of them left the store. I stayed real still for about ten minutes more just to make sure they were gone.

"Then I got up, got my gun, and locked the front and back doors. I never turned on the lights, so I didn't know how bad the stab wound was, but I knew I was bleeding. The white powder was burning my mouth and throat. I knew it was rat poison and I knew it was just a matter of time for me. I thought I'd be dead by morning, if not sooner.

"After that, I sat at the front door for hours, waiting for the men to return. I had my gun and was ready to shoot anyone who came through the door. But they never returned. They thought I was dead.

"The next morning, customers were banging on the door, but I stayed in the back room until I heard your voice, which took me out of my trance. Then

13

I thought, 'can't let her see me like this.' That's why I told you to go home. I wanted you to hold me and tell me you forgave me. But I couldn't face you. I felt I had failed as a man."

My dad told my mom, "For now, we must take the vow of silence." It's called the omerta, a vow of silence in the Mafia that is punishable by death if not upheld. "We must never speak of this to anyone. We will come up with our own storyline. Ro, you will tell everyone I committed suicide so they will never come after you and the children. They are cruel people who don't care who they kill or maim. I am afraid for our four sons. Get the family away from this as soon as possible."

Dad told Mom that it hurt him to have to explain what had happened, but that it was necessary. He would be leaving her behind and had to do the best he could while he was still alive to help his beloved family. "We will tell people that I tried to commit suicide. We will say that the police were trying to get me to tell them what happened the night of the shooting in our store and the mob wanted me to go to prison for them. We will say that I couldn't take the constant pressure from both sides. It was too much for me to handle. The only way out of this was to kill myself. We can never let the cops know the true story of why it went down this way.

"I will handle everything with my family. I will talk with all of them and make them promise to never breathe a word about this. This is the only way I can protect you and the children. If I am dying, let this be my last wish—to know that none of you will get hurt or even killed because of my stupidity. I thought I could handle anything or anyone coming at me. I know now how wrong I was to think that. My first thought should have been to take care of you. I made many mistakes in my 53 years. Now is the time to make everything as right as I can. With your help, I believe we can change the story to make it believable to everyone." Mom agreed to lie all her life for her husband. There wasn't anything my mom wouldn't do for her Brownie.

Mom told Dad to rest, saying she would come back later. "I have to go home and see the kids and put dinner on the table. I will think about everything we talked about and come back with a better view of everything. I need time to step out of this nightmare." She kissed him and quickly left so she wouldn't break down in front of him.

From that moment on, Mom knew she would never be the same person. She also knew she had to be strong to make the lie about her husband believable, not just to the family but to herself. At that moment, Mom vowed to never let anyone into her family who could hurt us. She would become our protector. Her thought was: You have taken him from us, but you will never get any more from this family as long as I am alive.

That night, when Mom visited Dad, my three uncles were already there. Dad was telling them this is done and that's it. "You all have your own lives to live and your own children to take care of. What has happened is now done. Let me pay the price. We will never talk about this again, and I want your word that when you leave this hospital room, it is sealed." They realized their hands were tied—there was nothing they could do except give their word to honor their brother's last wish. First Uncle George, then Ralph, and then Nick walked over to kiss and hug him. The group of five now had a pact, something they would carry with them forever: They would never speak the truth about my dad and his last five days on earth. Each one carried the secret to his grave.

This group had a lot of love for my dad, and they all trusted one another to be quiet to the end. That is how the lie in our family history began.

The next day, Uncle Nick showed up at the hospital. When he walked into the room, there were three men in suits around Dad's bed, talking low to Dad so no one could hear what they were saying. When they saw Uncle Nick, they stopped talking and walked out of the room. Nick wanted to know who they were, and when my dad told him they were IRS men, Nick asked, "What would the IRS want with you? Come on, Mike, tell me. I should know, shouldn't I?"

"No, Nick, you shouldn't, so leave it alone."

The last time my dad and mom spoke, they talked about how she would take full responsibility for our family's love and care. Twelve children—what a task for anyone to take on! Dad was giving her directions about what to expect and how to handle each and every situation he could think of. Talk about over-load—to know the end is near, yet still have so much to do on this earth. But there was no stopping what was going to happen. Dad had to go with it and try to remain strong for his loved ones.

Mom was saying, "I can't leave you. I must go with you. I can't live without your love for me." But she knew she had to do just that. So they made a pact that she would raise us. She would make the moral decisions, use her good judgment with our upbringing in this world. She would do this job to her liking and ask no one for their input. Dad knew that no one other than my mom could or would be up to the task of raising us.

"Get the girls married by 21," he advised. "That would be the right age. At that age, they will have a good head on their shoulders. Get the boys out of South Philly so that they don't get caught up in the same thing I was. Get this done and I will wait for you to be with me. Please, Ro, remember, you must raise all the children. You can't leave any of them behind without you. They will no longer have me. It's just you now… Am I asking too much of you? If I am, please forgive me. I don't know how else to do this. But I will always be with you. I will always be with the family. I will love all of you forever."

Dad lived for five agonizing days. The nurse found him dead in the hallway in front of his room, sitting in a rocking chair. This is when confusion came into our lives, and became part of our lives for some time.

This is How it Began

At this point, I should really go back to the beginning. My mother's name was Romania; she was born in Rome, Italy, on either September 16th or 17th in 1907. She was never sure of the date—her marriage certificate reads September 17th, while her death certificate says September 16th. When I was little, she told us she didn't know which day to celebrate. We asked her to choose one; she did, and we began to wish her a happy birthday on the 17th of September.

In 1912, when she was five years old, my mother crossed the ocean to America with her mother, Grace Pescatore. She told us she remembered being on that ship with her mom. My grandfather, Pasquale Pescatore, had been here for two years before their arrival.

My mom didn't get much education. She dropped out of school in the middle of the sixth grade because her father wanted her to help with household chores. Growing up, she never had friends because her parents felt she should stay at home with them, and she wasn't allowed to bring anyone home. Her only friend growing up was a mouse!

Eventually, Mom got a job as a seamstress in a South Philly factory, close to where her family lived in an Italian section of Philadelphia. They lived there to be around their own kind and speak their native language.

Her father was a shoemaker but didn't like to work, and her mother was in and out of the state hospital for mental illness. So my mom had to work, cook, and clean the house. Whatever turmoil she felt, she kept inside. With her hard work and good soul, my mom was the person who kept the family together.

When Mom was 26, she fell in love with the guy who sold produce on the street corner. His name was Michael Pasquarello, although his family called him Brownie, because he was so dark. Up until then, Mom had never had a boyfriend, or even dated. Her father wouldn't allow it. While working, Mom would get lunch with the girls from the factory because it would allow her to walk by my dad's produce cart. Finally, at age 26, she had a crush on someone. The girls would tease my mom and say, "Let's go see Frankenstein." My mom would laugh and go by his cart just to see him.

Mom and Dad had been dating for three months when they were on a trolley coming home from the movies and Dad kissed her—her first kiss ever. Mom told Dad he would have to marry her, and he did. My grandfather, not wanting to lose her salary, wouldn't have allowed this, so my mom ran away to many him without her dad's permission.

They married on November 7, 1932, and in August of '33, Mom gave birth to their first child, Ralph, named after my dad's father. Who could have known then that there would be eleven more of us?

My mom wanted lots and lots of kids because she had been so lonely as an only child, and my dad was more than happy to oblige her. They were happy together, and three years to the day after Ralph was born they had their second child, a girl they named Trudy, after my dad's mother. Dad would sell produce on our corner at Sixth and Hoffman Streets, while Mom would stay home to clean, cook, and take care of their small house. Then came number three, a girl named Grace (my mom's mother's name). Grace was born in August, just like her two older siblings.

Everything was going along great until the red-haired *puttana* (whore) showed up on the corner. My mom would see her every day flirting with my dad. One day, Mom told him that he had better get rid of her. But she would show up again and again.

So here's what Mom did: She asked Jimmy, my dad's helper, to move her and the kids from South Philly to North Philly. Dad did not know of her plans to take the children and leave him. Off she moved. When my dad came home that night, the house was empty except for one of everything in the kitchen—

one plate, one fork, one knife, one cup. She had left Dad to make him realize that she and the kids—not the red-haired girl—were the important people in his life. (The red-haired girl was what my mom would call her when telling us this story. But if she was upset, she would call her the red-haired *puttana*.)

It took my dad three months to convince Mom to come back to him. He would show up at her apartment every Sunday afternoon, stand on the street, and shout to her on the second floor. She would open the window and say, "Leave the money on the steps. When you leave, I will come down and get it." He would ask if he could come upstairs to talk with her and see the kids, and her reply would be, "I know what you want, and you're not getting it." He would show up every Sunday, but Mom wouldn't budge.

Finally, Dad showed up on a Sunday in a taxi with his sister. Aunt Mary said to Mom, "Ro, listen—Brownie wants you and the kids to come home; he misses all of you. And the redhead is gone for good!" With that, my mom went home with my dad and life as they had known it resumed. Mom never forgot what had happened, but she did forgive him. She loved him and wanted a happy life and family with him. I thank God she went back with him. Otherwise, the next nine kids wouldn't be here to hear their love story.

The fourth child was born, a girl named Christine, after Dad's aunt, and soon after came Patrick (the name of Mom's dad). Mom and Dad were busy with life and their five kids in their small house on Hoffman Street. Then she became pregnant again with number six, a girl, Rosemary. Our house was becoming busier and busier. Whenever Mom had a new baby all the kids were packed up and shipped off to an orphanage. We would stay there for ten days whch was when Mom came home from the hospital with the new baby.

But it was not chaotic—my dad disciplined us. He was tough; you had better listen to him when he spoke—or else. Mom let him rule the house, but in a sense it was she who had the power. She ran the household. And she was the best cook! She would make us a pot of gravy (Italian-American for tomato sauce) and meat every Sunday, Tuesday, and Thursday, and, boy, was it good! To wake up on a Sunday to the smell of the gravy and meatballs frying was the best thing. I still love my gravy and make a pot of meatballs and gravy now and then.

Every meal was homemade. Mom had fresh produce each day from my dad's store. By now he had a storefront on Seventh Street, about two blocks from where we lived. He would get up at four a.m. and go to the docks to buy his produce. If you got there first, you got the pick of everything. Then he'd be off to the store to sell his produce for the day. He was such a hard worker. Actually, both my parents worked very hard every day of their lives. And they were a team.

My grandmother (Mom's mom) died in the state hospital, but her dad lived 15 years longer. My grandfather was Mom's only family besides us, and he would come over every Sunday to eat his meatballs and pasta and to see all of his grandchildren. He loved his family, and we all loved him. He would take the older siblings to Atlantic City and to the zoo. He would even take them to Holy Cross Cemetery to our grandmom's grave, and allow the kids to run around while he would sit and talk to Grandmom. He died two years before my father.

Mom became pregnant again with number seven and gave birth to a boy called George, and soon after George came John. They were having baby after baby. Mom was using a method called *her way*—nine months of being pregnant and nine months of breastfeeding. Then she would start all over again. Here we go with number nine. It's a girl named Carmella. And right after her, number ten, is me, Josephine. The last six of us are all 18 months apart. Number eleven is Antoinette and number twelve, Anna. Anna was mom's "lazy baby"— that's what Mom called her. Anna was born with the doctor's entire handprint on her back. That's because the doctor had to push hard to get her to move and come out.

You would think after an experience like that you would say to yourself, I am done. Not my mom. She wanted more kids. At 44 years old, she still had all this energy to want to take care of more babies. I believe she found her answer to why she was on this earth—to be with Brownie and make lots and lots of kids. She was very happy and content with life.

But little did she know that her life was about to change drastically for the worse.

How Would We Survive?

After Dad died, my mom managed with no help from her family because she was the only one left. Her parents had died by then and she had no brothers or sisters. Nor did she receive help from her husband's side. My father's family had been really good to us while he was alive, but once he died, all that changed. That was sad for us. His eight sisters and brothers never offered emotional, financial, or any other kind of support. I always felt that my dad's family thought of us as a burden. They recognized that we were their brother's family, but that was as far as it went. They kept their distance from us, and I felt like a stranger around them.

My mom was now left alone with the task of caring for twelve children—what a task for anyone to endure! My heart broke for my mom. But she was resourceful, determined, and courageous. Once she realized that she had to keep our family together without any outside help beyond a small social security check, she figured it out. We were a big family, and everyone of working age could contribute. The oldest children, who already had jobs by then, would give $20 a week to the household. Then, whenever one of the girls turned 16, she would leave high school, take courses at a secretarial school, and find a job so she could bring money home. Once they got married, that would all stop, but my sister Christine worked and lived at home until she married at 30. A decade older than me, Christine was like a second mother, and she helped us out a lot. The younger boys, besides going to school, would work at an Italian bread factory some nights. They would bring home cash and a dozen rolls each that we would eat on weekends.

• • •

Not only was my family grief-stricken at the loss of our beloved father, but we were also without a means of financial support. My mom knew she had to make a plan for our survival. Somehow, she had to find a way to make us money to keep the family together. At first, some of Dad's siblings tried to help by offering to take the middle three boys for a while. Mom considered this, but after much thought and talk she realized she couldn't live without her boys, who were close to her heart. Maybe it was because each son, in his own way, reminded her of Dad? Patrick had his nose, George had his forehead, and John had his entire face. Mom couldn't live without seeing each of them every day, so she said no to that plan.

My father's family then started to put a second plan into action. The middle three boys would go to Girard College, a boarding school for white boys who were poor, orphaned, or fatherless.[1] The school, which had been in existence for about 150 years, was right there in Philadelphia and would give the boys a wonderful education. But Mom wasn't happy with that idea either, and she put a halt to it. She informed my dad's family that no one was going anywhere. The boys were going to stay with the family. We would stay together and take care of ourselves. We would all eat together, or we would starve together, but together we would stay.

My mom had big problems in her life right now. In addition to money problems, there was no man in the house to keep the boys in line. Poor Mom! I sometimes wondered, "Does she really know what she's doing? I hope so!"

Mom *did* have a plan she thought would work, in terms of keeping us all together. We still had the store; we just needed someone to operate the business. Mom couldn't take care of the business and raise all the children. It was out of the question. She had to be at home. But Ralph, the oldest child, recently discharged from the army, was now, at age 21, the man of the family, so he would run the business and bring money home to the family. That way, we would be able to pay the bills and put food on the table—three home-cooked

---

[1] Girard College opened its doors to black boys in 1968 and to girls in the 1980s.

meals—not just sometimes, but every single day, with each and every meal made by Mom.

Now that a general plan had been made, Mom put together an action plan. She would send Ralph to the waterfront every day to get produce. He would then go to the store and sell the produce to our customers. Some customers disappeared after my dad's death, but the loyal ones would still come around, and we would get new customers, people who knew our story and wanted to help us out.

At first, everything went as Mom planned. Mom would give Ralph ten dollars each morning to go to the docks to get the fresh produce—lots of fruit and vegetables—and Ralph would sell it at the store. At the end of the day, he would come home and give all the money to Mom.

Unfortunately for the family, that didn't last long. Soon, Ralph started to give back only the ten dollars that Mom had given him at the start of the day. He felt the rest of the money should be his. After all, he was the one working at the store. Oh boy! If my dad were alive, Ralph would be dead for being so selfish.

Mom told Ralph that we couldn't survive as a family if he was going to keep all the money. "Me giving you $10 a day and you giving me back $10 a day isn't going to work," Mom pointed out. "How do you expect me to be able to buy food and pay the bills in the house and store? And I have all these kids to take care of."

Ralph didn't seem to care about how the bills would be paid or if we had food for the family. As a result, Mom eventually had to sell the store. We survived on the Social Security she received for herself and us children after Dad's death. Also, Trudy had a job at the bank and gave Mom $20 a week.

My older siblings were furious at Ralph for not caring about the family, and especially for not caring about our mother. But she forgave Ralph for everything he did no matter how large or small because Ralph was her first-born and a son, which in an Italian family meant he was all-important.

Not once do I remember Mom having harsh words with Ralph, even though he stole from us time and time again. I remember the time my older siblings told Mom that Ralph took our grandfather's ring, a thick gold band with a ruby and two diamonds that my father had worn every day. I would see Ralph wearing this ring, and think about my dad when I was a little girl.

Nor did Mom say anything the time Ralph took Dad's large coin collection, as if it belonged to him. I would have liked a coin or two, to have something my dad once had. But the entire collection? Absolutely not. We were twelve kids. All of us would have liked a part of that collection because it was something our dad loved. It would have been so special for all of us. We never got to see the collection, though, because Ralph always denied having it. It was originally kept under my parents' bed, and after my dad died, it went missing.

But my mom knew Ralph took the coins. When the older children would talk to her about it, you could see the hurt and shame she felt at the thought of her son stealing from the family. After all, she had taught us to be honest. Ralph also took other family belongings. I guess you could say he was for himself. Surely, he didn't have us in mind.

Despite evidence to the contrary, Mom wanted to believe Ralph was a good son who would take over as the man of the family. But he didn't want that responsibility. Sixteen months after our dad died, Ralph married Lee, which got him off the hook as far as being expected to help us out (though I believe he never really was on the hook with my mom). He married for love, but he also wanted to get away from us all. We were in his way, and he had no interest in our well-being.

There was talk in the family about a lawsuit being brought by Ralph against his eleven brothers and sisters. I don't know what he was going to sue us for, but my older siblings were fighting mad about this. My mom was trying her best to keep a lid on this pot. She didn't want it to boil over.

Mom called my dad's attorney, Mr. O'Neill. He would help Mom out when things became too overwhelming to handle. Mom had Mr. O'Neill draw up some papers for the children to sign. The papers said that we could never sue Ralph for taking anything from the family. That made me wonder: What the hell did he do that I don't know about? Others wondered too, and that became the big question in our house. We knew Ralph did something, but what? Was it something really big? "Wow! What is it? Just tell us, Mom. We all wanna know. Don't we have the right to know? What did he take from us?"

Mom wouldn't tell us anything. All she said about the papers we were supposed to sign was, "If Ralph takes sheets from the house, you can't sue him later in life." A set of sheets? I knew this was a lie.

I was about nine years old when this was going on. It was flying all over the house. My older siblings were really angry this time. They wanted a battle with Ralph, and they wanted to win it. As for me, I didn't like this at all. I felt like my family was going to fall apart. "Please God," I would pray, "don't do this to us again. Can't we forget about Ralph? I don't want everybody fighting and my mom sad all the time."

As it turned out, Ralph won again. I came home from school one day and Mom looked at me, pointed to a chair in the dining room, and said to sit down, Then she said, "Sign this paper now. Put your name on this line." I said, "Mom, you really want me to sign this?" She nodded, and I did what she told me. You could see her agony from it all—I would have signed everyone's name to keep her from hurting. She got each of us younger kids to sign that paper. As for the older siblings, I don't know how she did it, but she convinced them to sign too. And so that crisis was put to rest.

We all knew that if Ralph had my mom call Mr. O'Neill, Ralph was up to something. He was trying to cover something up and make us look like the bad guys. What can I say except, shame on him. He will have to face my father in death with the weight of this upon him.

We never spoke about that matter again with Mom. Even when things would become unbearable in our family, we never spoke of it. The only sounds about Ralph and what he had done were heard in whispers, and only by my sister Christine at first. Under the rug this trouble went, along with many other stories never told.

There were many more jolts coming our way, but we did ultimately survive the loss of our dad. The fact is that all of our lives could have turned out quite differently than they did, and maybe for the worse.

Martha, Bertha, and Why I Needed Them

After my father's death, we knew we had to get on with life. There was so much to get together. We had to go back to school—only to find out no one wanted to play with us. I remember thinking: I guess we are diseased. Our neighbors won't play with us, no one likes us anymore, now we have only each other. Oh well, I guess I can handle that because I have eleven sisters and brothers. So I don't need anyone else to play with. But … my mom … the neighbors won't talk to her. Actually, about the neighbors' silence, I knew my mom was thinking, so what? You're not that great of neighbors anyway, because if you were, you would allow your kids to play with mine. Just maybe you could ask how I am … just maybe My dad's not here to help us with this … it's all up to Mom to decide what to do next. But that decision wasn't made by her. In fact, no one really knows who did make that judgment.

It happened when my mom had to go over to school to talk to a couple of the nuns. My brothers had been acting up in their classrooms … but what would you expect from them at a time like this? Have some compassion—we all just lost our dad! Are our brothers really that bad? No, now the nuns don't want us either. Oh boy, my family, my family—are we falling apart? … No one likes us anymore …

My mother had gotten me out of my classroom when she came to school that day, so I was with her when she talked to the nuns about my brothers. She asked the nuns to let her speak with her boys about their misbehavior. But the nuns told Mom it would be best if she took them out of school. And not only the boys—all of us had to leave school—and it was because of our father's suicide, which, in the Catholic religion, was a mortal sin.

Maybe all of us Pasquarellos should run through school and out to the street, tagging everyone we see and yelling, "Now we have given you the germ SUICIDE! Now what are you going to do—run and hide, or become the pursuer and tag the next person you see?" I really felt diseased. And what does that feel like? It hurts real bad.

Mom cries and says to the nuns, "Give the boys another chance. I will make sure that they won't make any more problems for you."

But Sister Maria says to her, "No, Mrs. Pasquarello. Today is Tuesday. This Friday will be your children's last day in our school." Then she tells Mom she has to get back to teaching, but she will walk her to the front door.

With that, my mom is holding my hand and she's holding on really tight. She looks down at me and says, "Come with me."

I certainly don't want to stay here any longer, even if my brothers and sisters are here. I just want to be with Mom. She cries a lot and stares at nothing all the time. You talk to her but she doesn't answer you … you could stand right in front of her but she doesn't see or hear you.

Please, Mommy, I want to go home with you. She looks down at me and sees me crying and agrees that I can leave school now; we will go home and on the way we will pick up my two younger sisters, who are staying at Mrs. Jordan's house. Out the front doors of the school we go, walking without saying anything to each other. My mom is so upset she is shaking all the way to Mrs. Jordan's.

I can't stand Sister Maria for making my mom cry and telling her that all of us kids can't go to school there. On the other hand, I think, good! Now I can stay home all day with my two sisters and my mom; I don't have to go back to school.

We stop at Mrs. Jordan's house to get Antoinette and Anna. Mrs. Jordan is probably the only neighbor who still talks to us. She liked my dad a lot; he would send food over to her and her kids because Mr. Jordan didn't work. Dad felt bad for her and the kids, so he would give them food from our store. I would hear him say to Mom, "Who will help that black family if we don't?" My dad was a tender and sweet man. Why did he have to die?

We pick up my little sisters. When we get to our house the back door is wide open and Mom says to us girls, let me go in first. We girls wait outside until Mom calls us in. There's an envelope on the kitchen table. Mom picks it up and we see that on the front of the envelope it reads MOVE. Morn opens the sealed envelope and inside there is lots of money. Now she is shaking and walking back and forth in the kitchen. You can tell she's thinking real hard … But what is she thinking? I don't know, but I do know that shortly thereafter we were out of our house in South Philly and on to a different house in Southwest Philly.

Oh boy, who gave us that money and why did they want us to move? I guess everybody hates us now, because of how my dad died. They seem to think you can catch a germ called suicide. Actually, I am happy that we're moving away from the people who think this. GOOD-BYE to them!— and lesson learned from so-called friends and neighbors! I am ready to go look for friends and happiness someplace else.

• • •

We four younger sisters are in a cab with our older sister Trudy. All we know is that we are moving to a new neighborhood. It's a long taxi ride but we are having so much fun—Trudy is always saying and doing entertaining things, like making funny faces at us. When she's around we laugh, and forget about our sorrow and how much we miss our dad. The taxi has stopped on this big street—it has cars going up and down it, plus there are cars parked on the sides. We get out of the cab and Trudy says, "Look behind you. That's our new house." I am so excited—I can't believe the size of our new house—it's a mansion! But then Trudy laughs and tells us, no, we should look across the street. She points to our *real* new house—it's a row house, one of 29 on that side of the street. (The one she had originally pointed to was the Presbyterian old-age home for females. It has a stone wall that's about four feet high that goes all around the entire city block. It's a fortress. I would later spend a lot of time walking on top of that stone wall.)

When we get inside the new house, my mom and the others are already there. While far from a mansion, the house is big, with hardwood floors. Upstairs are four bedrooms and one bathroom. Downstairs, the rooms are large.

We start running around and sliding on the floors. Soon Mom wants us to stop sliding on the floors because we will ruin them, but we can't help ourselves—we are having so much fun in our new home. We're happy that we moved from the old one. Except for my sister Christine, that is. Christine is 16 years old and is attached to a boyfriend called Cough Drop. She's crying and telling Mom she hates this white neighborhood. "It's all harps [slang for Irish] here," she says. "I want to be with my Italian friends—they are like me." Mom tells her to give this new neighborhood a chance—she will meet new friends. And she can always go downtown to see her old ones. But Chris tells Mom that if she goes back there she is not coming back here.

Now my brothers are running upstairs to the top of the banister and sliding down on their butts. John, ever crazy, wild, and laughing, jumps off the handrail just before it ends. "Oh, I like this house a lot!" he tells us, as we watch him come down one more time.

Then Mom says, "This is Friday. On Monday, all of you are going to a new school—MBS."

"What's that?" John asks. Chris tells him that stands for Most Blessed Sacrament Catholic School. It's only two blocks away from our new house, so we all—those in elementary school—will walk to school together on Monday. That sounds pretty good to me—we will have the six of us together.

On Monday we have breakfast and Mom accompanies all of us as we walk to MBS. A nun opens the door and takes me to a classroom. There, she says to a Sister Margaret, "This is Josephine Pasquarello, and she will be in your first-grade class." Sister Margaret puts me in the last row and the last seat. There are 95 kids in this classroom and I am so lost in here—I don't know anyone, and no one looks like me or my family. In the old school all the nuns were Italian and so were all the kids.

How did I get here? I do not feel welcomed by the nun or the kids. But I decide I will fake it through. The big question now becomes, when will it be time to go home for lunch?

Finally it's lunchtime, and I feel like running home. Outside the school building, I see that my sisters and brothers are waiting to walk home with me. We get home and have lunch and I do not want to go back to school. But Mom tells us to wash our hands and face and go back. The only ones who get to stay home with Mom are Anna and Antoinette, who are not old enough to go to school. They are lucky! They don't have to go to that school. It's just too big and there are too many kids, and all those nuns and priests. But I won't say anything about my feelings because I don't want Mom to know about them. She has so many problems right now—she doesn't need any more.

From that moment I realized that I would disconnect myself from my mom. She had so much happening for her, she really had no time to breathe her own air. Life was truly nonstop for her. So this is when I started to act out in my life. For instance, in third grade I made the decision to play hooky—for ten days. I don't know where I went, or even with whom. Sister Cecilia Francis, the nun who taught my class, called my mother and told her about my absences from school. I was home at the time, and I re member my mom telling Sister Cecilia Francis on the phone that she should teach me not to lie anymore. As she was on the phone with the nun, my mom turned to look at me. She gave me one of her "Don't Ever Do This Again" looks. And that was it for me—I knew I could never pull that again. I knew I must go to school and get an education, not that I was happy about it.

Life went on. I wished I could tell my mom how I was feeling about things, but I couldn't. Isolation would be a great word to express my hiding inside of myself during a lot of my childhood. I only broke out of that isolation in my home with my family, at times. To carry the guilt of suicide is to have a heavy weight on one's soul. I started to have an imaginary friend named Martha. She was tough to deal with; she had her fists up all the time. I was afraid of her. But I needed Martha on my side. So, to soften Martha up, I had another imaginary friend named Bertha. Bertha was too shy and sweet, but she balanced Martha, helping her to be a little more gentle. Not too much, though! Together with Martha and Bertha, I was alright—I wasn't so afraid with my two friends. They would always be there for me, no matter what. My mom and my two younger sisters knew of my friends. Mom would walk through my bedroom as I was talking to Martha and Bertha, and she'd never say anything to me. My sisters did tease me a lot about them, and we would laugh. I loved my two friends and had them with me for many years. They helped me get through life—I could tell them everything and they were with me always. They know I am fine now, but if I need them they will come running to me. See, they would never abandon me. Never.

As for my mom, I don't know what her feelings were about my friends. I do know that I thought they could help keep the weight of my problems or thoughts off her shoulders, and this would make her life a little easier.

The Busybody

We have just moved into a house in Southwest Philly. We've been there for just a few days, so everything is all new to us, and we are still putting our home together. All eight of us girls are fighting about where we will sleep. Who will sleep together? Who will share a room?

I tell my older sisters not to put me in the same room as Antoinette and Anna. They still wet the bed because they are babies, and I am six-and-a-half years old! My older sisters laugh and say, "You will sleep in between Antoinette and Anna forever." I am upset and crying when Grace comes over and tells me, "We're only kidding. Come on now, stop crying; it's all gonna be fine. Just give us older sisters some time to put it together, so you can sleep in the same bed as Carmella." Now I am happy—I get to sleep with one of my older sisters!

Mom's calling to us to come into the kitchen because it's time for lunch. You can smell the pizzas baking in the oven—the aroma of the seasoned tomato sauce, mozzarella cheese, and pepperoni. Sometimes Mom makes the crust thin, and sometimes she makes it thick; today the crust is thin and well done, so when you bite into it you can hear it crackle. Actually, I don't care which crust it is—I will happily eat them both. We all want a slice of the pizza because it's bubbly and hot. On top of the cheese is a generous sprinkling of my favorite herb, oregano.

I sit next to Grace on my left, and John is on my right. I love to sit next to John because he always has great stories and jokes for us. He makes us all laugh, but sometimes he is disgusting. He will walk by you and fart in your face and then run. I cry every time he does that to me. It's nasty! He won't do it when Chris is around because she'll smack him and then he will cry. And then I will go skipping through the house singing, "Johnny's a sissy boy for crying!" Of course I have to be careful when I do that because if he gets me I will pay dearly. I'll be dead.

We're all enjoying Mom's homemade pizzas. No matter what she serves us, it's the best. Mom loves feeding us, and we love eating everything she makes. She cooks not only with her ingredients, but with all her love. That's what makes it so good.

Now George is yelling for everyone to be quiet. He's saying something, but because George sometimes stutters, we don't immediately understand what it is he's trying to tell us. Patrick tells him to calm down and tell us again, but this time slower. I think George is trying to say that someone just opened our front door. But we don't have to wait for him to finish his sentence, because we are now all startled to hear the living room door open. Mom tries to keep us in the kitchen, but that's not happening. Everyone runs toward the dining room to see who is here in our house.

I see a lady with a big smile on her face walking from the living room toward our dining room. Mom comes rushing in to stop her from coming any farther into our house. Mom asks, "Who are you, and what do you want in my house?"

The smiling lady looks at Mom and says, "I live on this street and thought I'd stop in to say welcome to the neighborhood and ask if you like your new home and neighbors."

Mom calmly answers, "I like my new home, but if the neighbors are like you I don't know what the answer to that question will be yet."

You can tell my mom is not happy with this lady. Mom asks, "How did you get into my house since both my two front doors are always locked? You didn't ring the doorbell or knock on the front door. Don't you think that was rude?"

The lady laughs, and we all look at her. The lady tells Mom she has the keys to our two front doors because the people we bought the house from gave them to her in case of emergency, when they lived here. "Good," Mom tells her, "I would like those keys from you now." The lady, still smiling, hands the keys over.

Mom asks her name, and she introduces herself as Mary Kelly. Mom doesn't have any more patience with her—you can tell by the way Mom's body is getting tense, and she's saying something in Italian, which is always a bad sign. We know what it means in this case—Mary Kelly, you'd better run and run real fast!

Trudy goes over to Mary Kelly and says, "Well, it was nice to meet you. Now let me walk you to the front door."

Chris then yells out to Trudy, "Bring her to the back door, so she can walk the alley with the stray cats!" The rest of us are frozen in place. What will happen now?

Mary Kelly asks Mom, "So, how many kids do you have? Looks like you're running a school in your house."

It's Trudy who answers: "We have twelve children, and no, we are not running a school in our home. The kids all go to Most Blessed Sacrament School."

Then Mary, still smiling, asks Mom another question: "Where is your husband?" My mother looks at this lady.

She replies, "My husband is deceased."

Now Mary questions her on when he died and how. That second question, the one on how he died, is the million-dollar question. We kids are standing there, waiting. Mom says her husband died of a heart attack just a few months ago. Why did mom say heart attack? I wonder. I thought he committed suicide. Did my dad really have a heart attack? That was the one and only time I ever heard my mom give that explanation. Was that because Mary, that busybody, was asking too many questions?

Mary looks at us kids and says that's so sad for you and your family. Then, Mary comes in close toward Mom and says, "Is there a man living here with you?" But before Mom can answer, Mary says, "You know, and so do I, that you can't take care of twelve kids on your own. Are you sure you had a husband?"

Grace grabs Mary's arm and tells her it's time to go. "Don't talk to my mother like that," Grace says. "She is a lady." Grace doesn't give Mary any time to reply. She pushes her out the living room door onto the front porch. Then Christine follows them onto the porch and you can hear Chris telling Grace, "Push that slob down the stairs!" All of us kids are laughing because the fact is we would love to hear Mary screaming as she tumbled down our cement front steps. Christine yells at Mary, "The next time you go to someone's house, knock on the door and introduce yourself. Get yourself some manners!"

Christine comes into the living room and says to Mom, "That lady never even asked what your name was.

Mom tells Chris, "Who cares? Now when I see her on the street, I'll just keep walking like she doesn't exist."

Mom tells all of us to go back to the kitchen and eat our lunch before it gets cold. We are still laughing as we talk about Mary and eat pizza. We laugh about the idea of Mom hitting Mary over the head with her pizza roller, which looks like a small wooden baseball bat. But my mom would never do that—she'd never hurt anyone on purpose—even if they were rude. She would never go down to their level; she would always stay above their ignorance.

We hoped that day that Mary had gotten the message and would keep her nose out of our business. Our lives were complicated enough and didn't need any more ugliness. When you already feel poor and lonely, you don't need anyone to trigger any more negativity in your life. So when you see evil, you tend to go the other way, even—or especially—if it has a smile on its face.

For the next 15 years that we lived on that street, the only thing ever said about that woman was that Mary Kelly should find something productive to do with her time.

A Better Side of Our Big Brother

Despite our difficulties with Ralph, there are also good memories of my oldest brother and his family. I was seven-and-a-half years old when he married Lee, so I don't have much to go on, but I do remember that he wasn't living in our house anymore and that, on Sundays, he and his family would come over to visit. He would play cards with the boys and some of our brothers-in-law. Ralph wasn't all bad, just pompous at times. Was that because he was my mom's firstborn and a boy? She did adore him.

Mom always had her Ralph to talk with when she was in doubt. Maybe he soothed her? Maybe he eased her uncertainty in difficult situations? He was a smooth talker, and maybe, with the force of his personality and his superior attitude, she could relate to him. In a sense, they were a great duo, as Ralph helped her fix problems that the family was facing. As I grew older, she would talk with Ralph or the other older siblings about what was happening and then handle the situation on her own terms. She really was remarkable in her ability to hold all of it together that way. I've never met anyone else who could have done that.

Until her death, Mom and Ralph were on good terms. She looked at him differently than she looked at any of us other eleven. He gave her something that none of the other children could. And for that, I am truly happy. Maybe I didn't understand their bond. But who was I to question a mother and son's love for each other? If she was content and he enjoyed lending the force of his authority to her, then they had a great relationship. Maybe, in the long run, he helped more than I will ever know.

• • •

I think we all felt that, when Ralph married Lee, he changed. Now he was the man of his house. My older siblings would say that Ralph became a man on his wedding day. He took his love for Lee, and his commitment to her, seriously. And Lee had that same attitude toward Ralph and their marriage. Ralph and Lee always remembered us kids with special gifts. For instance, on Christmas, they always had a gift for us last six kids. We four young sisters, who were known as "the babies," were always given a pair of pajamas. Wow!—a brand new pair of PJs just for me! I didn't have to share them with my sisters, and that was a wonderful thing—they were for me alone. We weren't given such an opportunity but once a year at Christmas, thanks to Ralph and Lee.

Lee would come into the house with the Christmas gifts in a shopping bag. She would take out one at a time, calling out the name of one of us girls. We were all so excited to receive a gift like this—wrapped beautifully in red and green, complete with ribbons and a large red or green bow.

I was so happy that I would cry when Lee would call out my name. This was sheer delight—to know that maybe Santa really did love me and my family. This was the one gift we could count on every Christmas, and it was given to us with love.

Another special occasion was Easter Sunday. Mom would be in the kitchen cooking since six a.m. She would put on her pot of gravy with meatballs and pork. And she would make ravioli filled with ricotta cheese, which we were sure was the best in town.

In the late afternoon Ralph and Lee would show up with their usual big white box. When the two of them would walk in the living room we kids would all jump up. We'd been waiting all day for the contents of that box.

Mom would come out to the dining room with one of her large meat platters. Then she would open the white box with all of us kids crowding around her like a pack of hungry dogs. There was no barking, but our tongues *were* hanging out of our mouths.

There it was—a five-pound chocolate-covered coconut cream egg—beautiful as ever!

It was decorated with white sugar lace around the entire egg. On top, there were sugar flowers of spring colors. You could snap off part of one of the flowers and you would have a piece of candy that would last in your mouth for quite a while. It was all pure sugar, "of the best." The egg could last for about a week, although most years it was gone by midweek. Every year, even though we knew what was in that box, the excitement, and the feelings of happiness and love, returned.

On the holidays, knowing that Ralph and Lee would be coming over was always pure joy for us as a family. Those gifts for Mom's younger ones were Ralph's way of showing my mother that he indeed did love and respect her above all else. And he would help with the family as best he could, even though he was starting his own family. He would be there for us, and was. What else could you ask for?

Oh, What a Night

One night—it must have been when I was about ten—five of my sisters and I were in the living room watching television and talking and laughing with two of our brothers. Another brother, George, was not feeling well, so he was upstairs sleeping. One of my sisters said we should paint George's fingernails bright red, and my two brothers egged us on, daring us to go into his bedroom and paint them. Our brothers teased us—we were too scared, they said, because George might wake up and kick our ass. So naturally, the six of us took our brothers up on the dare.

We were telling each other that George thinks he is so good-looking and cool that we need to do this to him to bring him down to our level. Later, we could tell all his girlfriends what we did to him, and he would get really mad. That would be funny.

My sisters and I went upstairs to George's room, and found him sleeping. We tried to be quiet as we started painting the fingernails of his left hand, but we couldn't keep from laughing because he was lying on his right hand, and we didn't know how we were going to get that hand from underneath his head. My older sister Christine tickled his nose with a feather, and he started to rub his nose. We were laughing like crazy, which woke George. Startled, he said, "What's going on here?"

My brother John was laughing hard as he told him, "They painted your nails with red polish. Let them paint your other hand." George looked at his hands, threw off his blanket, and started cursing. My sisters and I bolted down the stairs to Mom. Right behind us were our brothers, with George shouting, "I'm gonna kill you girls!" Our other brothers were encouraging him to get each and every one of us to make us pay for what we did. Oh … my … God!

George really wanted to get us. We made it downstairs and into the kitchen, thinking it was a safe haven because my mother was there. No way. The boys were right behind us, yelling that we are dead or close to it.

Mom told them to leave us alone. "Don't hurt the girls," she said, "or I'll hurt the three of you." This was unusual because in an Italian household mothers usually treat their sons like kings, even though sisters see them as a pain in the ass.

Mom was trying to settle us down, but we were so full of energy that she backed off. We girls were running all through the house, trying to get away from the boys. Christine grabbed her cans of silver and gold hairspray and started to spray the boys. We were grabbing cans from her, including some cans of Reddi-Wip. Now whipped cream and colored hair spray were flying all over the place. The boys were trying to get the cans from us and managed to do so without much effort. Still, Christine had more hairspray cans in the closet. The house became a war zone.

In this war of the girls against the boys, Christine was a great help to our side; she even got George and John to cry. She generally took no crap from the boys and would fight them like a cat, scratching and pulling their hair. I loved watching her beat them down because she was the only girl in our family who could control those two.

Mom entered the living room, sat in her chair, and said, "You can do what you want tonight, but tomorrow you will get the house looking spic and span." We agreed to her terms. Tomorrow we would clean, but for now, we would go back to our battle.

I remember that for a very long time, we ran around yelling, laughing, and spraying anything and everything we could find. For the first time since our dad had committed suicide, we were all having fun and laughing. Mom allowed us to enjoy what was happening and was laughing too. Sitting in her chair, she watched us as if she was watching a television program. That night we released a lot of sadness. It's as if we said we've had enough of the darkness. We had to get a little crazy and start to live again.

Suddenly, my brothers Pat and George grabbed me by the arms and started spraying whipped cream at me. George put the can in my mouth and sprayed as cream shot all over the place. It was in my eyes and on my face and head. It was so much fun that we couldn't stop laughing. This is what brothers and sisters do to each other to show their love, and it is what we were all in need of. There is a saying, "United we stand." The ten of us were standing together, letting go of our pain.

I do have to admit that that night, although my sisters and I gave it all we had, our brothers won the fight. Still, it was such a joy to be a happy, laughing child again.

By the end of the night, our house was in total devastation from our craziness. The next morning, we all kept our promise to put the house back together. We washed everything—the furniture, the floors, and ourselves. It was like starting over as a family. Finally, it felt okay to not have our dad there. We knew it was better to move on without him than to feel the sorrow of losing him every day of our lives. Besides, Dad would like for us to live happily. Now happiness could be a part of our family life again. We would always love our dad and never forget what he meant to us. And I knew in my heart that my mom would never forget him, that he was with her every moment in her heart and mind. At this moment, perhaps she, too, felt more complete and ready to take on anything.

This is the moment I started to feel more at ease, knowing that my mother had our lives under control. She would guide us to be good, honest, and trustworthy people. I felt safe knowing that my mom would protect me from harm. Now I could feel secure in my being because I had the most powerful lady by my side.

Just an Ordinary Day

Morning: An Early Start for Mom

Mom wakes up early—before 5 a.m.—to start her day. The house is quiet when she goes into the bathroom to wash and dress. If she's lucky this morning not one of us will bother her, and she'll get to wash and dress without one of us on the toilet, or trying to convince her that we are sick and shouldn't go to school. But today she's not lucky—it's my turn to try to con her.

She never believes our claims that we are sick unless we have a high fever. She'll touch your forehead, then look into your eyes. If you aren't weak and delirious, you are going to school. More times than not she'll say, "Go to school. If your nun sends you home, then I'll believe you are sick." Of course I always think there's no harm in trying to put one over on her, so today I try. I'm not successful, though, and as I go back to bed I'm thankful that I still have another two hours before I have to get up.

Mom goes downstairs and out the front door. She's off to church to pray to God; she needs His guidance to make it through her day. All her prayers are for us. She has to keep us safe and it's a hard task because, with so many of us, it's impossible for her to know our every move. So if He could help her that would be a tremendous weight off her shoulders. When she finishes talking to Him, and thanking Him for His help, she leaves church and walks the three blocks back to our house. Mom doesn't drive a car so she walks everywhere unless she catches a PTC vehicle (that stands for Philadelphia Transportation Company).

45

I hear the front door close … straight to the kitchen she goes. She's getting ready to prepare breakfast for us. The main room in our house is the kitchen. It's the largest room; we can all sit at one of the two tables, and there's plenty of space for us to move around. So the kitchen is where it all happens for our family. This room serves as our everyday conversation area and our problem-solving area. And of course in any Italian home the kitchen is where it all happens with eating. To keep us happy my mom always makes sure this room is filled with lots and lots of good food. In our kitchen we solve all our problems—and create much of our happiness—with food and drink, no matter what time of the day it is.

I hear Mom walking up the stairs. Each step has its own sound from the weight of her body, so I can always tell exactly where she is on the stairs. When she gets to the top step I tell myself to wake up. I am thinking, I don't want to go to school. But she won't let me get away with not going. Remembering that I've already tried making my pitch at the crack of dawn and it didn't work, I make my decision to be good today, to keep my mouth shut and go to school. Deep down I know my mother doesn't have time for one of us to stay home with her—she's too busy with everything there is to do in the house. I'd feel bad for Mom if I pushed the issue.

Mom always wakes the boys first. She has to walk through Antoinette and Anna's room to get to the boys' back bedroom. I can hear her telling the boys to get out of bed, and to get washed and dressed for school. "As soon as you're finished, go downstairs for breakfast," she tells them. "Your sisters need the bathroom, so hurry."

Next she walks back into Antoinette and Anna's room. I hear her getting louder with them. She is saying to them that they have to strip the bed so she can wash their bed sheets. They have to stop wetting the bed, Mom tells them—making the point that they are big enough to get to the toilet in the middle of the night. She's getting louder, saying, "I've had enough of your peeing in the bed. Please stop! That's all I do—wash your sheets and remake your bed! But from today on you both are going to take care of your bed. I just don't know how to handle this any longer."

Now Mom is knocking on the third bedroom door, because it has a lock on it. It's the only door inside the house with a lock. Trudy had Pat—at the time her fiancé—put the lock on the door because someone was stealing the dimes from her bank. She was saving her dimes to buy linens for her hope chest. Now, Grace and Rosemarie are in that room. Grace runs out of her bedroom to get to the bathroom before Christine. If you get there after Christine the door will be closed for a long time. She doesn't like us sisters to see her naked. She's the only girl in our family who is like that, and you might have to wait 10 or 15 minutes for her to be finished in the bathroom. That's too long in the morning, when we all have to rush to get downstairs for a hot breakfast. Sometimes we yell for Mom to come upstairs and throw Christine out of the bathroom, but that doesn't always work.

Here comes Mom to get me and Carmella out of our warm bed. The front bedroom is the last room upstairs. Christine is already up and Carmella and I are hiding under the blanket.

Mom is putting her index finger into my shoulder and pulling on the blanket. She's laughing because this finger-poking is kind of a joke between us— it's Mom's last straw way of trying to get me up, and we both know that it works. Mom tells us to get up and come downstairs for breakfast—she'll be serving bacon and eggs.

I say I'm not hungry this morning. She holds my face in her two hands and says, "Come on, Josephine, I'll cook whatever you would like. You have to eat—you're so small and thin." I smile back at her, as I think, *I guess I'll eat something to make her happy*. I tell her I would like some cream of wheat cereal, with lots of butter and sugar. Now she's happy because I will eat something. Anything I eat will make her happy. Mom's causes for happiness are so small— she never expects anything big in life. I could never be happy like her with all of us to take care of—it would be too much. She smiles at me and tells me to get out of bed. "Go get washed and your hot cereal will be waiting for you."

I get up and go into the bathroom. I join Carmella at the bathtub to brush my teeth. Rosemarie is at the sink washing her face. Antoinette is on the toilet and Anna is jumping up and down waiting her turn. As we finish we go to our bedrooms and get dressed in our Catholic school uniforms.

When we come downstairs we pass Christine in the dining room. She's in front of the large oval mirror putting on her makeup. Below the mirror is a large serving piece in which Christine has stored all her hair products, along with lots and lots of makeup. She could be in front of that mirror for half an hour.

As we enter the kitchen we see the three boys at the first table, gobbling down their breakfast. We girls sit at the second table and Mom serves us our breakfast.

As we eat the boys jump up and run out the front door to walk to school. Grace and Christine rush into the kitchen, kiss Mom, and tell her they're running late. They will see her at 6 p.m. for dinner.

We youngest five girls stop at the mirror to see if our hair looks good. Antoinette grabs Christine's gold hair spray and sprays the top of her head. She looks cute with a big gold piece of hair running along the crown of her head. Mom's yelling, "You five will be late, so stop playing with you sister's hairspray. Get to school!" The five of us grab our schoolbags and run out the door.

Finally, Mom has a moment to herself! She sits down and has her breakfast and a cup of coffee, reads the paper, and plans her day. Then she goes back upstairs to strip Grace and Rosemarie's bed. She takes all the towels from the bathroom, along with the sheets, down to the basement. First for the washer are the sheets. Then she puts the towels into one of the laundry sinks. Now it's back upstairs to clean the kitchen, the dishes, and the pots and pans. All of this is done by hand. She dries everything and puts the dishes in the cabinet to the left of the sink. The glasses go to the right.

While doing the laundry, Mom times her washer, because it's a wringer machine. After washing and rinsing, every item must be hand-cranked through the wringers. Going back upstairs she carries the clean wet sheets in her laundry basket, straight out to the backyard to hang on the clothesline to dry. Mom always says she loves the smell of clean air-dried clothes. But perhaps that's because she can't afford a clothes dryer. A dryer would make her life a lot easier. She wouldn't have to go up and down the stairs all day, which is certainly tough on her body. She must go up and down to do the laundry at least 15 to 20 times a day.

Mom goes into the living room to dust and to sweep the hardwood floors. We'd better not have left any of our belongings anywhere. If we did she will be upset. She tells us it makes the house look sloppy, and slows her down in her cleaning. Off onto the enclosed front porch she goes to put all our snow boots in a straight line, matching them together. Outside on the front steps are cigarette butts that she sweeps down to the sidewalk. With her dust pan she picks up all the butts and other trash. She puts the trash into a brown paper bag from the grocery store that she carries with her as she sweeps.

A neighbor, Mrs. Green, stops to talk to Mom about the family. She questions Mom on how we all are. Mom and Mrs. Green speak for a moment, each smiling at the other. Mom asks if Mr. Green is back to work after his car accident. Mrs. Green replies that all is well with Mr. Green and her family. Walking back up the steps, Mom tells Mrs. Green she must go in the house. "My kids will be home soon from school," she says. "They will be expecting the leftover pasta from last night's dinner. I may have a war on my hands at lunchtime!" They both laugh as Mom walks back onto the front porch.

It's into the kitchen now to set the two tables and put the large pot of pasta and meatballs on the stove. It's 11:15 as the eight of us come home for lunch. As usual, Mom feeds the boys first. Most of the time we girls don't say anything about her boys; we are accustomed to Mom's way with her sons. We girls do hope that the boys don't eat all the pasta. Today we're in luck—there's enough for all.

Afternoon: We Learn Some Family History
After we finish our lunch it's back to school for the eight of us. And back to work for Mom—not that serving lunch for eight hasn't been work! Mom cleans the kitchen and all our lunch dishes as she eats a bowl of pasta. She has to get to the store for more food before we return from school. She walks six blocks to the Penn Fruit food market, pulling her wire cart behind her. She gets food for dinner today, and for breakfast and lunch tomorrow. For tonight we'll be having beef stew, salad, and lots of Italian bread. We will all be happy with this meal. Mom pulls her cart all the way home, stopping a few times to catch her breath. When the cart is full, it's heavy. Mom must really be strong because she does this every day.

She's in front of the house with the cart, and this is the hardest part of her trip. Mom has to pull the cart up the twelve steps to the front door. Then it's through the house with the cart and into the kitchen. She makes a cup of tea, sits down, and catches her breath before she starts on dinner. Before she knows it, it's 3:15, and we're back from school. Then all eight of us are in the kitchen for an after-school snack. On the tables Mom has set a large plate of celery, along with a couple of plates with olive oil and salt and pepper. We all enjoy this for a great snack. We love our olive oil with any fresh veggie.

It looks like today our after-school conversation will involve storytelling. Mom often has great stories for us, and today it seems the story she has is about her and my dad fighting. Dad always thought he won every fight, she says, laughing. Here comes the story, and we kids are now listening intently because she has never spoken to us about the two of them fighting. I never thought about my parents fighting because my older siblings told us younger kids that our dad was the boss. Whatever he said to do, we all listened. I guess except for my mom. I am loving this story—it seems our mother didn't always listen to our father!

Now John and Antoinette are eagerly encouraging Mom, "Come on, tell us how Dad and you fought." John says, "I know you were an obedient wife." At this, my brothers laugh, and Mom rolls her eyes. Carmella yells for the boys to shut their big mouths. Wow—sometimes all this noise is so exciting! It keeps us happy. I think we fight and yell just for the fun of it. But I notice it is always the boys against the girls in our house.

Mom tells us to settle down or forget about the story. "No Mom," I beg; "I wanna hear about you and Daddy! Please tell us!"

The kitchen becomes quiet. Mom begins. "One Sunday, late morning, me and your dad were drinking coffee. He said, 'Sit, Ro. I need to talk about something really important.'" (Three months before, Mom had just given birth to John, their eighth child.)

Mom tells us that then, Dad said, "I think having eight kids should be enough for our home. Besides, Ro, you're getting up in your years. How many more do you have left for childbearing?"

We're all looking at Mom. Oh, boy, her face is bright red … all her blood seems to have rushed to her head. She looks like she's ready to explode any second.

She catches her breath … looks around at all of us … and says, "Can you imagine your dad saying that? After all, if I would have listened to him, you last four girls wouldn't be here." Then a big smile spreads across her face. She tells us that when he said that to her, she could have killed him on the spot. But then, she thought. *First of all, I am not that old,* she thought. *I am only 38. And second, I will have as many kids as I want. Just maybe a few more…*

Mom let Dad know her wishes, and he was not happy. She goes on, "He thought if he got more stern with me, I would back down and give in to him. But I told him I had a solution to his problem. I said that on Sundays, when it was our special time, we should no longer spend time together."

Listening to this, my 10-year-old self is thinking, *What's "special time?"* So, I ask. Pat and George tell me to keep quiet and that it's none of my business. Just sit there and listen, they say.

Mom is laughing so hard that her stomach is jumping up and down. Then she says that she told Dad he could sleep in the bed with the four boys. And that's when my dad goes off! He's yelling at the top of his lungs that no woman will ever tell him where he will sleep. Oh boy, Mom loves this story! She's out of her chair, walking around, asking if we know what she said to him. I am thinking, *I don't know what you're talking about.* But I'm not going to say anything because then the boys will call me stupid and tell me to shut up.

Mom sits back in her chair and reports, "I won that fight. Carmella was born nine months later. I showed him who was boss!" We all laugh—even me, although I still don't get it.

Mom tells us to go out and have some fun before dinner, so we kids all run outside to play. The girls usually play jacks or jump rope, and the boys play stickball. Then we all come back in for the 5 o'clock movie on TV—that is, if we aren't still busy outside.

Evening: Dinner, Dishes, Homework, Kisses

Mom is in the kitchen preparing dinner. Tonight it's beef stew; another common dinner for us would be chicken cutlets, baked potatoes, and corn on the cob. And always we have salad and our Italian bread. Mom's busy in the kitchen until 6 p.m., which is when dinner is served.

When Grace and Christine return home from work we gather in the kitchen. The ten of us sit down and start talking about our day. Mom serves us our meal, then she sits at the head of the table next to the stove. All of us laugh and talk.

As soon as we finish our meal, Mom tells us to go into the dining room to do our homework. We get our schoolbags and pull out our books. As for me, you can keep this homework. I don't do it that often. But I sit with everyone because I will laugh and talk until someone tells me to shut up.

It's Carmella's turn to do the dishes this week. Mom puts the leftover food in the ice box. She puts on her coffee pot for anyone who will join her in a cup of coffee. Then, she goes to the living room to sit in her favorite chair and watch some television. She turns on channel 10 to watch her favorite newsman,

John Facenda. She can finally call it a day—as far as her physical labor is concerned. Now it's on to her other responsibilities.

She starts with "How was school?" for each and every one of us. "Did you have any problems with your nun or the other kids?" Actually, if you gave your nun a problem, you had better run, because Mom will kill you.

"Make sure to do all of your homework," our mother tells us. "Get washed before you go to bed." We have to be in bed by a certain time; each year older will get you a half hour longer to stay up. We all know our bedtime but we also hope she will fall asleep in her chair. When this happens not one of us will wake her up, because we want to stay up longer.

After we are told to go to bed, Mom kisses us goodnight. Sometimes, we go to her in her chair, taking turns with kissing and hugging her. She loves it when we tell her we love her. You can feel her happiness.

Once we are all in bed, Mom turns off the lights downstairs, and the TV. You can hear her in each bedroom counting heads, just like my dad did when he was alive. After her headcount you hear her in the bathroom. Then, in our bedroom, I watch her dress in her PJs, all the while talking to my dad about her day, at times with joy and at other times with sadness. As she sits on our bed, I feel the weight of her body. Then she lies down and you hear her praying and thanking God for his help.

Tomorrow it will start all over.

Mixed-Matched Gloves

It's a Saturday morning in February. There's a big snowstorm today, so there are no deliveries—that means no milk, juice, bread, or donuts today. We get those delivered because we are a very large family, with twelve kids, and even though three have moved out by this time, we still eat a lot of food. In addition to the deliveries, Mom goes to the food market every day, and today she will certainly have to. She tells us four youngest she'll be home in an hour. She's going to Paul Brothers Market, only two blocks from our home, and we are to watch cartoons until she gets back. We four sisters are happy—we can watch television, plus there's the anticipation that when Mom gets back she'll have lots and lots of food for us. We're really hungry. The older five kids are still asleep upstairs.

Before leaving the house, Mom puts on her heavy winter coat, her boots, and that big wool scarf of hers that wraps around her face and head. From the door she yells to us that she will be back in an hour, so we should be good.

We have a great time, laughing and watching our favorite cartoons—Mighty Mouse and, after him, Minnie Mouse. I really love Minnie. We are glad that the older siblings are still in bed. That's a good thing because we don't have to share the television with the boys. Once they come downstairs, it's over for us girls. They control the TV, and we little ones have no choice but to listen to them. So right now we are happy that everyone else is asleep. Please stay in your beds, we wish—and they do. We are lucky this morning.

It's over an hour now and Mom isn't home yet, so we're getting nervous that something has happened to her. I go to the front door to look outside for her, but I can't see anything. It's a whiteout. I go back to the living room to tell my sisters you can't see anything. And we start to think maybe Mom fell down and can't get back up. Mom is real tiny. I don't even think she's five feet tall, and she always looks pregnant. (That's because she was pregnant twelve times, so that's nine years of her life being pregnant!)

Finally, we hear the porch door opened and now the living room door opens and it's Mom. She's covered with lots of snow, especially her head. She's so cold, her face and hands are numb. But she has some black lady with her and the lady's four small kids. And they are all covered with snow. They have no boots, hats, or gloves on. Their little faces and hands are numb, just like my mom's and their mom's.

Mom tells us to get up and help the kids get their coats and shoes off. We do that, putting their belongings on the radiators throughout the house. So, we are all helping the kids, but they won't talk to us or even smile at us. Now Mom tells us that this is Mrs. Jones, and Mrs. Jones introduces us to her four children.

Mrs. Jones's oldest girl, Pauline, is seven years old. Her second oldest, Sherry, is five. Her third girl, Peaches, is three-and-a-half years old, and then there's little brother Joe. Even though Joe is Peaches' twin, he seems to be the baby of the group, whom the girls all love to take care of. He seems to enjoy his sisters' mommying him.

Now my mother introduces all of us by name: eleven-year-old Carmella, ten-year-old Josephine—that's me, eight-year-old Antoinette, and Anna, who's seven. Mom tells us, "I want you girls to take care of the kids while Mrs. Jones and I get breakfast for all of you. Her kids haven't eaten since last night, so they are very hungry and tired."

While Mom goes with Mrs. Jones, the eight of us stay in the living room watching cartoons. But the Jones kids don't talk—not to us, and not to each other. We sense that something has happened to them but we don't know what it could be. We silently ask ourselves questions: Where did Mom find this lady and her kids? Why did she bring them home to us, to feed, and to get dry and warm? We realize that our mom must have a big heart to help this lady she doesn't even know. After all, we are poor ourselves. We're always behind in paying our grocery bill; we pay Paul Brothers on the third day of every month because that's when we get our Social Security checks. We get one check for Mrs. Pasquarello and another for the Pasquarello children.

After a while, all of us kids do get to talking. And even laughing. Although we Pasquarellos still don't know where these children came from, we notice some things. We can see that the Jones kids are happy right now—so unlike when they first came in. We learn that big sister Pauline worries about her sisters and brother. She wants to take good care of them. Sherry, on the other hand, is mad at everyone, especially her mom. Sherry looks at Mrs. Jones with such anger you can tell her heart is broken. Peaches and Joe are so happy and cute. Their eyes are still young and full of stars. (In a way, I could see all of their lives through their eyes because we twelve were the same with our eyes through our lives. You can see pain or happiness in the eyes, but you must live your life and find happiness somehow. Even if you know life stinks, you still have to find something that smells nice.)

The moms say, come, get breakfast. We all jump, especially our little friends. We have hot chocolate with whipped cream, along with my favorite Italian bread, warmed in the oven and with lots of butter. Now all of us kids are eating, talking, and laughing, sitting together at the same table. And the moms are sitting at the other table talking, but real quiet and whispering to each other. My mom's really serious as she speaks with Mrs. Jones, and Mrs. Jones is listening to every word my mom is saying. You can tell Mrs. Jones needs someone to listen to her story. They are becoming the best of friends.

Now that we are in the kitchen, I can see the bruises on Mrs. Jones's face, and that her left eye is swollen. Clearly, someone has beat her up. More questions arise. Where is Mr. Jones? Is he dead like my dad? Is Mrs. Jones on her own like my mom and us? Is that why my mom is helping her—because we are all alike, with no man to protect us?

After we eat breakfast, we kids are feeling better. We go into the living room to watch more TV. We're having a nice time together. Our four little friends are getting comfortable with us and are now talking up a storm.

Our moms stay in the kitchen for a really long time talking, talking, and talking some more. After a long time, they come out to us. My mom says, "Help get the kids ready. They are going to Mrs. Jones's mom's house." We look at mom, and she says, "Get the cardboard box out of the closet and find scarves and gloves for the kids." The box has gloves, more than half of which don't match. But so what? They keep your hands warm. We kids call that pile of mismatched gloves "mixed-matched," and we are not particular about fashion.

Help to get the kids' coats on. Put the scarves around their heads and faces. Even if the gloves don't match, put a pair on their little hands. Dress them as warm as you can, my mom keeps telling us. My mom gives Mrs. Jones her own gloves and her wool scarf to help keep her warm for her long journey to her mother's house, which is about 15 blocks away. You can walk that in the spring or summer. But on a day like today! Also, with the four little kids! But Mrs. Jones says she will be able to get to her mom's house. And we all believe her. This is probably because my mom has told us, just about daily, that there isn't anything you can't do if you put your mind to it.

Now our older siblings are coming downstairs for breakfast, but my mom tells them to go back up. When she's ready, she will call them. So back upstairs they go. Mom can't feed them now; she has to get Mrs. Jones and her kids ready for their journey through the blizzard.

We four sisters are upset to see our little friends getting ready for the walk through that storm. But it has to be done. We can't call anyone for help because we don't have a telephone. We ask them, "Why don't you get a bus or something?" But mom says in this storm no buses or trolleys are running. If you must get somewhere, you'll have to walk. So Mrs. Jones will walk her way through the storm with her children by her side.

Why was this happening to them? we were still wondering. And where was Mr. Jones?

Mrs. Jones goes over to my mom. Hugging my mom, she starts to cry as she thanks Mom for talking with her, and for being there when she was in such need. And then, as quickly as they came into our lives, out they go. We stand at the door watching as they walk down the front steps. For a few seconds, we feel the wind blowing and the snow blowing in. And then they are all gone. Just like that.

Now my mom says to us kids, let's go into the kitchen and I will tell you her story. As we go into the living room, my mom calls upstairs to my older brothers and sisters to come on down for breakfast. Soon all of us are in the kitchen. The older kids want to know, "Who was that black lady and those kids?"

My mom says, "Sit down. I will tell you."

At first, my mom thought Mrs. Jones was lost because this neighborhood was white, and she was black. And the people around here don't take kindly to black people. Not that my mom cared about anyone's skin color. We Pasquarellos looked somewhat dark ourselves, and our old neighborhood had had Italians, Jews, and blacks, and everyone got along. This part of Philadelphia was different, though. It was white, almost all white, at least until we Pasquarellos showed up with twelve dark-skinned kids and our dark-skinned mom. So when she first saw Mrs. Jones and her kids on the corner of our street, 58th and Kingsessing Avenue, my mom was worried.

When Mom returned to our corner after almost an hour of shopping, Mrs. Jones was still standing there with her four kids. They all looked terribly wet and cold. Mom said to Mrs. Jones, "Are you waiting for a bus?" and Mrs. Jones replied, "Yes, I am." Mom told her that in this blizzard no public transportation would be running today.

My mom noticed the swollen eye on Mrs. Jones and asked, "Are you okay or do you need help?" With that, Mrs. Jones started to cry. That's when my mom said to her, "Come home with me and let's get you and your kids warm and feed them some breakfast." Mrs. Jones was so happy to hear this—she had been out there for almost two hours already.

When they were in our kitchen talking, Mrs. Jones told Mom her story. That Mr. Jones had come home about three a.m. that morning and told her that his girlfriend was moving into their house. That Mrs. Jones had said no way. That he had then started to beat her, punch her, kick her, and pull out her hair. She told Mom her husband would get drunk every weekend and lots of times came home with no money from his paycheck. The night before, all she had had to feed the kids was two cans of soup. She couldn't take it any longer, and she couldn't have her kids around him any longer. "What kind of man does this to his family?" She asked my mom that question about a hundred times.

Mrs. Jones told her husband she was going to leave him. No, you're not, he said, because I'm going to put you and the kids out of my house right now. So, she went upstairs and woke the kids, and put their coats on. At the same time she was saying, "Please, don't do this now. It's the middle of the night, it's winter, and it's snowing."

Mr. Jones said, "Put on your coat, or I'll put you out without a coat on you."

Mrs. Jones and the kids started their walk at about six a.m. that Saturday morning. It was about eight when my mom ran into them. They had already been in that storm for about two hours, not that they were dressed for a storm, and not that they had any food in their stomachs. So how could you not help a lady and her kids get warm and put something hot in their stomachs? My mom said that if it had been her, she would want someone to help her and her kids. It was as simple as that.

There were many lessons learned that morning. For one, there was a lesson in sharing, in giving all you've got. Our box of mostly unmatched gloves was our box of gold. After all, if we didn't have dry, warm gloves, we couldn't go out to play in the snow. But it was about more than the gloves; we had in fact shared everything we had—our food, our house, and our love—because this family needed them more than we did.

Another lesson that stayed with me forever was how kind my mom was to people she didn't know and would probably never see again. Also, for the first time, I realized that our family wasn't alone. Other people had hardships too. Realizing this helped me believe that we could and would overcome our own obstacles. After all, we had the help and strength of my mother. With her, we would make it through anything.

I like to think that Mrs. Jones learned something that morning too. By the look on her face when she first entered our house, Mrs. Jones had been frightened, but after being with my mom, I believe she wasn't so scared. I don't know if Mrs. Jones knew how similar our family's circumstances were to hers, but she probably sensed that there was no father's presence in our home. And who better than my mom to let her know that you, a lone woman, can take care of yourself and your children? And that you can always, always hold your head high as you walk through life. And that you can and will get there, and not to let any person or anything hold you down. You can walk through the fire with pride and dignity and a sense of self-worth.

We never again spoke of that Saturday morning to each other, probably because my mom never encouraged us to talk about hardship and pain. As the saying goes, out of sight, out of mind, and as a child, you take the lead from your parents. So I learned to keep things inside.

Still, Mrs. Jones and her children were often on my mind. Probably, had we been encouraged to talk about what happened, I would have felt better. Perhaps it would have helped me understand our family's situation. Still, I learned that everyone carries a weight in life. The grass is not always greener on the other side. There will always be a crisis in your life. Learning hard life lessons at a young age can be a blessing in disguise, because when you are older, you are able to handle just about anything.

We never did hear from Mrs. Jones or her children again. But I know that they are all in our hearts and we are in theirs. And that it was one of God's blessings when our mom ran across them on our corner as they waited for a bus that never came.

The Loss of a Friendship

Annmarie was my schoolmate in second and third grade. She was pretty, with blond hair and blue eyes. She was an only child, treated by her father, mother, and grandmother like a princess.

This was my first true friendship with someone other than a family member. We hung out a lot on weekdays; I would go home with her for lunch, and after school we would be together. It was fun being at her house. She had a large house that was always quiet and clean, unlike my own house, which was always noisy and somewhat messy. With all of us kids running around, it couldn't have been otherwise.

Something amazing to me was that Annmarie had her own bedroom. She slept in a big bed, by herself. Boy oh boy—things were different at her house! Her clothes were always new, and so were her shoes. She had a lot of everything—her family, I thought, must be rich. But I didn't feel poor around her, because she made me feel good and I knew she liked me.

Annmarie's grandmother, who sometimes visited, was another story; she was mean-looking and she didn't like me. Well, too bad for her, I thought—I don't like her either. Sometimes her grandmother would be at the house when we went there for lunch break. That woman was too stiff for my taste—her hair was never out of place. I remember how she kept her false teeth in a glass on the kitchen counter. It would gross me out to have to eat my lunch looking at those disgusting teeth, which somehow seemed to be looking back at me.

The feeling I got from that woman was the same one I had for her: "Don't like you." But that didn't stop me from hanging out with Annmarie. We were inseparable, forever talking and laughing at anything. We were kids having fun and enjoying life together.

Annmarie's parents both worked, so they weren't home much. We were free to do as we pleased. Sometimes we would go to the corner market to get lunch. The family had a house account there, so Annmarie would get lunch and doughnuts for the two of us. A few times that's all we ate for lunch—the chocolate doughnuts. There was nobody to know. It was fun not having so many people around. I could do what I wanted and no one knew. To me that was the best feeling—the freedom of being away from my family and all of our problems, even if it was only for a lunch break or after school. I did start to stay longer and longer at Annmarie's after school. At times it would already be dark when I walked home, not knowing if this would be the time my mom would kill me for being so late. I really didn't care, though, if she did kill me—it would be worth it, being able to enjoy a longer time at Annmarie's.

One day after school, when I went home to change my clothes before going over to Annmarie's, my youngest sister, Anna, asked if she could come with me. I was eight years old and Anna was five. I said yes, and off we went. I forgot to tell anyone I was taking Anna with me. When I realized, I reasoned that, ordinarily, I never told them I was leaving, so why did I have to tell them I was taking Anna? This was a big, big, mistake.

At Annmarie's, we had fun. We played pin the tail on the donkey; Annmarie helped Anna turn around, but not too fast, so Anna didn't get dizzy. Then we all decided to get some ice cream and pretzels. This was fantastic— I could never do it at my house because it would be too close to suppertime. But here, there was no one to see us—it was great!

After our snack, Annmarie's dad came in and told us that Anna and I needed to go home. It was dark outside, he said, and my mom would probably be worried about the two of us. So we said goodbye.

Off we go on our long walk home—it's about five blocks long. We go straight down 58th Street past Springfield Avenue. It's dark and cold out tonight and I can tell by the lessening traffic that it's after dinnertime. This is a problem: In my house you'd better not be late for dinner or come home after dark. So I've already broken three rules of our home—those two and the one about not taking the little ones out without telling anyone. I'm in trouble now.

We're walking on our street, about ten houses away from ours. I see Carmella and John running toward us. They're yelling at me, saying Mom is going to kill me. I took her baby with me and never told her. "What is wrong with you, Josephine?" they say. "Don't you care? Mom is really upset with you—she's crying." There was more—my older sisters and brothers were also going to kill me for this one.

But I'm thinking to myself, "Who cares?—just kill me. Because I am going back to Annmarie's tomorrow; I just won't take Anna with me." Yes, that's what I will tell my mom—don't worry, I won't take your baby again—anywhere. That's my plan about how I'll avoid getting into trouble.

I go inside, straight to the kitchen where the entire family is waiting for me and Anna. My mom grabs Anna and kisses her all over her face. I know I am dead—for now. So I keep quiet and let this battle start and just take the blows. Because ... well ... I am wrong ... but I did what I did. I'm thinking, stupid!—why did you take Anna with you? Next time, leave the baby home! Spare yourself the trouble, and you won't get *into* trouble.

My mom and sisters tell me to stop going over to Annmarie's house. They instruct me to come straight home from school and play here.

The next day, straight from school, I go over to Annmarie's. She tells me she wants to show me some books in her parents' room. I am leery because I've never gone into her parents' room. It always seemed like a room I shouldn't be in. But she says, "Come on—I'll just show you something, and then we can go to my room."

She goes to the side of the bed where her dad sleeps. She goes under the bed and comes out with some magazines in her hands. Laughing, she says come over here and look at this. So she hands me one of the magazines ... I open it ... and there are naked men! I've never seen a naked man before, so I am amazed. I'm going through the magazine ... and now it's men and women. And they're having sex. Now Annmarie is explaining everything to me. We're laughing so much my side is hurting me.

I tell Annmarie I never knew how sex was done. This is something else! She makes me promise never to tell anyone we were looking at these things. So I promise, but I know I have to tell my older sisters. Just in case they don't know about sex, I need to let them know about these magazines. The only time I saw a naked man was in the medical book we have. But it certainly doesn't show you people having sex. It doesn't scare me, but I wonder—who came up with that? Who wants to have sex like that? My mom and dad? No way! It's too strange for me to understand—I am only eight years old. Why did Annmarie show me her dad's magazines? Why does he have them? Why don't we have anything like that? I plan to stay away from Annmarie's dad. He's weird!

I can't wait to get out of Annmarie's parents' bedroom. I tell her I have to get home. I get home and run upstairs to my sister Rosemarie's room. She's in there brushing her long hair—she does that every day—one hundred strokes. Roe can tell I am up to something. She tells me to come sit next to her on her bed. So I do, and before I know it I'm telling her about the sex magazines. Now Roe is starting to get upset with me. She's only 13 years old, so does she know about sex? Has she seen the pictures?

Rosemarie tells me to stay in her room and she'll be right back. She goes downstairs, and while I'm waiting for her to come back I'm starting to worry that maybe I shouldn't have told her anything. So now what to do?

I hear my mom calling upstairs for me to come down to the kitchen. That means only one thing—Roe told Mom on me about the sex magazines. I go downstairs, and as I walk toward the kitchen I hear Mom, Roe, and Christine talking about the magazines. I walk into the kitchen, and Mom points to a chair next to Roe. "Sit."

I look at Roe but she won't look at me. She's looking at Mom, who seems to want to do more to me than just kill. Again, I am dead. This was a big mistake. "Dear God," I say, "would you help me get out of this mess? I'll pray more, if you help me. I promise—at least for today."

All three of them start with the interrogation about what I knew about sex. NOT A THING. But they won't believe me. They seem a little happier when I tell them that I am never going to do that. EVER. Then, they all smile at me and tell me to stay away from Annmarie. She's a bad influence.

I don't say anything, but I'm thinking, "Are you kidding? I have a great time with her—she's my best friend. She's teaching me about life!" My family didn't understand my friendship and love for Annmarie. They didn't get that she was practically a sister to me—we just didn't have the same blood in our veins.

I did stay away from Annmarie for a couple of days, until things at my house cooled down. But before we could get back together, something went wrong, and it was terrible for me.

Annmarie came to me at school and asked if she and another girl could walk home with me. I pointed out that she and the other girl lived in the opposite direction, but I said that if they wanted to walk with me that would be fun. So after school the three of us met in the schoolyard. We started to walk down Kingsessing Avenue toward 58th Street. We all laughed and talked until we got to 57th Street, near the drugstore. And then—boom!—they both started to pull my hair and shove me back and forth from one to the other. At first I was shocked that Annmarie would attack me, but after a few seconds I absorbed the fact and started to defend myself. I started to push back at them and pull their hair.

Between pushes, I asked Annmarie, "Why are you doing this to me? Why are you beating me up?" But she never said why. She said nothing, and I had to think of a way out of this. About 25 feet away, on the side of the drugstore, was a phone booth. I thought that if I could make it to the phone booth, I might have a chance. I managed to run there, get inside the booth, and close the door against them. I braced myself up against the inside wall with my back and put my two feet against the bottom of the door.

They kept pushing the door, but I wouldn't let my body get relaxed in any way. Finally, a man came walking by and told them to leave me alone and go home. They started to run down 57th Street, and once they disappeared, I walked home. As I walked, I had only one question: Why?

I didn't tell anyone what had happened because I was embarrassed that my best friend—a friend I had loved as a sister—had turned on me. I was crushed. I decided to cut Annmarie out of my life—I would have nothing to do with her—was finished with her forever. As for the other girl, I never had anything to do with her before or after.

The next day at school, Annmarie and I didn't talk. She never came to me to apologize or explain, and I never had words with her again. By the end of third grade she was gone—she had transferred to another school.

Another girl took her place in my heart. Patty had come to my school in the middle of third grade, and she and I stayed friends for many years during our school years. Patty and I had a great friendship.

But it took me some time to get over the loss of my first true friend. In fact, I actually do still love Annmarie and will always cherish our friendship. At one time, she meant the world to me.

Friends Behind Fences

My city block, on 58th Street near Kingessing Avenue, had 30 row homes. If I looked out the window of our house, I could see the home for old ladies across the street, a big, stone mansion that took up an entire block. Close by, on 58th between Kingessing and Chester Avenues, were two very large orphanages surrounded by cyclone fences, though only one was in use.

If I and my friends went onto these properties—and we went often—we had lots of room to play. The old ladies loved having us to talk to, and the orphanage kids loved playing with us. We weren't really allowed on either of these properties, so we would sneak past the guard at the old ladies' home and past the counselors at the orphanage and hope that no one would see us. It was fun to see if we could get away with trespassing again and again.

At times, the guard at the old ladies' home would run after us, yelling that if he caught us he would lock us up and call the police. We would yell back to him, "Catch us if you can!" He was big and fat, and we knew he couldn't catch us even if we walked.

It was different at the orphanage because there were a bunch of lady counselors there watching everything. Many times, as soon as we would get inside the grounds, we would immediately get chased out onto the street. I would say, "I don't care. I'm coming back tomorrow." We would go back the next day and try to get in again. It was fun.

One day after school, I and a few of my girlfriends went over to the orphanage to play with our friends there. We snuck in the gate and were running around on the grounds, playing on the swings, talking and laughing and chasing each other. Then, from behind the large, brick building, at least four meanlooking ladies emerged. We were frightened and we all started to run, even the orphans. The orphanage was a city block long, so we had a lot of running to do to get to the front gate. We were running and screaming because we were scared but also because being chased was exciting. The counselor ladies really wanted to get us because we were coming onto their grounds all the time and this was driving them crazy.

We all made it to the front gate, even the orphans. In the past, we had asked the orphans to come outside the gate with us, but they never would, telling us they would get into trouble if they did. But this time was different. Today they were staying with us. We were all good friends now, and they trusted us. They knew we girls liked them and that we would never hurt them in any way.

So there we all were on the sidewalk, outside the front gate, talking and laughing about how we had just gotten away. The counselors were yelling at us that we were in big trouble. If my mom had been saying that, I would have been scared, but their threats didn't faze me. Good luck, ladies, I thought. First you have to catch me.

It was a beautiful warm day in the fall. The sun was strong and the leaves were turning colors. It was just a great day for friends and playing—that's how free we felt. Not so for our friends who lived in an orphanage with a fence around the entire block. There was no way to enter or leave except through the front gate. (Of course, if my brother John had wanted to get in, there would have been no stopping him. He could climb anything anywhere!)

We were all talking and laughing, unafraid of the counselor ladies, who weren't venturing outside the fence to confront us. They simply stood inside the fence and told the orphan children to get back in. But the children didn't listen. Instead, they asked us many questions about our lives and families. They had questions and so did we. We all just talked and talked and talked.

I fell in love with those children right there. They had such sad lives, and yet they were so interested in us. They wanted to know if we all were fine and happy, and they really seemed to care. I guess if I had ever wanted to run away, it would have been with them. They took good care of each other, and they weren't even blood relatives. Still they were family, just like me and my family, there to help and care for one another.

At one point I talked to one little girl, who was about my age, eight or nine, with big, bald spots all over her head. I asked her what that was all about. She was so cute and shy, with big, blue eyes, really white skin, and blonde hair, the 50 percent that was left on her head. She spoke softly and had a sweet way about her. She was my favorite of these children.

She told us that whenever she got upset and really nervous, she pulled her hair out. She said she felt better after doing that. I was thinking there was no way I would ever pull my hair out of my head. This kid must have been nuts or something. But I didn't care if she was. I loved her anyway. I knew that if it ever came to it, I would help her, and she would help me. She was my new friend.

But now something was happening—the counselors were telling us they were going to call the police. Well, what does a city girl do when she hears the words, "I'm going to call the police?" She runs!

We said quick goodbyes to the orphans and that we would see each other soon. We told them we hoped they wouldn't get into too much trouble because of us. They didn't seem to mind if they did or didn't.

I ran across the street to my house to tell my mom about this. There were two reasons why. One, if the cops came to our house, it would be better if she knew now what I had done; and two, I just had to tell my mom about my new blonde-haired friend.

I ran through the living room to get to the kitchen and report my news. I was nervous, but not too much. Mom was cooking chicken cutlets, mashed potatoes, and corn. I was so hungry. But first things first. I started by saying, "Mom, you know the orphanage across the street?" She looked at me with a big question mark on her face. I started to laugh and tell her I had friends that lived over there.

She said, "When did you go over there?" "Today." She stepped toward me and asked, "When today? Josephine, you'd better stay away from there. You know they don't want you kids in there."

"So what, Mom," I said. "Who cares what they want? The kids there like us, and we like them. Mommy, they are just like us, right? Everyone is equal, no different than anyone else. That's what you always tell us."

Mom looked like she wanted to hit me on the side of my head. "They will call the police on you. You will get in trouble."

"But Mom," I said, "you tell us you don't like the cops, so who cares? Let them come to our house. You'll take care of that."

"Listen to me. Stay away from those kids and those grounds. I won't tell you again, Josephine. Now that's the end of it."

If you want my mom on your side, just give her a story of injustice. Knowing that, I said, "Wait, Mom—I wanna tell you about my new girlfriend from over there. She has blonde hair, blue eyes, and white skin. But, Mom, she has really big bald spots all over her head because she pulls her hair out all the time. She talks real low, like she doesn't want you to hear her at all." I knew that when I told my mom about my friend, she would fall in love with her also. Her heart would open to her and the others. And you could see that it was happening—my mom was getting upset about the kids over there. She wanted to cry but didn't want me to see it.

"Alright, go get your sisters and brothers. It's time for dinner."

We were sitting at our two kitchen tables eating dinner and everything was nice. We were laughing, talking, and some of us were yelling out jokes. I started telling the family about my day across the street, and soon I had the entire family in an uproar about the orphanage. We were voting on whether I should go over there anymore or stay away. Of course, going over there won out. I knew it would because the twelve of us could have been living in an orphanage ourselves after our dad's death. I had this fight in my pocket twelve-to-one because we knew that without Mom we could have been living across the street, too.

But now, how do I convince my mom on this matter? I was looking at Mom and waiting to hear what she thought I should do. Finally, she told me, "You can go over there and play with your friends whenever you like. But if the counselors tell you to leave, you must come home. Do you promise me that you will do that?"

"Yes, I will do that, Mom."

I believe the reason I was able to go there and never get in trouble with my mom was that there were kids out in the world worse off than us. I had a mom and eleven siblings to live with. Those kids lived in a dormitory with different kids all the time. I couldn't imagine going to bed and not being able to kiss my mother good-night.

Whenever we kids went over to play with our friends, we always had a good time. At times, we were still chased, but that was alright. As long as Mom knew about it, everything was fine.

That is, until one day when four of us girls walked across the street toward the front gate and there was a big lock on it. We could no longer get inside to play with our friends. We talked with them through the cyclone fence a few times. Shortly after that, we found the place empty. We didn't know what happened, but everyone was gone.

The building remained empty for a long time. At times, I would walk by and look inside and wonder whatever happened to my blonde-haired, blue-eyed friend. And I wondered what had happened to the other children who passed through those gates. I hoped they were all doing okay. And I hoped that my blonde-haired friend stopped pulling out her hair. Maybe she eventually found some peace … maybe even happiness.

Mom's Way

It was a Saturday morning in September 1959, when my sister Gracie, who was then 21, first met her husband-to-be, Carmen. We were waiting for Patrick to come home from work; he was working the overnight shift, so when he got home he'd be bringing a dozen hot, long Italian rolls. We could have them for breakfast with lots of butter, and some hot chocolate.

Pat worked at Mattero's Bakery, not too far from our house, in a section of Southwest Philly called Little Italy. He'd been working overtime because two of the guys at Mattero's had gotten into a fistfight over who could make better rolls. When the boss heard the commotion, he tried to stop the fight. But one of the guys threw a punch and hit the boss in the mouth, so that was the end of those two workers.

Pat took up the slack and was happy to be making the extra money. He liked buying clothes, and always looking nice and neat. He would ask me to press his pants, which I was happy to do because he paid me a nickel and then I could buy a Hershey's chocolate bar. They were the best!

This Saturday morning, Pat's friend from work, Carmen, drove him home. Pat was tired, and it would have been a long walk home. When Carmen brought Pat straight to the front door, he was watching as Pat ring the bell to our house. He was watching as Grace opened the door and, well, it was love at first sight for Carmen. And he seemed a perfect match for our family—he was Italian, his dad was dead, his mom worked, and he had one sister. He'd fit right in!

That night at work, Carmen told Pat that he was interested in Grace and that he thought she was beautiful. He wanted Pat to help him get a date with Grace, and Pat did just that. Then, before the family knew what was happening, Carmen proposed to Grace. Her reply: "Yes, yes, I will marry you!" Grace couldn't wait to start a family of her own. And—it was wonderful—after only six months of knowing Carmen—true love!

Grace's plan was to save money to pay for the wedding. They wanted an engagement party and a nice wedding with friends and family—and ours was a large one. Mom's reaction to Grace's announcement was one of happiness, but also of concern. Mom decided to sit Carmen and Grace down to discuss how they were going to manage. But what we did not know was that Carmen wanted my mom to pay for the wedding. And that idea was nuts—because where would my mom get the money? Would she rob a bank? Not feed us for a year?

Mom was talking with Carmen and Grace, questioning Carmen on his finances, on how they would pay for everything, and on how they would carry on after the wedding. All was fine until Mom asked Carmen to please bring his bankbook over to the house. She wanted to see what he was worth. She put it in the only way she knew how: "I don't believe you. I want to see the bankbook tomorrow to see what you have."

Oh boy, we knew that was going to start a war with Carmen because he was a momma's boy and no other woman was going to speak to him like that. The war did, in fact, begin.

I remember being in the kitchen and my mom being downstairs in the basement. In came Grace and Carmen, and he was mad as hell. Both of them marched down to the basement and it started. You could hear some words, but Carmen was yelling so loudly I couldn't really hear what my mom was saying.

We four young girls are sitting at the kitchen table. We don't know if we should run, so we sit real still and just listen to the fight. After the battle, Grace and Carmen come upstairs and walk right through the house and out the front door. Boy, you can hear that front door slam!

Mom is still downstairs fighting, but with whom is she fighting? I eventually realize she's by herself down there, still very upset. You can hear her saying, "I don't have the money. I have all these kids to take care of." Now she's crying and saying, "You're a bitch!" Hold on. My mom doesn't curse. So when you hear her say "bitch," you better run because that's when she's had enough. She's done with Carmen and Grace, with trying to figure out what she can give them.

We hear her walking up the wooden stairs. She's breathing real hard. None of us girls can say a word—we are all shocked at what happened down in the basement. Where are the boys when you need them? We girls could use the help.

But Mom's in the kitchen trying to act like nothing just happened. So, who other than Antoinette to say, "So what did Carmen want from you, Mom? And did Grace stand up for you against him?" Those are two really good questions that we all want answers to, but Mom looks exhausted.

Into the kitchen comes Christine. Antoinette fills her in quickly, telling her that Carmen and Grace just had a big fight with Mom, and Mom was crying and cursing in the basement.

Chris wants to kill, and we are all behind her on this one. "What the hell did he want from you?" Chris asks. Mom's trying not to get Chris upset. But Chris says, "Okay—I'm gonna call Ralph and tell him Carmen has you crying." As Chris goes into the dining room to grab the phone, you can hear Mom crying.

Mom eventually explains a little more. "Carmen wants me to get a second mortgage on the house to pay for their wedding because traditionally the bride's family pays. But I told Carmen I don't have any way to pay back the loan. Carmen told me he didn't care if I paid back the loan or not—that was my problem, not his. He wants a big, fancy wedding—on me. But I can't do this. What is wrong with them? Can't they see how I struggle every day to have food, heat, and water in this house? I still have nine kids to feed. I don't have the money for their wedding or anyone else's."

Chris is telling Mom, "Who cares what he has to say? What about Grace? Isn't she one of us?" Mom pleads with Chris to be quiet and just let it rest because she's not paying for the wedding and that's that.

It took some time for this to settle down in our house, and eventually the bridal couple did end up paying for their own wedding. But that wasn't the only time Carmen tried to push my mom around. Luckily for him, Mom wasn't the type to hold a grudge. She just knew who and what you were—she never spoke a word about it but she did keep an eye and ear in your direction at all times. She was like a cat in that way.

I have to mention that there were good times too with Carmen and Grace. When we kids were still little, they would take us over to New Jersey to Holiday Lake, a summertime swimming and picnicking spot. They'd also take us to drive-in movies. One movie they took us to on a Saturday night was quite interesting. On Sunday morning, we dummies asked Mom, "Did you know that girls kiss in the movies?" Mom gave us such a strange look and asked us to tell her about the movie, so we did.

We never got to see girls kissing again like that, although we still got to go to the 61st Street drive-in movies when the boys came with us. They got into the trunk of the car so we wouldn't have to pay for them. When we parked the car, Carmen or Pat would let them out of the trunk. It was great fun watching my brothers climb out of the trunk. That lasted for a couple of years until the entrance attendant caught on and would walk behind the cars to see if anyone was in the trunks. So that was the end of free movies for the boys. We started to go on Tuesday nights, when it was $2.00 a carload. There would often be six or more of us in a car.

We did the same thing at Holiday Lake. Carmen would find an isolated road and pull his car over. The boys would then jump into the trunk. We would drive onto the grounds of the lake, and as soon as Carmen parked, the boys would yell, "Let us out! It's so hot in here!" Some days, it could be 90 degrees outside, and I can't imagine what temperature it reached inside the trunk. We did that for years and never got caught. These were the fun times as a kid with our older brothers and sisters and their sweethearts.

On other occasions, Carmen really put distrust in my heart toward him. For one thing, he had a tendency to gamble their money away. At one point early on, Gracie packed up and came to live at home with us, although she did go back to him.

Another time, Grace and Carmen had me over for dinner at their apartment on Woodland Avenue, not far from our house. They were cooking a really good dinner together and I was sitting at the table waiting for it to be done. Carmen liked to cook and bake and he was good at both, maybe even better at these skills than Grace.

All of a sudden, Carmen is yelling at Grace, and you can see fear on her face. He's telling her that the money they are getting back from the income tax is all theirs, while Grace is trying to explain that a portion of it goes to Mom. But Carmen won't allow Grace to give Mom any of the money.

Grace is telling Carmen to please keep quiet and let her explain how this works for all of us. "The two of us put a couple of the kids on our tax return, meaning that they are our dependents, so we can collect some money back. Whatever money we get for my siblings goes to my mom. She needs the money to help my family." Carmen is so mad that he is screaming at Grace. When he does that, it scares me.

Grace is looking at me. She knows he frightens me, but she can't control him when he acts like a madman. The only thing she can do is try to talk low and sweetly to him. This time, it works, and he calms down. Grace tells Carmen that it's time for dinner, and they will talk about the IRS check later.

I couldn't wait to go home and tell my mom about the fight they had over my mom getting money for us. When I got home that night, I ran into the house, calling, "Mom, where are you?"

She rushed into the dining room. "Josephine, why are you so loud?"

I blurted out the news about Carmen and Grace fighting over the money, but my mom told me not to worry about Carmen. We all know he has a temper, she explained. "So, tell me again what was said by Carmen and your sister." After I told Mom everything I could remember about their fight, she laughed.

I said, "Mom, what's so funny about Carmen trying to keep your money? He was acting like a crazy man. Gracie was really scared, and so was I."

Soon everyone in the house was in the dining room with us. Mom told all of us that there was no way Carmen would keep her money. "He can talk to your sister like that, but as for me, I won't take that from him. After what he put me through—all that crap about a second mortgage—he won't get to me ever again. It will be a cold day in hell if I don't get all my money."

Mom never spoke to Carmen about the money. She did talk to Grace, telling her that when she got the check, Mom would be expecting her money. When Gracie received the check, she came over with Mom's portion. We never spoke of that, or the outburst of rage from Carmen, or his attempts to push Mom around. She never did cave in to his demands, or anyone else's for that matter. My mom always carried out what she felt was the correct way to handle a situation. I call it Mom's way.

Three Down, Nine to Go!

Our family is up early this beautiful Saturday morning in September. Grace is marrying Carmen today! Grace is the third sibling to marry and leave us. First, it was Ralph, who married Lee, then Trudy, who married Patrick. All the weddings were in September, when it was still warm and sunny, just as we were going back to school.

The house is clean and decorated with white bells and streamers everywhere, even on the chandelier and down the railing of the living room stairs. At the bottom of the railing hangs a huge white bell covered with silver glitter. The front door is adorned with white and purple flowers and greenery all over. The inside of the house is newly painted, and the living room and dining room have wallpaper with big flowers. It looks like a princess is getting married here. For today, our house is beautiful and filled with joy.

All of us are really happy for Grace. She is 21 years old, the age Mom wants us girls to marry. Mom thinks what girls should do is get married and have babies—lots of them—and she thinks 21 or 22 is the right time to get started. Grace wants to have babies as soon as she can, and I know she will be a good mom because she is gentle when she talks to us and never yells or hits us. She understands us younger kids.

What pressure my mom put on us girls! The way I look at it at age ten and a half, all my older sisters and brothers can marry. I just want a lot of nieces and nephews to babysit and play with. I am already an aunt to Mona and

Michael, who are so cute, I just love them to pieces. But don't wait for me to have babies. I only want one kid, and that's if I have to have any at all. Actually, the thought of having babies makes me sick. I know how you make babies. Who came up with that idea?

Carmella and I are talking about Grace and Carmen making babies. We can't believe they would do it. We wonder, how many times do you do it to make a baby? Carmella says to me, "Let's go ask Mom." I always follow my older sister's lead, so into the kitchen we head, looking for Mom, who is going crazy with all she has to do, which includes cooking eggs and bacon for us. We go over to the stove, and we watch Mom turn the bacon. She's telling us to get something to eat because today is a really busy day for our family. Carmella says to me, "Go ahead, Josephine, ask her now."

Mom looks at me and says, "Ask me what?"

I am really nervous because I have never asked questions about sex before. Well, here goes. "Mom, how many times did you and Dad have sex?"

Her expression doesn't change, as she looks into my eyes and says, "How many kids did we have?"

Carmella and I look at her and then at each other with an expression that says, "WHAT?" Before we can say anything else, Christine grabs us and says to get something to eat now. Then she bends over and whispers to us so Mom can't hear, "Are you two stupid or what? Don't ever ask Mom that question again."

"But, Chris," Carmella says, "you know Mom and Dad had sex more than 12 times."

Christine repeats, "Are you stupid? Just eat your breakfast so we can get dressed and ready for Grace's day."

Grace comes into the kitchen to tell us that everyone is coming back to our house after the ceremony for lunch and refreshments, like Mom's home-made eggplant parmesan, meatballs, and sausage and peppers. There will be beer, wine, and anisette liquor. We always have wine with Sunday dinner and anisette on special days like Thanksgiving or Christmas or a wedding. Everyone looks forward to those treats.

Grace is so nervous she can't eat her breakfast. She likes her coffee and has three cups in a couple of minutes. "Slow down," Mom tells her, "or you'll be nervous all day. Just calm yourself down, and no more coffee."

Now we must all get dressed and be on our best behavior or Mom and the older siblings will kill us. We'd better be good and proper. Our brothers are teasing us girls and saying that they will drink and do whatever they want because Mom will be too busy to have her eyes on them this day and night. My brothers are in their teens now, so they think they're big deals. We girls tell the boys they are jerks, with Christine topping that with some more choice insults. We love it when Christine insults the boys! That's because not one of them will mess with her. She goes on for another minute, telling our brothers they better not tease their sisters. Antoinette and Anna are sticking their tongues out at them. Those two little ones are funny and silly. How could the boys beat them up? It would never happen—we wouldn't let them get away with that. Besides, they'd look like sissies if they hurt the babies. We still call the last two babies, even though they are now seven and nearly nine years old.

We warn the boys, "If you drink today, we'll tell on you." They just laugh at our threats and couldn't care less about what we're saying. They would never hurt us girls. So, sometimes we push them over the edge for the fun of seeing them get mad.

I ask my brothers, "Can I hang out with you guys today?" They generally think I'm a pain, but sometimes I get them to give in to me. Not today, though. Pat, George, and John are laughing at me, and George tells me to get lost in the crowd. Now I'm crying and telling George I'm going to tell Mom that he's planning to be with "those girls" at the wedding.

"And when you go to the reception tonight, you're going to get those girls drunk," I say.

Patrick comes over to me. "Come on, Josephine," Patrick says, "let us brothers have some fun." As usual, when Pat tells me something, I just listen. I don't ever give him or Ralph a hard time because these two oldest brothers stand in for my dad. George and John, though, are another story. They're always doing something wrong, and most times, my mom doesn't have a clue. These two get on my nerves, but I'll keep my mouth shut, and hopefully, it will be a peaceful day for Grace and Carmen.

Mom's yelling at us kids, telling us we better all be dressed in the new outfits that she, Grace, and Christine have bought for us. Each one of us has a new dress or suit for today so that we'll look really good for our big sister's wedding.

81

Pat, my brother-in-law, is going to drive us four youngest girls to the church. He's telling us how pretty we all look. Antoinette says she hopes there are cute boys at the reception. You never know, though, if Antoinette wants to kiss them or beat them up, so Pat tells her to be kind to the boys and not scare them away.

We are on our way to the church for the wedding. Oh, you should see the church with all the flowers at the altar, the stained glass windows, and the marble—it's beautiful! The Most Blessed Sacrament parish is one of the wealthiest in the nation, not because the people are rich, but because it has over 4000 parishioners. The church has two floors, with mass going on upstairs and down. Mass starts at six Sunday morning and goes on until noon. A lot of people give their money to the church.

Here comes the entire Pasquarello family marching to the pews. On the right side of the church is Carmen's family. On the left side is ours. People sit real close to one another, filling every available space. It's fun to watch all of my family, and, like my Mom, today I am truly happy to see them—uncles, aunts, and cousins—almost 100 in all—all here to celebrate with us.

Here comes my mom with my brother Patrick. He's so cute with his jet black hair and his pretty-boy smile. The Irish girls love my brothers a lot. They're always knocking on our door looking for one of them. To tell the truth, I find the girls stupid and annoying. But I can see why they are after my brothers, who are good-looking and fun.

Oh boy, my mom looks stunning walking arm-in-arm with Patrick, her head held high. Mom looks like a movie star; she is sparkling. Her dress is lavender with lots of clear beads on the bodice, and she has a hat to match the dress, made by Connie, a lady from South America. She carries a small purse containing a lipstick tube and a tissue. That's all she ever carries. If she has any money, she carries that inside her bra because she worries that someone will steal her purse.

Mom is amazing—she does not seem tired from cooking all her special dishes for today's party. She hasn't stopped working all week, although we all did help her with cleaning the house. But I know my mother won't stop working today until everyone leaves the reception hall tonight.

Now Patrick walks Mom over to the first pew so she can sit in the front to watch Grace marry Carmen. Her face shows happiness at Grace having found her true love, but at the same time, there's sadness showing, because Grace does not have her dad here.

Now comes the bridal party. This includes my sisters Trudy and Christine, who wear deep purple dresses with big flowers on the left side of the waist. Trudy and Christine are so pretty with their dark hair and red lips, and they have lots of black eyeliner on to make their big eyes even bigger. Trudy is beautifully rounded; this is partly because she has been breastfeeding her daughter Mona, my darling four-month-old niece. Christine is tall and thin, with long, black, straight hair. The boys like Christine and she really likes the boys. There is always some boy at our front door looking for her.

Here comes Grace now, with Ralph, walking toward us. Grace looks beautiful and she can't get that smile to settle down. Oh, she is so happy, and I am happy for her. Her dress is white with little pearls everywhere. Her arms show through see-through sleeves, also with pearls. And the skirt is so full she needs two crinolines under it.

Carmen is watching her walk toward him, and you can see he's over the moon. Ralph gives Grace's hand to Carmen, and Carmen takes her to the altar. Grace cries; you can see it in her shoulders. This gets all of us girls going— one cries, then we all cry.

When the ceremony is over, and Carmen and Grace walk out of the church, we all throw rice. We're laughing and talking to them and calling Grace, "Mrs. Carmen Castalino." The bridal party goes to Cobbs Creek Parkway for photos. Mom's telling everyone to come to our house for food and wine. It's going to be loud and fun with lots of laughs, the kind of party we Italians love. What I want is some wine. I'll get one of my brothers to give me some, and not just a little like we get on Sunday.

There are about 75 people at our house for the festivities. They are talking, laughing, and telling funny stories about my dad's family. On this great day, it's sheer happiness. Everyone seems to be enjoying the food. The house smells so good from the meatballs and gravy. And my God—those cookie trays are huge! They're filled with Italian cookies from Termini's Bakery— the best.

Now I go after my brothers, who are drinking with those girls. If they are drinking, then so can I. I know my brothers are going to kill me tomorrow, but today, I don't care. So, I tell them I want some liquor. "If you don't give me some, I will rat you out," I tell them, though I would never do that. I just want to drink with them because they always seem to be having fun.

To get me off their backs, they ask if I would like to smoke a cigarette. "Oh, yes, of course I would, with the three of you."

"Sure, come with us down the alley," John says. I follow the three of them and Pat lights a Winston. "Now inhale and blow out the smoke." We pass it around a few times, and I feel a little sick in my head and my stomach. They are laughing at me and take me home.

We come in the back door, and Mom asks me, "Where were you?" Pat tells Mom they caught me smoking a cigarette in the alley.

I can't believe what he told her—he dimed me out! Mom tells me to wash my mouth. She says she will get me tomorrow (although that never happened). My brothers are laughing at me and running through the kitchen to get to those girls. I still don't know who "those girls" are, whether they are friends or family.

We are getting ready to go to the reception. It's in a big place with lots of people I don't know, so I stick with my sisters. Us Pasquarellos are there to party, and that's just what we do. What a great time we have, with music and dancing going on all night. I dance most of the time, in between getting food and wine. I never do get any liquor, thanks to my brothers.

Between our house party and the reception, we eat a lot of food. We have salad, ravioli, veal, and lots of Italian bread. When it's time for Grace and Carmen to cut the wedding cake, everyone is excited, not only to watch them cut their Italian rum cake, but to eat a big slice. It's the best cake ever, with vanilla and chocolate custard. That's the cake my dad got for us on our birthdays. I always had to share my March birthday cake with Anna. In fact, we all shared a birthday month with another sibling, so we all had to share our cake. But it was fun.

It's time for us to go home and watch Grace pack for her honeymoon. They are going to Niagara Falls for a week. I know when she comes back she'll have small gifts for us, and chocolates. She thinks of us, and we will all miss her.

Mom and Grace are hugging each other goodbye and crying again. Carmen has no patience for that kind of stuff and says, "Let's go now." Mom gives him the evil eye, but doesn't let him see her doing it. She wants a few more moments with her daughter before letting go of her.

Carmen doesn't understand what my mom is feeling now. Only we girls know, and we don't want Grace to go either. There are only nine of us here with Mom now. It's sad to see our siblings get married and leave; our family is dwindling. Who will be next to leave? I don't want anyone else to go, but I know as we get older we all will. When I get older I will leave and live my life too, but it may not be in a marriage. When I am ready, I will go and take on the world. I will try really hard not to break my mom's heart when I leave. On the one hand, she'll be happy for me, and on the other, she will be sad. She will eventually have to let go of all of us. That will be twelve aches in her heart, but it also will be twelve most happy events. Mom will gain many grandchildren from these transitions. She will witness her family growing every year. Mom has much to be happy for. Deep inside, she is thankful for her life and ours. She will celebrate with us, and for us.

She will wake up tomorrow and start all over again. Let no one or anything stand in her way. She is plugged into her God's ear and speaks to Him often. She knows in her soul that she will watch us grow and marry because she knows He will answer her prayers. She is doing on earth what He sent her down here for.

• • •

Oh, one more thing. "Those girls" turned out to be cousins, and George got caught making out with one of them. She was a first cousin, and my mom wanted to kill him. We sisters laughed when she yelled at him. "Of all the girls," she said, "you had to go after your first cousin?!" We all teased George for a very long time.

Whatever It Takes

I am so embarrassed. It's my turn to go over to the convent tonight. I hope Sister Cecilia doesn't answer the door. She's my third grade teacher over at the Most Blessed Sacrament School.

My hands are sweaty from nervousness. But I ring the doorbell anyway, and who answers the door? Sister Cecilia! The stern expression on her face is enough to make me turn and run. But I'm not going to allow her authority to scare me away. It's always like this—if I want the food I have to pretend I'm not affected. Usually it's two of us who go over to the convent. But tonight no one else was home to walk over with me. I am by myself and I certainly do feel alone. Why do I have to do this?

Sister looks down at me and says, "So you're here for food again."

I am so shaken that I could throw up—my stomach is jumping up and down. I want to get away as fast as I can. But also, I am thinking to myself about what I would ideally like to say to Sister: "Take your food and stick it!" Of course if I said that I would only feel worse than I already do, plus my mom would kill me.

So I reply to Sister only after she shuts the door in my face as she goes inside to get the food for my family: *Oh no, we don't need any food or help from the church. We like to go to bed hungry and wake up hungry.* I know I must keep my thoughts about this situation to myself. As a matter of fact, I keep all my thoughts about life to myself. That's what happens when your family carries

87

the suicide stigma. My shame as a result of my father's actions causes me to want to protect myself from the world, because no one can understand why he did what he did.

Inside my head I go round and round with the same thought: I wish I wasn't here.

I wait for a long time before Sister Cecilia opens the door. She motions for me to come inside. As I walk over the threshold into the foyer, I can see the jars and cans of food. I bring the wire cart in with me—it's the shopping cart my mom uses for her everyday food shopping.

Sister tells me to be careful of the gallon glass jars. "If you drop one of them they will break." As I load the cart she advises me to put the cans on the bottom. I notice that she's given me two one-gallon glass jars of pickled beets—my favorite! Also two 48-ounce cans of baked beans. And four boxes of pasta. The cart is soon full with food.

I look at Sister as she brings the cart down the two steps out front. I have never been this close to her before, and I can see her beautiful blue eyes and the blond downy hair on the sides of her cheeks. Her habit covers her entire head, and I think—how can you stand that thing on your head all the time? I am also thinking that Sister Cecilia is pretty. And she's being really nice to me. She's helping out my family with this food. I see all of her for the first time. I think she knows I am fragile, and she only wants to help.

I turn to her as I wait for her to give me the food cart. She tells me to go straight home. "You know, Josephine," she says, "you should have had Carmella walk with you. Why did you come by yourself? I want you to get home before it gets dark."

I tell her Carmella's home doing the dinner dishes. I don't mind walking home by myself on this warm spring evening. It will give me time to think.

"I hope you did all your homework," Sister says. I smile but don't answer, because I can't stand doing my homework. I thank Sister for the food and for helping me get the cart on the ground. She says, "God bless you," and off I go for my walk home.

On my walk home the embarrassment returns. Mr. Bradley sees me and stops to ask, "Where did you get all that food?" I want to tell him it's none of his business, but, again, my mom would kill me if I spoke to a neighbor like that.

I can't tell him the truth because Mom always says, "What goes on in my house stays in here." Also: "Keep the outside world out there." So I smile at Mr. Bradley and keep on walking, hoping that I don't see anyone else I know.

I like to be by myself, and I like walking. It's quiet and I don't hear anything but my own thoughts. This state of affairs doesn't usually last long, so I must enjoy it whenever I can.

When I turn down 58th Street I can see my brother John. He's standing on our front steps talking with his friend Dick, our neighbor.

"I can't pull this cart anymore!" I yell to John. He yells back that he's coming to help me. He takes the cart from me and tells me I can't do anything right. He and Dick are laughing at me. I tell John I only weigh about sixty pounds and this cart must weigh a hundred. It's too heavy for me to pull.

"John, you should be the one going over to the convent to get the food," I say.

John laughs at me and says, "That's girls' work. Us boys don't do things like that."

Now, John and Dick are both calling me "Olive Oyl"—she's Popeye's love in the cartoon. We're all crazy about Popeye, and I actually like when they call me Olive Oyl. I think Olive is cute. I can't let them know that, though, because then they will switch to another nickname, and it won't be nice. That's just the way boys are—they're a pain, and worse when they are your brother. But I love my brother John and I like Dick, who is always nice to me—even nicer than John at times.

John tells me to go in the house and let Mom know I'm home. He and Dick will carry the cart into the house, because, he says, "you're too skinny to pull the cart up all the steps." I turn toward John as I run up the steps, calling him an asshole only as I reach the porch—so I can run inside and lock the door behind me if he tries to get me. I laugh at him. Sometimes I wish I could beat him up, but I could never really hurt him—I love him too much.

I walk into the dining room and Mom comes out from the kitchen. She has a big smile on her face and questions me about what food they gave us this time.

"Pickled beets and baked beans," I tell her, "but I don't know what else … Mom—open one of the jars of beets for me—I want some before I go to bed. I love the taste of the vinegar!"

Mom tells me I should just drink the jar of wine vinegar that's in our kitchen. I tell her I need some of those beets now.

Mom tells me to run bath water for me and Carmella—we both need a bath tonight. Then I can come down for some beets. "For being a big help and going over to the convent," she says. She smiles and kisses my check and gives me a hug. I love when Mom hugs and kisses me. That's her way of saying, "I love you." I know that in her eyes I did good today.

Carmella and I get ready for our bath. I have the bathtub half full with warm water, and there's Ivory soap. I get in and Carmella says, "Josephine, you have to wash my hair tonight. I was at Cobbs Creek today and fell in the water. My hair smells like dirt."

"Come on, Carmella, get in the water—I don't want to be in here all night," I say. She gets in the tub and the water is suddenly almost to the top of the tub lip. She tells me to turn off the water, and when I wash her hair I can turn it on again to rinse her head. When I start to wash Carmella's hair you can see the dirt coming out into the water. I call her a dirtball for playing in the creek water. Carmella laughs and says, "Not too loud—we don't want Mom to know what I did."

The water is turning brown from all the mud coming out of Carmella's hair. "I'm getting out of this tub," I say. "You can finish rinsing your own head. You stink like a dead fish!"

As I wrap myself in a towel, in walks Anna, who wants to brush her teeth at the sink. Antoinette's right behind her. Our bathroom is always busy—our big family only has one bath but luckily we girls have no problem sharing it at the same time; we are totally comfortable with one another.

Now Mom walks in, looks at Carmella, and asks her why she smells so bad. "Don't tell me you were at the creek today!" We three younger girls are laughing because we want to see what Carmella says to get out of this. Our mother thinks Carmella is such a good girl, but we know better. She's just a good liar.

Carmella tries to change the subject, asking me whether I went to the convent by myself. I don't want to answer because I'm eager for Mom to "get" Carmella for being down at the creek. After all, if that was me, Carmella would rat me out. I don't rat on anyone, but I won't help her out of this. When I don't answer, Carmella turns toward Mom and asks, "Mom, how did you ever get the nuns to give us food?"

The bathroom gets instantly quiet. We girls are all looking at Mom. We want to know how she got the Immaculate Heart of Mary nuns—the nuns known for being strict disciplinarians—to help us out. I am thinking that my mom is not afraid of anyone. I wish I was more like her. She just does what needs to be done and doesn't care what anyone thinks of her. She does whatever it takes.

Mom closes the toilet seat cover, sits down on it, and begins to tell the story. She tells us that she went over to see the school principal, Sister Alphonsus. I'm wondering—she went to see the principal? When? But Carmella beats me to the punch with the same question.

"About the beginning of January," Mom says.

"Come on, Mom, what did you say to that wacky nun?" That's my sweet sister Antoinette saying it just like it is. She has such a way with words.

Antoinette is at the sink; Carmella's getting out of the bath. I'm getting ready to wash the tub because Anna and Antoinette have to get their bath now. I love the way we girls in our family are so comfortable with one another. We have a bond no one can break, and we can feel it.

Mom continues with her story. She stopped at school one day and asked at the main desk to see the principal. Sister Regina Patricia, who was at the front desk, asked Mom if she had an appointment. Mom said no, she didn't, but could the principal see her tomorrow if not today? Sister Regina told Mom there was a free slot available tomorrow at 10:00 in the morning.

So the next morning Mom came to school to have a talk with Sister Alphonsus. She arrived fifteen minutes before her appointed time, feeling quite nervous but at the same time hopeful that there would be help given to our family.

When Sister Alphonsus came out to greet Mom, my mother sensed instantly that the meeting might not go well. Sister's face was stone cold. But my mom decided she wasn't walking away empty-handed.

After Sister greeted her, she said, "Come with me, Mrs. Pasquarello," and led my mom into her office. She closed the door behind her.

"What can I do for you?" Sister asked. Mom asked Sister if she could sit down and have a little of her time. She had many troubles in her life right now, she said, and she could use some help from the church. Sister motioned for Mom to take a seat across from her. As Mom sat down, Sister inquired as to what the church could to for her.

Mom watched as Sister, sitting straight back in her chair, folded her hands on her desk. The nun held her head high as she looked at my mother through her eyeglasses. "Just like a statue!" Mom laughs, as she tells us the story. Mom says she couldn't believe how that nun was always so stiff.

Antoinette jumps in and says, "Sister walks around all the time like she has something in her butt!" We all burst out laughing, because Antoinette is so right.

Now Antoinette is asking Mom, "Why were you there?" and Carmella's getting mad at Antoinette for not following the story.

Carmella says to us three younger sisters, "If you can't keep up with the story, then go to bed. I want to hear what happened, so please shut up and listen."

Antoinette retorts, "Maybe you have something in your butt!"

I know Antoinette is going to go for Carmella's hair—you can tell by the way Antoinette is eyeing her. Carmella's hair is like a mop head, which is in fact what my brothers call her. She cries every time that they do. Now, if Antoinette gets her fingers around those hair strands, there's going to be some excitement! This is becoming fun to watch.

"Okay," Mom says to us girls, "no fighting tonight, or I won't tell you the rest of the story." So we all sit still and listen as Mom continues her story.

"Well, Sister, if you can help me out I would appreciate any kind of help," she said to the nun. "As you know, I have twelve children. My three oldest are married. When my children get out of school and find a job, they give me $20 a week for room and board. But now I don't get any money from the three oldest, which means I am down $60 a week. My fourth oldest is the only one helping out financially with the $20 a week. The problem is—I still have nine kids and myself to feed. I don't think with Social Security and $20 a week there will be enough to carry us through.

"Patrick is getting a job at the bakery," she continued, "but that won't start until summertime. From now until then I won't have enough food. If I could work outside the house, I would, but I can't. There would be no one home with the children. They need me around to watch over them, to make sure they are not bad kids. As much as possible, I need to be there to raise them properly."

Then Sister leaned toward Mom. Staring right at her, she said, "Well, Mrs. Pasquarello, what are you asking for from me? You know this is not a bank."

Antoinette interrupts. "That makes me sick! I hope you got up and walked out of her office! We don't want or need anything from her! We don't want her help!"

Now little Anna is crying and Mom is rocking her back and forth in her arms while she sits there on the toilet lid. Anna has her arms around Mom's neck, and we three older ones have to laugh because it looks like Anna is choking Mom. Even Mom sees the humor in this—she's laughing too.

Then our mother gets serious and looks at us girls and says, "If I had walked out of there, what good would that have done for our family? We need help and I'll fight for it whenever I have to. I can't let my children starve! What mother would?"

I am running the bath water for Antoinette and Anna. I am upset, but don't want my mother or sisters to see my face. I certainly don't want my mother to feel worse about the situation than she already does. I tell my two sisters to take their clothes off and get into the tub. "That way you can wash yourselves while Mom tells us the rest of the story about *Sister the Witch*."

Oh boy! Now my mom is yelling at me. "You will never call Sister a witch again!"

I look at Mom and see the hurt in her eyes. I shouldn't have opened my big mouth. I tell Mom I am sorry as Carmella jumps in with a question. "Were you asking Sister for money?" Carmella points out that they *do* collect a lot of money on Sundays. At each mass the basket goes around twice.

But Mom explains, "I didn't want money. I wanted food to feed you. All of you."

"Is that what you said to Sister?" Carmella asks.

"Yes. Exactly. But then Sister told me they didn't have any extra food at the convent."

"You will have to find another way to get food for your family," the nun had told her. "The church can't help you."

Mom tells us that when Sister said that to her, all her blood seemed to rush to her head. She thought she was going to faint! But she caught herself and forced herself to sit up straight in her chair. She looked at Sister eye-to-eye and said …

But now we can't hear Mom because Antoinette is yelling from the tub, "Did you tell her off?!"

Carmella walks over to the tub and says to Antoinette, "If you open your mouth one more time …" With that, Antoinette jumps out of the tub and grabs Carmella's hair, yanking her to the floor. Carmella screams for Antoinette to let go of her hair.

Now Anna and I are hugging each other and laughing as we watch the show put on by Carmella and Antoinette. But Mom breaks up the fight almost as soon as it starts. She's upset with Antoinette for starting the fight—she doesn't like when any of us get physical.

"Do you want to hear about the rest of my visit with Sister or not?" Mom demands. "If you do, be quiet."

We are quiet. So Mom goes on to explain that she told Sister the following: When we lived in South Philly, St. Nicholas's parish was our church, and we sent food over to the convent about four or five days a week—it was food that came from our store. It was our food, but we shared it with the nuns over there so they would always have fresh fruits and vegetables. We never charged them a penny. "Now," my mother told Sister Alphonsus, "I need your help with food for my children."

And Mom had more to say to the principal: "Also, Sister, the Catholic Church is the one to say many times to me and my husband that we should multiply … Have many children for our Church. We need to have a large flock to continue our beliefs and traditions.

"Well, I and my husband honored the Church and its beliefs to the fullest. Now, I need help for a short amount of time. Whatever you can spare from your pantry would help my children. It's not for me—it's for the kids."

My mom doesn't cry much, but in front of Sister the tears came. The truth was, she had nowhere else to go for help.

Sister sat for a moment considering what Mom said. Then she told her that every Thursday we should come over to the convent; that was the day the deliveries were made there. She could give us canned and jarred food. And as soon as our brother Patrick started to work, that help would stop. My mother agreed with Sister. She told her how much she appreciated her kindness. My mother stood and shook her hand. "God bless you, Sister," she said.

As my mom is talking to us, I am thinking, *we get the government's orange cheese, Social Security checks, and now food from the church. We must be really, really poor.* But I don't say anything. I keep it all inside of me.

• • •

We did get food from the church for about six months. It really did help us in our time of need. I remember going over to the convent and how every time it felt like it was my first time. There was always the embarrassment. I had to go into their large dining room, where the table was always set with elegant china and crystal. It was beautiful and quiet … and I was always embarrassed.

My mother always spoke nicely about Sister, saying she didn't know what she would have done without her help. She was forever grateful.

But I guess you never get over that awful feeling of ringing a doorbell and asking for food. All of us younger kids had to take turns. When my mother told us that we no longer had to go, it was such a great relief!

After a while we were still poor but we were fine, not needing any more outside help. Christine was working. Patrick was working. Rosemarie was in business school, which meant she would be working soon. The atmosphere in the house got much lighter, with the entire family much more at ease. Most important, we knew that our mom could get us through anything.

Old Man in the Shack

It's a hot summer morning in Philly. The weatherman said today's going to be a scorcher—around 95 degrees, with lots of sunshine. The news is on the television; my mom listens to it every morning and every evening.

My mom and I are the only ones awake in the house. Everyone else is still asleep. I already had my breakfast, some Wheat Chex cereal. It's really good when you pour ice-cold milk on top. It's nice and crunchy—if you don't wait and let it get soggy, which I never do.

My mom is telling me that today is going to be a hazy, hot summer day, with high humidity. Then I say, "Mom, today would be a great day to buy a fan for us." That way, I say, we'd be able to cool off a little. She's laughing at me because I bring up this same subject every day during the summer.

Her standard reply is: "I'm not wasting the electricity on a fan." So, that's the end of that.

We are having fun teasing each other. It's so pleasant to have her all to my ten-year-old self. I like it when it's just the two of us. We really don't get much time together; there are too many of us for her to give each one special attention very often. I take it whenever I can.

I know she really loves me when she tells me I have my dad's hair. Her eyes are sparkling with love when she looks at me. In this moment of having her in the palm of my hand, I know I can't do anything bad in her eyes. I'm so happy she's my mom!

She tells me to sit quietly and turns off the TV. She runs into the kitchen. I hear the refrigerator door open and close quickly. She comes walking into the living room with that government cheese we get. It's a five-pound block of orange cheese. We are so tired of this cheese that when Mom takes it out of the refrigerator we all say the same thing: "Please, not again." We eat so much of this cheese that we have all come to dislike the taste of it. We dislike the color too—just the sight of it turns our stomachs.

Mom comes over to me and whispers that I should get up and follow her. So I follow her lead from the living room onto the front porch. Then out the front door we go and down the cement steps. We turn left to walk down 58th Street. I ask, "Mom, where are we going?"

"Never mind where we are going," she says. She tells me we have to do this before any of my sisters or brothers wake up. "Keep up with me and walk fast," she instructs. Off we go down 58th Street toward Woodland Avenue. It's so hot and humid with the sun beating down on us. Actually, this is the kind of weather I like—the sunnier and hotter it is, the happier I am.

Hardly anyone is around. It's so early, I haven't seen a bus or trolley go by yet. I ask Mom why we are out so early doing whatever it is we are doing. She doesn't answer.

Are we going to the Penn Fruit food market with that cheese? No, she says—we aren't going that far. "We are almost at his shack," she says.

Almost at whose shack? ...What shack? "Mom, where is there a shack around here?" But she is not answering my questions.

We cross over 58th Street to the other side, going toward 59th and Woodland Avenue. We pass the Prince's Pizza joint. But there isn't anything on this entire block, except for a very small house. The rest of the block is an empty field. So this must be the shack she means, I think. I've seen it before, but I never gave it much thought.

It's a small house made of wood—one floor and maybe just one room. The place is quite rundown; I don't even know if there's running water. And there may be no electricity because I've never seen any lights on in there.

As we get closer to the little house, Mom looks at me. She tells me to listen to her and stay down on the sidewalk while she goes up to the front door. Still holding that block of orange cheese, she knocks on the door. I'm wondering: Who lives in this house? Does my mom know who is in there? Does anyone even live here? This place is so old and beat up—how *could* anyone live here?

My mom turns around and tells me to wait there for her. Then she knocks on the door again. This time she's knocking real hard. Her knuckles must hurt because they sound like a bat hitting the wooden door. I hear the door creak as it opens just a little bit. I can't see who's on the other side because my mom is in the way. Then I hear a man's voice say, "Good morning, Mrs. Pasquarello. It's nice to see you again."

Mom says, "Good morning, Mr. Walker. How are you?" Then this Mr. Walker mumbles something to my mother and they both look at me. Mom tells Mr. Walker that this is one of her daughters, but she doesn't tell him my name. He smiles at me and I smile back. I notice his eyes are all red.

I walk up closer to the front door to see the old man. He has no teeth. He looks strange. He has to lean against the door frame to stand up. He's small, thin, and bald.

My mom is telling him that he has to eat and not drink so much liquor, because if he doesn't eat he will die. I am feeling sick to my stomach because I'm so sad for this man. I start to cry for him.

He is also crying, and telling my mom he knows he can't live much longer like this. But he doesn't care, Mr. Walker says, because no one else cares for him—not his family or his ... well, he has no friends.

Mom tells Mr. Walker not to worry about anyone else. "Just take care of you—then you can help others. Then you will start to feel good about yourself. And say some prayers to your God."

Mom gives him the cheese and asks if he has any bread or crackers. He says yes, he has some bread and juice to drink. He reaches out to shake Mom's hand and they say their good-byes. She turns to see me behind her and nods for me to head back to the street. We walk to the sidewalk and I take her hand.

Then I hear Mr. Walker saying loudly, "Thank you again, Mrs. Pasquarello." I look at Mom and she's smiling.

She asks me if I'm alright, and why am I crying? "I feel sorry for that man," I say. "No one likes him or loves him." Mom explains that he made his decision that he liked liquor so much that he was going to put it before anything or anyone else. Now he's paying the price—he is all by himself. But, she goes on, that is no reason people shouldn't help if they can. He made the wrong choice, but he is still a man and a human being. He just can't stop the drinking.

Mom looks at me and says, "I want you to do me a really big favor."

I am still upset about Mr. Walker, but I ask, "What is it?"

"I don't want you to come back to his shack ever. Promise me you won't, for any reason." I tell her I will never go back to see him. Then she tells me why she's made this request. She suspects I might try to bring Mr. Walker something to eat, and she's afraid he might hurt me because he's drunk all the time. She tells me to pray for him, and that that will help him. Hopefully, God, knowing that life is hard for Mr. Walker, will have mercy on his soul.

• • •

We continued to get the government cheese but we never ate it again. I believe Mom gave it to Mr. Walker. This went on for a couple of years; then it just stopped. As with many things in life, this just disappeared.

Queen for a Day

"How would YOU like to be queen for a day?" In the 1950s and '60s, this was the opening line of *Queen for a Day*, a popular daytime television show that featured women who had fallen upon hard times. The show would start with host Jack Bailey interviewing competitors individually about their emotional and financial difficulties. Each contestant would be asked what she needed most and why she wanted to be queen for a day. A woman might request a wheelchair for her husband, for example, or bunk beds for her children. An applause meter, measuring audience response, would determine the woman most in need of help. Then the lucky lady's name would be announced, and she would be handed a dozen roses, a jeweled crown, and a red velvet cape. With tears in her eyes, she would march to her throne to the music of *Pomp and Circumstance* and be showered with gifts—things she had asked for and so much more. *Queen for a Day* was, in fact, one of the first big prize giveaway shows. The segment would end with Mr. Bailey saying, "Wishing we could make every woman a queen for every single day."

Although I can't remember one story from that show, I can recall as a child feeling that the winner was happy and honored. It was fun to see the queen so excited about being chosen. Some women were embarrassed, while others would grin from ear to ear. The show would be on for half an hour, and we would watch it after school every day.

I would often imagine my mom on that show. I would imagine her on more than one segment, probably an entire week of shows. She would compete with contestant after contestant and always win.

Mr. Bailey would ask Mom all the normal questions he asks everyone. "Why do you want to be queen for a day?" and "How can we help if you are chosen?" Mom would smile and laugh and answer all of his questions, until the really big one. "So, Ro, you are a widow?"

With that, my mom would look serious and reply, "Yes, I am."

"How long has your husband been deceased?"

Mom would say, "Four years now." Mom would start to get visibly upset as she anticipated what Mr. Bailey would ask next.

Then the most difficult question of all: "What did your husband die from?"

Mom would give Mr. Bailey a mama bear look that said, "I want to tear you limb from limb!" But just in time she would pull herself together, put on her big, pretty smile and say, "My husband had a heart attack and died at the age of 53."

"Oh, Ro, I am so sorry to hear that! Now you are left with all these children to care for on your own. What a wonderful job you're doing keeping your family together." Mom would smile once again, knowing she had Mr. Bailey and the audience understanding the severity of her situation. She would know he wouldn't be asking any more questions about her husband, and that would be more than fine with her.

Mom couldn't be honest about the way her husband had died. She would never let the audience know that her Brownie had killed himself, even though this fact was always on her mind. Of course it was. But she bottled up her feelings, expressing only those things that had to do with the bright side of life.

I could hear Mom saying to the audience that she loved being a mother. Being a mom is such fulfillment, she would tell them, a blessing from God not to be taken lightly. Mom would say how she thanked God every day for what he had given her. And for having received so much, she was eternally grateful and humble. This was the truth, for Mom went to six a.m. Mass every day to thank God for giving her twelve children, all healthy and happy—well, as happy as anyone in our situation could be.

No matter who competed against my mother, the result would always be the same. The applause meter would go off the charts for Mom, making her the obvious winner. I can see her up on the stage trying her best not to grin too broadly. She wouldn't want you to think she was pompous. Mom was never pompous, just sure of herself. She wasn't rude to anyone, and she didn't have any desire to gossip. Her attitude was that talk should be to help, not hurt.

The show's pretty models would hand Mom a dozen fragrant, red roses. Mom would look so cute on her throne with a crown on her head, holding her sweet-smelling flowers. She would be over the top with happiness, not needing anything else at that moment. *Pomp and Circumstance* would be playing as Mom cried and all of us children cried along with her to see her so happy. Even though Mom would know she had a tedious undertaking to perform for the rest of her life, she would still have a big smile on her face. She would take on her burden with love.

After my mother is chosen as queen for a day, Mom chats with Mr. Bailey, making him feel at ease because she is pleasant to everyone. They talk and laugh, with Mom making Mr. Bailey's job more fun. She tells him how to make a delicious pot of gravy and meatballs, "talking up" the Italian way of doing things. (Mom wanted all of us to marry someone Italian, and I would tell her, "Mom, not me. I am not going to have some Italian guy telling me how, when, where, and why." Mom would get mad and say there was something wrong with me. In my head, I would think, first, that I didn't want to get married and, second, that I didn't want to be bossed around by some guy, Italian or not.)

While my Mom truly deserved to be queen for a day, I am sure many other women deserved that honor as well. I always thought it was a wonderful show for honoring the women, like Mom, who stayed by their families through hard times. My only wish was that they would have gotten to the core of each con-testant, to let the audience see much more pouring out from their souls.

From backstage, I would watch Mom go on and on about us. It was never about her, always about her twelve kids. Mom would never complain about all her chores, about having to get up early and go to bed late, with so much going on in between those hours. Whenever you walked into the house, there she would be at the kitchen sink, either washing dishes or making a meal. Nothing was from a box; everything was fresh and homemade. If she wasn't at the sink, then she would be downstairs doing laundry. With 13 of us, there was lots of dirty laundry every day. She would hang the laundry outside to dry, and the clothes would get to smelling like fresh air. In 20-degree weather, she would hang the clothes outside. The clothes would be frozen, stiff as a board, but they would smell great.

Now all of us kids come out on stage. We are laughing, hugging, and kissing Mom. She is so happy to have all of us around her. We are a strong and happy family, and no one can bring us down. We all have each other's backs, no matter what, because that's what Mom has taught us. We will take care of the younger ones, and the older ones will take care of us. That's the system Mom developed. She had a system for everything. Without those systems, our lives would have fallen apart, and she never would have allowed that to happen.

After Dad died, we were shunned by neighbors, friends, and family. That's the hand we were dealt. But Mom was a great example to us. Rather than hold a grudge, she made our circumstances work for and not against us. If Mom could hold her head high and forgive other people, then we kids could do the same. Shun me, but I won't shun you. Mom taught us that we are all born equal; no one is more or less than anyone else. We learned to treat everyone with respect.

Mom also taught me my most powerful lesson in life—to forgive my father. I didn't understand where she was coming from until I was much older. I used to be so angry at him. How could I forgive my dad for taking his own life and leaving his wife and twelve children to carry on without him? Didn't he know how much we needed him? We needed his support and missed hearing his voice and talking to him. I missed his holding me and saying that he loved me and would protect me. How could I love a man who abandoned me and our family? How could Mom love and respect him? But she did, forgiving him and carrying on with her life. That gave me my cue: If she could do it then so could I.

The audience is on its feet applauding and cheering for my mom. She heads for the nearest exit until the host grabs her arm. Mom turns toward Mr. Bailey and says, "I have to go home now. But thank you for a lovely time and lots of laughs."

"Not yet," he says, "We have more surprises." Mom wonders what those could be. Now Mr. Bailey is laughing at her bewilderment and all the confusion. "Please sit down for one more minute. I have some exciting prizes for you and your children." I'm thinking how great this is, knowing we are all going to be happy with whatever we receive. Mom's having a hard time breathing. She's clearing her throat so she can say something—anything to make her appear not as overwhelmed as she is.

Mr. Bailey sits next to Mom and says, "Well, Queen Ro, look to your left."

As we all turn to see what is there, Mom screams. She's shaking and asks, "What's all that food doing on the stage?"

He says, "That food is for you and your children. Starting today, your family will receive a year's worth of food." Mom can't believe her eyes. Look at all that food! Cans of Contadina puree and tonno (tuna), boxes of Ronzoni pasta, and lots of other Italian food.

I'm so excited I yell, "We will take it all!" and Mom says to Mr. Bailey, "Are you kidding me? Is this a joke?"

"No way, Queen Ro, this is all yours to enjoy. We would like to help make your life a little easier. What's more, look to your right." A door slides open and two models gesture graciously toward a Westinghouse washer and dryer. Then another door swings open and out slides an Adler sewing machine in an oak cabinet. Mom wins a vacation in the Poconos, a point-and-shoot camera with a slide projector, and lunch at The Four Seasons restaurant.

Mom smiles, saying "Thanks, Mr. Bailey, but no thanks. We don't need these things, but we will take the food with your blessings."

With all this good food, we feel rich. Maybe now, Mom won't need that orange government cheese we've been getting every month? Mom made some really good dishes with that cheese, but after four years, we are tired of it. The government can keep their cheese. Now we can move up to white American cheese—I can't wait to have some homemade macaroni and cheese made from that!

It's the end of the show and we have to say goodbye to everyone. It was magical to be treated like we are an important family and to receive special care and love from people who we didn't even know. We are all feeling so good about ourselves, especially my mom, who is looking and acting ten years younger than she is.

Announcer Mr. Bailey and my mom are backstage talking about how wonderful everything turned out. This is when he says to Mom, "You know, I am half Italian."

My mom says to him, "I know."

With a look of surprise, Mr. Bailey says, "How did you know?"

"Because of your beautiful brown eyes." She's flirting with him.

"Mom, Mom," I am calling to her. She turns, and I say, "Time to go, Mom. The taxi cab is waiting for us. We gotta go now."

She smiles at Mr. Bailey and out the back door we exit, feeling so good and happy, and very rich. We don't have to buy food for a year. And now the world knows just how smart my mom really is. She is the CEO of our family organization.

I sometimes wonder what large company my mother could have run in the outside world. It really doesn't matter, though, because she ran the most important organization in her world, her family. She always knew what each of us was doing, and she gave us feedback—some good, some not so good. She would tell us if we made good grades or needed to do better, if we were helpful enough around the house with chores, or needed to do more. If we were being lazy, she would let us know. Or if we stayed out late, that didn't go over big. She would clobber us and you would think twice about being disobedient again. She was the one person in the world all of us could trust to be honest. And to always be there for us.

We are in the taxi—Mom, me, Carmella, Antoinette, and Anna. Mom always took the four of us with her and called us her four babies, which I hated. "I am ten years old," I would say, and she would laugh at me. She's telling us that she is so happy that she was on the show and that we received all that food. Now she won't have to worry about having enough money to go food shopping.

Mom tells us they will be delivering the food tomorrow, and Carmella asks what is on all of our minds—how they are going to fit a year's worth of food into our house? Mom laughs and tells us not to worry because they will deliver a week's worth of food at a time, each Thursday morning. That's great, I think. Each Thursday, our dinner will be the best meal of the week.

There were some times the meals weren't that great, like when Mom couldn't afford to buy beef, veal, and pork for our meatballs and would make a pot of gravy with chicken instead. Or when she made mashed potatoes and poured baked beans over them. Mom's facial expression showed that she wasn't happy putting that in front of you, even though it was tasty. When Dad was alive and we had money, Dad conveyed sheer delight at every meal Mom cooked for us. But since his death, with no support from anyone on the outside, there were times she didn't have the money to buy good food.

Now we are all driving down our street, and our taxi stops in front of the house. Two more taxis with the rest of the family are behind us. We all go into the house, and someone says, "Let's put music on and let's sing and dance." Christine turns on the record player, and we yell, "Play Dion, or the Shirelles!" She puts on the Shirelles' song, "Mama Said," and all of us are singing and dancing along, even my mom. Oh, how good it feels to be alive and not worrying.

Singing and dancing was our release from life's hardships. We would sing and dance the blues away. Most nights, it was our cocktail after dinner. We would take turns and put on a show. Carmella would tap dance and I would dance ballet. We were good at dancing. Those were my happiest moments with the family.

If I'd had it my way, I would not have gone to school. I would have stayed home listening to that wonderful '50s and '60s music and dancing all day and night. But that thought remained locked in my imagination because there was no way my mom would have allowed me, or any of us, to stay home and not do something with our lives. She would always tell us to be honest with ourselves and to do whatever we wanted that would bring us happiness. But not going to school was not an option.

Mom truly belonged on *Queen for a Day* for all she accomplished in her life. Surely, she was the queen of our family. She had her domain, and she would fight until the end to take care of her family and to keep Dad's memory alive in our minds. For me, my mother was a queen every day, not only in my fantasy but in reality as well.

Christine

When Dad died my sister Christine was 16 years old. She quit high school and went to a business school. That way, she could get a job and help the family financially. And Chris did that for us for almost 15 years. She helped to support us, while loving and protecting us from the world, just like a dad would do. That's the image she always had, from the day Dad died until she married and left our house. She was definitely a driving force in our home.

She was so pretty and smart. But at times Christine would act strange— so strange that we kids would wonder if she was crazy. We would tell Mom our thoughts about Christine. But Mom would tell us that Chris was simply under a lot of stress at her job with a large insurance company. That was believable when we were kids, but when we got to be teenagers it was less so. Chris was doing so many odd things that we sometimes stayed away from her. Maybe we felt we would catch her craziness if we were too close to her?

Chris took her job seriously; she always went to work and was never late. Until one day, when she did not come downstairs to go to work. Mom told me to get ready to go on the trolley. Mom said, "Get ready—you're going downtown with me. We are going to see your sister." I asked Mom what sister she was talking about. She said, "Christine is in the hospital and I have to talk with her and the doctor." I didn't know why Mom wanted me to go with her because, usually, it was my two younger sisters she took with her on her outings. I guess she thought I was older now at 11, and I would be of more help to her.

We travel on one trolley and one bus to get downtown. We get off the bus in front of a large, scary building. Mom looks at me; she knows I'm nervous about this trip. She takes my hand and tells me not to say anything to Chris. Just go to her and kiss her cheek when we get to her room.

This is my first time in a hospital so I'm wondering: What does she mean, "room?" Why can't I say anything to Chris? What's going on now?

When we get to Christine's room my mother goes in first. She walks over to Chris and gives her a kiss and a hug and whispers in her ear. I can't hear what she's telling her. Chris looks pale and is just sitting in her bed, looking straight ahead, scared. She doesn't see me. It's sad to see my sister like this. This is not my big sister who is wild and crazy, who's always laughing, talking, and dancing all over the house. My mom is really quiet when she talks with her, as if Christine will break if Mom talks too loud. All Chris does is nod. I don't like it here.

I go over to the bed and give Chris a kiss on her cheek.

Then this guy in a white coat enters the room. He walks over to Chris and Mom and tells Mom he is Dr. Ryan. My mom extends her hand to shake his. He looks over at me and says hello, then quickly turns to Mom and tells her Chris needs to stay here for two weeks. She needs the time to rest her body and mind. My mother tells the doctor that Chris is on too much medicine— she can't even think or talk. "Could you please give her just a little less than you've been giving her?" she asks.

Dr. Ryan tells Mom, "Mrs. Pasquarello, your daughter is really sick and needs all the medicine I am giving her."

At the time, I didn't realize that the floor we were on was the psychiatric floor. I found that out when we got home and everyone started asking where we had gone. Mom had told no one where Chris was.

My brothers were playing poker when we arrived home. When they saw Mom they started to question her about why she hadn't told anyone where we were going. "Tell us, Mom, where you and Josephine went," Johnnie said.

I told my brothers we had gone to see Christine in the hospital. She looks sick and can't talk, I reported. My brothers laughed because Chris was always talking. John teased Mom, jokingly saying that Chris was in the crazy-house and would never be coming home. He didn't realize how close he was to the truth.

Mom stopped him in his tracks. "You will not talk about your sister and her illness like that," she said. She told him how serious his sister's illness was and how she had to find a way to get Chris back on her feet.

John got sad and told Mom, "I was only kidding around. I don't want Chris to be sick. I feel bad for opening my big mouth. Is Chris really in the mental ward? ... Mom... is she?" John looked really upset.

"Yes, Chris is in the Pennsylvania Hospital mental ward. She might be there for two weeks. She has too much on her for such a young girl." Mom went on to tell us that Chris was only 21 years old, and needed to relax and have fun in her life. John suggested that Chris could find herself a husband, someone to love her.

But my mother shut him down on that idea. She needed Chris to help at home. If Chris could wait a few more years to get married, Mom said, that would really help the family. I was thinking, how come Mom wants us girls to get married when we are 21 or 22 years old, but Chris should wait? Wait for what?

We did actually all realize that Mom needed Chris to help her. So after that, no one said a word about Christine getting married. We never talked about Chris getting a boyfriend or a husband.

For now, we all had to help Chris get better, so she could bring life back into herself and our home.

Chris stayed in the hospital for the next two weeks. When she came home, she was still fragile. It took some time for her to get better. When she got her strength back, though—boy, oh boy!—she was now three times more wild than before.

All of us still at home watched from the sidelines to see what Chris would do. It was all in the name of fun, but sometimes really scary. Christine walked on thin ice, and she wasn't afraid to fall in. I don't believe it ever occurred to her how dangerous some of the situations were that she got herself into. She did manage to get herself out of some sticky situations, and always with a smile on her face and laughter in her soul.

Curbing the Creepy Caller

There were times when you walked into the house and you could sense the loneliness. Even with a house full of people, it would feel empty. We were all aware of the heavy, dark cloud hanging over us. It seemed to make everything still, like no one was around. The air was thick, so you would move slowly. Your thinking was almost at a standstill.

If Christine walked into the house and felt that dark atmosphere, she would go into overdrive to get us out of the gloom. She would put on music, turning the record player volume way up. Before we knew it, we'd all be singing and dancing. Even Mom would come into the living room and get to dancing. Our living room was our music room and our dance floor. The floor was hardwood, so you could move easily. We would do the twist and slow-dance together. We never cared what the beat was—all that mattered was that we were moving and laughing, getting rid of our depression. It was a healthy way of letting our emotions go.

Sometimes Chris would play the Moms Mabley comedy album for us kids. We would all gather around the record player and laugh the entire time at Moms Mabley's dirty jokes and the funny image she presented. This was another way our fun-loving sister Christine helped us lose our worries.

But it was different after Chris came home from the hospital. Right away her behavior started to get dark, and then darker. We had guys calling the house, knocking on the front door, always looking for Chris. We younger girls would question our mom on why so many guys came to our home asking for Chris. Mom always gave us one excuse or another. They are your sister's co-workers, or they are her new friends, she would tell us. We didn't quite believe it.

Christine started to go out a lot and stay out late. The clothes she wore got tighter and shorter. She was getting out of hand. Her temperament changed from sweet, nice sister, to something else, so that when she came home from work, you wanted to run to get away from her.

Now we were getting phone calls early in the morning, about 7 a.m., from this guy that asked for Christine but wouldn't tell us who he was. After three days of him calling, the calls got really dirty. He would tell us girls that he wanted to have sex with us—although he expressed this desire using the crudest of four-letter words. At first my sisters would laugh at him and hang up. But then he would call the entire time we were eating breakfast. Our mother told us not to answer the phone, but we would go into the dining room and answer it.

Mom would tell us he's a weirdo and not to talk to him. Then, hopefully, he would stop. But that didn't stop him from calling us every day—Monday through Friday, anyway. He would call us after Christine went to work. So we figured out it was us young girls he wanted to talk dirty to.

One morning, Antoinette tells us girls she wants to take his call today. We all agree—Ant's going to handle him. When the phone rings, Ant takes the call. She picks up the receiver and says to him, in a really sweet voice, "Good morning, good-looking."

Mom is standing in the archway between the kitchen and the dining room. She tells Ant to hang up because we girls will be late for school. As Mom heads toward the kitchen, we are not listening to her—we have to see what Ant's going to do with our caller. We wait. Then we hear Ant say into the phone, "Take your dick and put it in your mother's mouth." We girls are all laughing so hard—this call is becoming fun on our end! Now, Ant looks into the kitchen to check where in the room Mom is—because she doesn't want her to hear what she's going to say next. She's trying to whisper, but as loud as she can Antoinette is saying, "I bet your thing is really small." We girls are totally shocked, but we are loving how she's talking to this guy! As always, leave it to Antoinette. She can get down with anyone, and she is really good at it.

She's telling him, "If you call back one more time my four older brothers are going to find you … and beat the heck out of you."

Then Carmella says, "Look at Mom." We all look in the kitchen and Mom is laughing and laughing. She's leaning against the ice box so she doesn't fall over.

Antoinette tells the caller to come on over to our house. We four younger girls are all home today, she says—and so are our four brothers. We three are jumping up and down and asking if we can talk to the caller.

But all of a sudden, the call has ended.

Mom says that it's time to go to school. "I don't think this guy will ever call back," she predicts, "because he never wants to run into your brothers. Now forget him."

Off we went to school in our Catholic school uniforms. We laughed all the way to school. We told our friends about our phone call that morning.

We never did hear from our phone guy again. I guess he was afraid of our four brothers—who weren't home at the time anyway!

Christine's New Friends
... and the Song She Loved

The housewives on our street don't care for Christine. It's the green-eyed monster. They know their husbands all watch as Chris walks down the street. When she gets off the trolley car after work the men on the street watch her sway her hips. It's funny watching our neighbors—the men watching every step Chris takes. But the ladies are so angry at her for being young and pretty and having a great set of hips.

Chris adds fuel to the fire by wearing her skirts really tight—she knows this makes her moves more exciting. She's so amusing to watch as the men fall into her trap. She definitely knows what a man likes.

• • •

Christine had some strange male friends. I remember one sunny spring afternoon when I came home from high school. As I got off the bus I noticed three Harley motorcycles on our pavement in front of the house. I knew they were Harleys because my brother-in-law Pat always had one. He would take us for rides; my first time on a Harley was when I was seven or eight years old.

So I'm thinking that maybe Pat and a couple of his friends are here visiting Mom. I go rushing in to say hello to Pat because I like him—he was always kind to me. When I open the parlor door it's three guys sitting on our sofa, and Pat isn't one of them. I think they look like Moe, Larry, and Curly, the Three Stooges. But there is also something animal-like about them, and not in a good way. So I look at them in the same way they are looking at me. We don't say a word, but our looks are saying, "Who the hell are you?" Then Mom enters the room and says to me, "These are your sister Christine's new friends."

Well, okay, I'm thinking, that's what Chris needs—new friends. But then, as I'm walking up the stairs … all of a sudden it dawns on me … whoa!—these guys are from that violent motorcycle gang, the one that has a clubhouse a few blocks from us, on Woodland Avenue. It was kind of an interesting choice of new friends.

Then I hear Mom telling the guys, "I have eight girls, but you won't bother them or hurt them in any way." They sit and listen as she continues to instruct them. "This is my house, and in my house you do it my way."

The smallest of the three says to Mom, "Mrs. Pasquarello, we will listen to you—after all, this is your house."

I laugh at all this, and as Mom walks back into the kitchen I flip them the finger. I'm thinking, I can have fun with you in my house. But I don't want to go to your clubhouse. All the girls in the neighborhood know better than to do that.

The guys laugh at me and tell me to go get Chris because they want to ride their bikes. When I get upstairs I ask Chris, "Who's your friend down there?" She tells me it's the small, thin guy, called "Fox." He does look like a sly little animal, I think. She tells me he's really a lot of fun to hang out with.

That friendship lasted about one and a half years. She grew tired of Fox and moved on to something new and exciting.

• • •

One day we are all at the table eating dinner when we hear a lot of noise coming from outside. Some of us go running to get to the front door first. John wins this race and he's running down the steps. He calls up to us, telling us to come down, but that we shouldn't go on the sidewalk.

We look outside first before venturing down the steps. All you can see are Harleys on the sidewalk, flying by. Up and down the street they go, and we hear the guys on the bikes yelling, "Come on outside and beat one of us up now! Are you afraid, you punks?!"

Our neighbors are also on their steps watching this parade of bikes. But no one has any idea what's going on. Then Christine comes out of the house, asking, "What's happening?" One of the guys she knows stops to tell her what's going on, and we all go over to hear his story. It seems that about an hour ago, this guy's brother was riding his bike down Woodland Avenue toward the gang's clubhouse. When he stopped at 58th and Woodland for a red light, five guys from another gang grabbed him off his bike and beat him and stole his Harley, leaving him in the street. Now, his group is out to avenge this deed: They want the bike back, and they want to beat the hell out of those five guys.

It seemed that they succeeded, because the next day the bike was on the sidewalk in front of Christine's friends' clubhouse, and as long as we lived there they never had a problem like that again.

• • •

It's Saturday morning and Chris has the record player on. It's on its 20th time playing the same song, "The House of the Rising Sun," by the Animals. "Please Mom, get her to turn it off!" we beg. We are all going crazy from listening to this same song over and over. Last Saturday, she played it a total of 50 times straight. George is telling Mom he's going to break the record over Christine's head.

Mom turns the record player off, and for a few seconds we have no sound in our house … Until you hear Chris yelling, "You'd better not touch my record player!" Now we are all yelling for her to shut up or we will break your record player NOW!

We seldom heard that song played in our house after that. But these days, when I hear it on the radio, I always sing along. I have a big smile on my face as I flash back to that Saturday morning. I now understand, from Christine's soul to mine, why this song meant so much to her. It had to do with how the writers felt about family and life. That song let her know that we weren't the only family in distress. For Christine, this was soul comfort.

• • •

When Christine was in her late twenties she met Stefano Muzakitis, from the island of Corfu. He had come to the U.S. from Greece to work and make some money, in order to live a better life. Stefano was handsome, with beautiful blue eyes, They married and right away had a baby boy named Steven. But soon after that, Stefano was running around with anyone he could get his hands on. The truth of the story is that Stefano wanted a green card, and marrying my sister had given him what he needed.

They divorced and Chris took her son over to Greece for his father's family to raise, because Chris was starting to mentally lose it. She was under a lot of stress, and was working extremely hard to pay her bills.

• • •

Christine is working down in South Philly at the state liquor store. She looks really healthy and beautiful. Until one day she stabs her boss because she thought he was in the mob and wanted to kill her.

The police found her at 69th Street, running in the street, saying the mob was after her. They took her to Haverford State Mental Hospital. She was a violent suicidal schizophrenic, they said. She was totally gone.

When I went to see her in the hospital, I wanted to cry. Do you know how hard it is to see your kind-hearted sister looking deranged? To know she has to be on antipsychotic medicine for life? I realized then how much I loved her and that I wished her only the best. But what would be the best circumstances for her? And what kind of life would she be able to live?

While she was in the hospital Chris met a patient who had the same illness as she did. Bill was a big guy whom you knew better than to mess with. He adored Christine and she loved him. When they were released from the hospital they moved in together. Each one really helped the other. She was sociable and he preferred to be by himself. So they balanced each other out.

• • •

Chris died on July 29, 1994. She was 54 years old. She had a heart attack caused by the heavy medication she took for her mental illness. I was sorry to lose her love in our lives—my daughter's and mine, that is. We both loved her to pieces. She was the best sister to me and the best aunt to my daughter.

Six months prior to her death she called and asked if I would find the deed for the family plot. "I will get it for you, Chris," I said, "but why do you need the deed?" She said she wanted to be buried in our family plot. Without questioning her any further, I got the deed. When I told her I had the deed for her, she said she didn't know what I was talking about. I thought, what's up with Chris? What is she doing now? Why is she lying to me?

A couple of months later she was gone. She knew she was dying or she wouldn't have had me get that deed. I never did give it to her. But she's there in our family plot. She was laid to rest with the family.

• • •

The Animals' Lyrics

"House of the Rising Sun"

There is a house in New Orleans
They call the Rising Sun
And it's been the ruin of many a poor boy
And God I know I'm one

My mother was a tailor   *Mom was a tailor*
She sewed my new blue jeans
My father was a gamblin' man   *Dad was a gambler*
Down in New Orleans

Now the only thing a gambler needs
Is a suitcase and trunk
And the only time he's satisfied
Is when he's on a drunk
[Organ Solo]

Oh mother tell your children
Not to do what I have done
Spend your lives in sin and misery

In the House of the Rising Sun
Well, I got one foot on the platform
The other foot on the train
I'm goin' back to New Orleans
To wear that ball and chain   *I guess Chris was a prisoner of her mental illness*

Well, there is a house in New Orleans
They call the Rising Sun
And it's been the ruin of many a poor boy
And God I know I'm one

Writers: Eric Victor Burdon, Alan Price
Copyright: Keith Prowse Music Publishing Co. Ltd., Milwaukee Music Inc.,
Far-out-music Inc.

Fight with Connie

It was a hot summer Sunday when I was about nine, and we girls were outside playing jump-rope. We were all taking turns jumping and counting each jump out loud; the idea was that whoever jumped the longest would be the winner. I wasn't so great at this game because I always ran out of breath. I was asthmatic, not that I let that stop me. My mom told me repeatedly that if I would eat better I'd be stronger. Actually, according to my mother, no matter what your ailment was, it would improve if you ate better. My mom didn't believe in pharmaceutical drugs. To her it was herbs and food that were important. She meant only the best, but unfortunately she wasn't always correct. An inhaler would have been such a relief to me growing up.

On this particular day, I had to sit it out in the middle of the game. I watched my sisters jump and jump hundreds of times. It was fun just watching. We were all laughing and picking on Anna, the youngest. She would jump maybe 20 times and call it quits. We would call her lazy.

Now she's crying and telling us we are all mean to her. Antoinette is telling her to shut up and just jump. We continue laughing and Anna continues crying. Then, as usual, Anna runs into the house to tell Mom on us, and Antoinette advises us to act like nothing is wrong when Mom comes out. But neither Mom nor Anna come out, so Antoinette says it's a good thing Anna went home to Mommy—now we can really jump and turn the rope fast!

I am now back in the game with Carmella and Antoinette. Carmella is taking her turn when Connie Kelly comes over. Connie, one of Carmella's girlfriends, is about two years older than me. She asks if she can take a turn. I say sure—after I take mine. Connie says no—she wants to go before me. Carmella says that's okay—but it's not okay with me. I tell them I will go before Connie or I will kick her ass back to her house. The fight is on!

I really don't like Connie. The day before, she had called me names—names like "greaseball," "dago," "spic," and "nigger." She calls me those names because of my dark skin. She and her brother do that to me when I am alone. Her brother, who is five years older than me, calls me those names when he's with his friends.

When they do this to me, it hurts my feelings, but I pretend that it doesn't. I tried many times to be friendly with Connie, because Carmella likes her. But deep inside, I wish I never had to see her ugly face again, or hear her ugly voice. That's how much I dislike her and her rotten brother.

Today, I decide, I am taking no crap from her. I don't care what anyone has to say—I am ready for the fight. I don't even care if I win or not. Just standing up to her is worth it to me.

So I take my turn, and soon it's her turn to jump. Connie is complaining that I'm not turning the rope fast enough. Well, I am thinking, here you go, s—t-head. I begin turning the rope real fast now, and Antoinette, on the other end, follows my rhythm. Connie can't keep up with us. The rope smacks her across her legs and she is mad. As for me, I am loving every minute of this, and so is Antoinette.

Connie is so mad that now she's calling me a dago. Then she switches her insults to place me in a different ethnic group. "Who do you think you are turning the rope that fast?—you stupid spic." I laugh, telling her I don't know what she's talking about. Soon, switching the focus of her hate once again, she's calling me a nigger.

Well, I think, I've had it with you and your stupid name-calling. And I've had it with that a—hole brother of yours. I let her know I don't want her to call me anything but Josephine from now on.

To that, Connie says, "F—k you." She runs toward her house, with me following a few steps behind. I grab her by the back of the head, which is actually a trick my mom taught me. Near her house, we fall over on the ground.

She gets up and runs up the steps of a neighbor friendly to her family, Mrs. Broderick. She screams for Mrs. Broderick to let her in the house. I run up the cement steps and again grab the back of her head. We're fighting like two little cats—but I want her head. So I pull her down on the porch floor and I have her blond hair in both my hands. Then I let one hand hold her hair while I jump the railing that divides Mrs. Broderick's porch from the adjacent one. Once I'm on the other side, I hold her hair through the railing bars, wrapping it around my fingers, and try with all my might to pull her head through. Even though the bars are about four inches apart and her head is much wider, I am still trying to pull her head through. Why? Because I want to hear her head pop. Like my head pops every time she calls me a nasty name.

Connie is crying out in pain. But I can't let go of her hair. My sister Carmella goes over to Connie's house to get her mom. Soon I hear Connie's mother frantically saying, "Let go of her hair!" But I can't. Then her mother tries a nicer tone. "Please, Josephine, let her hair go. You are going to hurt her. Whatever this is about, we can fix it. Please, let her go now."

My fingers are hurting badly. I've had Connie's hair wrapped around them for so long, they have no blood flow. Still, I can't let go. I just want to bust her head wide open. I want her to feel the pain she's put me in with all that name-calling. And for what? Because I have dark skin.

Antoinette is pulling at my arms. She's whispering to me, "Let her go …You got her. She won't call you any more names again. And if she does—I will kick her ass. I promise you!"

I hear Carmella and my mom calling out to me. I feel my mom tugging at my shoulder, saying in my ear, "She's not worth this."

With that, I let go and I am really relieved to get blood back down into my fingers. My mom picks me up off the ground and she's hugging me. I am shivering because I just released three years of frustration, of having to listen to all that name-calling.

Connie never called me another name after that episode. Although we were never good friends, we did play games together at times.

Later on, I tried to look more deeply at this situation. How did Connie know those awful names to call me? She probably heard them in her house. We lived in a neighborhood that was at least 95% Irish, and in the '50s and '60s the Irish didn't care for the Italians, thinking they were a lower class of people. Not that that was an excuse for Connie, but I did think about something my mother said: "Look at where it comes from."

After that incident, my mother also told me: "Know who is good to you and who isn't. Put this all to rest and don't explode over this again. You are Italian and you should always be proud of where you came from. This will carry you through life."

I concluded that anyone can think whatever they like. But I know who I am and what I am. I don't need or want anyone to call me anything but the name my parents gave me at birth—Josephine.

It was difficult for all of us kids being Italian in an Irish neighborhood and coming from a home without a dad. It was doubly difficult believing that our dad committed suicide. I had to carry all this weight for a long time.

Round Two with Connie

The next time I had a run-in with Connie Kelly I was about 12 years old. It wasn't because she was calling me names—that had stopped after the porch-railing incident. It was all about defending my sister Carmella.

We were watching the Roller Derby show on TV. Roller Derby was my mom's favorite sports show. We girls would join her, and we'd yell like crazy when our team was winning. It was an all-female team, so we girls could relate. Those Roller Derby girls were tough—they slammed each other around like they were rag dolls. The game was exciting to watch, and even my mom would join in the yelling when our team was winning. Sometimes we'd scream when someone on the other team would hurt one of "our" girls. Mom would yell, "Kill her!" We loved this game!

So on this day we are all caught up in the excitement of Roller Derby, and it seems like we are even louder than the players. This is one of those times when you can yell a word like "hell" or "damn" and Mom won't react. Naturally, I am taking advantage of that.

Christine has joined us younger girls to watch the game. She's smoking a Pall Mall cigarette. Every time she places it in the ashtray, Antoinette takes a puff. We all smoke in our house—all of us except Mom. We younger kids smoke any kind of cigarette we can get our hands on—Camels, Kools, Marlboros, Winstons—they all taste good to us.

All of a sudden we can hardly hear the TV; there's a lot of noise coming from outside. What are the people out there doing? Christine gets up and goes to the enclosed porch to look out the front window. She yells for Mom to come see what's happening, but before Mom gets there we hear the door open and shut quickly. Christine is already down the front steps.

So we all go running to the front door and see Connie Kelly—she's at it again! There are about 20 people in a circle around her and Carmella. The people—many of them members of Connie's family—are cheering the girls on to fight. Connie is smacking Carmella in the face and yanking at her hair. But Carmella, as usual, is not defending herself—she's just standing there taking it, trying to talk her way out of it. Connie is not giving in—she's enjoying herself.

I hear my mom say, "Don't go out there" and I understand that she is saying that to me. I certainly remember that the number-one rule in our house has always been No *physical fighting*. But now I turn to look at Mom and she's asking me, "Would you like to help Carmella?" I nod my head yes. She tells me to help Carmella this one time—and only this one time.

Unsure, I ask her, "Are you going to 'get' [punish] me when I come back in the house?"

"No, Josephine, I want you to go save your sister. I allow you to do this. This one and only time now—go help her. End this fight."

I don't remember going down the 13 cement steps. I don't remember exactly how I—all five feet and 80 pounds of me—landed in the middle of that circle. But I do remember this: I grab Connie—who is two years older than me, and bigger—before she realizes it is me who has entered the circle. I am shoving her out of the circle and pulling her hair. Now, Carmella is nowhere to be seen. I guess she has run into the house. But my full attention is on Connie. Mrs. Kelly, Connie's mother, is yelling at me, saying that I had no right to jump in for Carmella. Mrs. Kelly is all mouth—just like her kids. She had been yelling before for Connie to beat Carmella's ass. But I don't care what she's yelling, because now I will beat Connie's ass.

Now Christine is yelling back to Mrs. Kelly to shut her mouth—or Christine will shut it for her.

Connie breaks free from the circle and is running into the street around the parked cars. I am chasing after her, not really caring if I catch her or not, because I got her good when we were in the circle. Now, my anger is gone, and all I feel is relief, and joy that I kicked Connie's ass.

I hear Christine telling me to come in the house. She tells me that I got justice for my sister, so it's over now. I walk over to her and she puts her arm around my shoulders. She walks me up the steps and into the house. "I can't stand those harps," she says, using a slang term for the Irish. "They think they are better than us." Then she asks, "Who's prettier?" She answers her own question: "We are!" We both laugh at her simple humor—and at our victory.

But we know this won't be our last fight. The color our skin, the fact of our being Italian, will mean that there will be others. And that's okay by me.

On the porch, our mom is waiting for us. She tells Chris to go in the living room and make sure Carmella is okay. Then she looks at me, and I am thinking she's going to "get" me for fighting. I know she told me to help Carmella, but I still fear this.

My mother looks at me—straight into my eyes. My mother's eyes are big and brown and they seem to be burning with anger. I am scared.

I hear "Josephine," and I stop in my tracks. I won't look at her. She touches the top of my head and says, "Do you know you have something really ugly inside of you? And it only comes out once in a while when you are angry."

I look at her and say, "Yes, I know that. It only comes out when I can't take it anymore. When I need to scream."

My mother tells me, "Josephine, you need to control that." I promise her that I will work on it. And to this day one of my New Year's resolutions is always to try to control my temper. That's one resolution I have been making for 50 years. Next New Year's Eve I will make my 51st resolution to control my Italian temper. Because it doesn't matter what anyone else thinks of you. It's what you think of yourself.

Kisses, Kisses, and More Kisses

"The cruelest lies are often told in silence."—*Robert Louis Stevenson*

Out of love and respect for my mother we would kiss her first thing in the morning. It was part of the kissing ritual in our home. It's an Italian thing.

Kiss her when you went off to school. Kiss her again when you returned for lunch. Kiss her goodbye when you went back to school for the afternoon session. Kiss again when you came home from school for the day. And maybe again if you were teasing her about all the kissing going on all day long! This was a pleasure for all of us.

But my favorite time was at bedtime. That's when I was at peace because we had made it through another day as a family. When I kissed and hugged my mom good night it was my way of saying, "Thank you for all that you did today. We are healthy and alive, so we can start all over again tomorrow."

All in all, we kissed Mom at least six times a day. Multiply that by twelve kids and my mom was kissing 72 times a day. She loved it!

If I would ever have forgotten to kiss my mom goodbye—which I don't recall ever doing—I would have felt empty inside. Something would have been missing from my soul. I always kissed Mom as if this was our last kiss. We Italians are so emotional! Well, my family was, anyway.

Even when Mom was upset with me, I would still kiss her. After all, if you didn't kiss her she would be insulted because you would be showing her disrespect. In an Italian household, respect is everything—you must give respect

133

and hopefully you will receive respect back. But disrespect can lead to excommunication from the family. No one in our family would have allowed any one of us to show disrespect to Mom in any way. So the kissing never stopped.

Even with all this emotion showing, we never really came clean about our one big, dark secret. We kept that completely hidden from the outside world. It was even concealed in our inside world, because, for years, no one ever spoke the truth. Yes, there was the lie that was spoken about my father's death—heart attack. But never the truth—at least the truth as far as we knew it at that point—suicide. My mother kept up that lie to protect us, especially the boys. They could have gotten involved with the wrong people, and ended up in a scenario like our dad's.

How did we manage with all this secrecy? I can't say how my siblings held it together during those long years. But as for myself, I would become unglued at times. I remember when, at the beginning of each school year, the nuns would pass out white index cards. You had to fill out your family information on them. It always started with the family name on the first line. Then, on the second line, which I hated, you had to fill in your dad's name and his occupation. My hands would perspire as I was filling out this line. I would write on this line, "Deceased." I hated that word. I would start to get uncomfortable in my chair. I always felt like everyone in the classroom knew how my dad died. And what would I do if one of my classmates questioned me about my dad? Would I tell them the truth? Or lie, like my mom did when questioned?

Why do we have to fill this card out every year? I'd wonder. Don't they know all the information by now? My head would be pounding, and all I wanted to do was run and hide. And never come back—never!

But each year, I would have to go through the same ordeal. When it went smoothly, I remember thinking, thank God! I can keep pretending that all is good. Nobody has to know how miserable and frightening my life is—and not only mine but my brothers' and sisters' lives, and my mother's. Nobody has to know how my mother was left all on her own with twelve children to take care of.

You hear women say they raised two children on their own, with help from no one. I say, good for you. But my mother didn't have two kids, or four kids, or eight kids, or eleven kids. She had twelve! And she managed to hang on to us and do an incredible job raising us. She was put on this earth to have this family. That was her purpose in life, and she fulfilled it gloriously.

Even when the Girl Scouts of America turned us away…

. . .

My mother walked home with the two of us from that meeting beaten down and sad. Carmella and I were asking her, "Why can't we join the Scouts?"

"How come they don't want us?"

"What did we do wrong?"

She looked at us, smiling. "It's okay that they don't want you," she said. "*I* want you!" I was crying—not for myself, because I didn't really want to join the Scouts. It was Carmella I was sad for, because she had friends from school who were Girl Scouts.

But deeper down, I was also crying for all of us. How many times were people going to reject us? Can't they leave us alone? Why did my dad have to die? Didn't he know this would happen to us?

When the three of us got home from that meeting we were emotionally drained. As soon as we walked into the living room Christine began asking Mom about the Scout meeting. "How did everything go? When will Carmella and Josephine join? What about the fees?"

I am thinking, please Chris, be quiet, because the three of us will start to cry. Then Carmella starts yelling at Chris to shut the hell up. Wow—Carmella never curses at anyone—she must really be upset. "Christine was just asking a question," I hear Mom telling Carmella. "Why don't you calm down?" And now here we go with an Italian fix—Mom is telling Carmella she's getting her a bowl of ice cream. Carmella caves in to the fix and settles down. But not me. I proceed to tell Christine about the lady at the desk who "helped" us at the meeting.

I start with when we walked into the front room of the building and were told by a lady sitting at the front desk that we should have a seat and wait. So, we sat and waited. There were lots of girls and moms there waiting for their turn. After a time a second lady came out from the back room, calling over to us to come to the desk. Mom sat on the chair across from the lady, who introduced herself as Joan Harrison. She told Mom she would start on the paperwork and would notify us in just a few minutes about whether we could join the Scouts. After the paperwork was taken care of she told Mom to wait at the desk and she'd be right back.

After a few minutes Joan Harrison and another lady came over to us. Their message? "We can't have your two girls join the Scouts."

Mom was startled! As she questioned Joan Harrison as to why her girls couldn't join, you could see her eyes practically popping out of her head, and the vein across her forehead was bulging out. Her breathing was hard as she jumped up from her chair. "Why not?!" she demanded. "I want to know now!"

You could see the two ladies getting nervous. They weren't going to answer Mom's questions, but they knew she wasn't going to walk away from this …

My mother leaves the living room for a minute, and Christine asks me what I think about all this. I am all too happy to tell her my thoughts—exactly. I tell her that Joan Harrison had a big fat ass. And she was a slob. I only say that to Chris because my mom has left the room and I know Chris won't tell her what I just said. I tell Chris I feel bad for Carmella because she was so excited about being a Girl Scout. As for me, I couldn't care less. "Christine, you know I don't want to join a club with a bunch of girls." Now Christine and I are laughing. Mom's back, and we head to the kitchen, where she will continue telling Chris the story. Now I keep quiet and listen as we all sit down.

Mom sits at her favorite spot at the table—the head of the table closest to the oven. She looks at Chris and her face becomes relaxed. No popping eyes or bulging vein. She tells Chris the rest of the story…

Joan Harrison gives my mom the reason her two girls can't join the Girl Scouts: There's no more room. Mom tells Joan Harrison, "I don't believe you! Look at all the girls that are waiting to join the Scouts in the waiting room. I know why my girls can't join—because they're Italian! Wouldn't that be right?"

Joan Harrison looks at Mom with a smirk, and says, simply, "Your girls can't join. Maybe another time. I will get in touch with you later."

Mom tells her, "I know I will not hear from you, or from anyone else in your organization. You're not a caring or a nice person. But that's your problem! As for my girls, they and I will walk out of here with our heads held high. Tonight in my prayers I will ask God to help you become a nicer and more understanding person. Goodbye, Joan Harrison."

Christine wants to go over there right now and confront "that creep." But Mom says this is not a fight worth fighting. We will let this one go.

So Christine smiles at the three of us and tells Carmella and me to get ready for bed. As we leave the kitchen to go upstairs, she tells us to remember never to act like Joan Harrison. And then she says—because if we do, we will all get a fat ass, just like her! We all laugh. It's a better way of ending this day than crying.

• • •

We are all here for a reason—no matter who we are or what we have to handle in our lives. We in our family had to handle a lot. First, we were thrown out of our neighborhood—by our own people—the Italians. Then we had to move into a new neighborhood with a different nationality—the Irish. We were not met with open arms. We were shunned for being different, for being members of the wrong group.

But that first time—to be told to leave our familiar surroundings was extremely tough on us. Why did it happen? Was it because my dad wouldn't give in to the mob? Maybe it was because the mob, who had done this awful thing to our family, couldn't bear to look at us or hear our voices anymore. They most certainly were cowards. They forced my dad to take his own life in a brutal manner, then sent us away. Was their belief, "out of sight, out of mind?"

I've often wondered if they ever had any sleepless nights, nights like my mother had on many occasions when she tossed and turned in fear because she didn't know if she could take one more day—if she could hang on one more day for her family.

I had a lot of hate and distrust toward the human race. Wouldn't you? It took me many years to be able to deal with it.

• • •

In the evenings, Carmella and I would go over to Mom to give her a last kiss of the day, our good night kiss. Mom would perk right up when a kiss was coming her way. She worked all day for her kisses and to her they were her reward.

The night of our rejection by the Girl Scouts, we kissed Mom and said good night, and she hugged us at the same time. She whispered to us to be kind to people and you will receive the same kindness back in your life. Maybe not tonight, she said, but it will come to you some day.

My mom never heard from Joan Harrison, and we never joined the Girl Scouts. But we had our own club—it was the Pasquarellos' Club. This club was just fine with me. To me, this was the finest of clubs to be a member of. This was where I belonged.

Dark Night, Deep Questions

Adversity came calling ever so often in our lives. I guess the universe wanted to know how much we could endure as a family. But little did the universe understand my mother and her determination not to allow anything or anyone to hold us down. She would withstand any hardship that came our way. And she would take and handle each blow as a lady.

Who's to say how a woman should act? Under whose watchful eye will she be judged? Actually, judgment meant nothing to my mom. She took it upon herself to know herself and how she should get through the stresses of living without her husband, the father of their 12 children, at her side.

What she didn't have inside her to begin with, she learned through living this new life. She knew she was capable of doing a great job. With her courage and honesty she believed she wouldn't fail. If she sensed she was in a retreat she would pull herself together and regroup for her next move. When she was in her quiet mood, that's when she would do a lot of talking downstairs in the basement. The basement was her cave for releasing private thoughts and feelings. It provided meditation time away from us kids … time with my father.

She spoke to him, and to her God. With the help of her two supernatural powers she could continue on. She believed in her God, but I suspect her strength truly came from her love of her husband. She knew each day brought her another day closer to being with him forever. Because of their bond of love, he was always by her side, and that was something that would last forever.

There must have been many, many dark nights in the 19 years without my dad, nights when she fell apart in her lonely bed, wondering if she could make it through another day. She tried never to let her children know how vulnerable she sometimes was, or how defeated she sometimes felt. Instead, she tried to keep moving in the right direction at all times. If she felt beaten down by someone in the family, or someone coming into the family, she had to keep emotionally strong for the rest of us. She couldn't let us know if she'd lost a battle.

One night, when we were all in bed, Mom went into the back bedroom, where the boys slept. There were two beds and a cot in there. Patrick, a teenager at the time, was in the bed closest to the cot, but he wasn't asleep. He kept still, pretending to be asleep, as he was thinking, "This is strange, for Mom to be back here in our room. She never comes in here except during the day when she's cleaning or changing the sheets."

Mom climbed into the cot and got under the blanket. Then Patrick heard her saying the "Hail Mary" to the Blessed Mother. She told the Blessed Mother that she was tired and not feeling well. Then she told her she knew she couldn't get sick or, for that matter, die. She knew she had a lot to do before God would take her from her family.

But she needed help, Patrick heard her say. She didn't know how much longer she could take all of this upon herself. She told the Blessed Mother, "I have no one, no family or friends to help me. How can I ask my children to help? They all have their own lives, now that they're getting older, and married. My three oldest are gone now, with their own families. Who can help us?

"Christine is still with me, and she *is* a big help. I feel bad at times, though, always asking for her assistance. Yet I have nowhere else to go. I'm a burden to her, but if she left me now, what would I do? Chris is a good girl, but she's fragile and sickly. Please—make her strong again so she can find happiness in her life. She is such a good person and a hard worker … I must try not to rely on her so much …"

Patrick couldn't let Mom know he wasn't sleeping. But he didn't know how much longer he could lie still. He thought, "Why is she back here anyway? She always sleeps in the big front bedroom with the girls." (Mom had her own bed, but one of us four youngest girls would usually be in bed with her, for comfort. It was a way you could have Mom all to yourself. You could feel safe then.)

My mom was staring at the ceiling … and she was talking and crying. Patrick was having a hard time understanding her. She was doing that thing when she's not together in her head. She was speaking in her language, Italian, and then going into English. So Patrick didn't understand her, other than to understand she was hysterical. Then she spoke in English—to Dad—and Patrick couldn't believe what he was hearing. "Brownie—why did you leave me? ... How can I do all of this on my own? ...You left me alone. WHY??"

Patrick was worried. This was the first time he had heard our mother question her ability to handle life as it was now. Maybe it was all too much for her? Patrick thought. Maybe Dad's brothers and sisters were right—we kids should have been sent to an orphanage.

We were in need of a man in our house—someone to love us and to come home with a paycheck. Not that we'd be getting any of that—no help would come our way. We would have to make it through life on our own because Mom wanted only one person by her side, her husband.

How were we to know that she felt isolated in her own grief, just as we kids did? The reality was that even though there were twelve of us, we were all on our own with our grief. We didn't know how to handle the loss of our dad or the way he died. But—to know that she didn't understand her grief— that, to me, is unbearable. To know she was lost like all her children! We were all swimming in the ocean of despair.

Looking back, there are a lot of "what if's?" I learned about this incident many years later, but what if Patrick had told us at the time what happened that night? What if we all could have spoken to Mom the next day? Then, maybe, we could all have cried together and released some of our pain. But then again, if Patrick had told us, we would have had many questions for Mom, and she never would have answered them. There's no sense in kidding our-selves—she never would have told us the truth. She kept that truth within her forever, because she would never betray her husband. So maybe sometimes things are best left unsaid, questions left unasked?

Mom must have had some anger toward my dad. He left so many burdens for her to deal with—the 12 of us, to begin with. So she at times must have had feelings of abandonment. But if she had any ill feelings toward him, Mom never spoke a word of them. She always spoke of him smilingly and admiringly, so everyone could see that there was a bond there that would never shatter. She kept her promise to him, and her word turned out to be a valuable gift, not only to him, but to herself, in her new life, and to everyone else in theirs.

A Perfect Philly Evening in 1961

It's a humid Friday night in July. The air in the Pasquarello house is hot and still. No breeze is coming in any of the open windows. This is typical of summer nights in the city of Philadelphia.

Mom is busy in the kitchen preparing our dinner. Tonight she has the oven on, making the kitchen twice as hot as the rest of the house. We don't mind, though, because we know Mom is cooking something all twelve of us kids enjoy, eggplant parmesan. It's dinnertime and we're all hungry. We younger ones have been outside all day playing in the sun.

We did have some relief from the heat this afternoon. Luckily, my brother Patrick had the wrench to turn on the fire hydrant. About 30 kids came around to enjoy the hydrant water. For about 15 minutes, that is, because that's how long it took the cops to come and shut it off. They told us that if there was a fire we wouldn't have any water to put it out. One of the boys yelled back to the cop, "But we are all on fire!" and we kids all laughed. It's fun to cool off in that water and play in the street. Two things you hope for: (1) The cops don't come right away; and (2) no cars come down the street, because they get in the way of playing.

Mom is calling us to the kitchen for dinner. She has the long Italian rolls. These are so good with the fresh eggplant and tomato sauce—the same tomato sauce Mom makes when she makes pizza. The sauce covers the eggplant and the mozzarella cheese; you take a delicious bite of that and then you take a bite of the hard-crusted roll and hope you can keep all of it in your mouth and not look like a slob. But who really cares?—we are all family. Sometimes the boys will call us pigs if we eat too fast. We can't help it, though—Mom's cooking is so, so good! Each day we can't wait for dinner to see what she's prepared for us. It takes the whole afternoon for her to cook the meal because everything is done from scratch with fresh ingredients. When we get to the table we twelve kids (eight girls and four boys) eat everything in sight. I guess you could say our brothers are right—we are pigs. But pig or not—I enjoy every meal Mom serves me.

Believe it or not, Mom did serve each and every one of us our meals individually. It was one of the ways she showed love. She enjoyed every way she could express her motherhood no matter how old we were, and you could say we were all spoiled by her every day—not with material things, but with her love.

Today Christine tells us she got some new records. After dinner she's going to play some for us. Mom tells Christine she has a large watermelon for dessert. Go play your music, she says—then we can get dessert. Put your record player on … have some fun dancing in the living room.

Christine asks Rosemarie what record she should put on first. George yells out, "Put on Dion and play 'Run Around Sue!'" We all love Dion's voice and songs. He's Italian, so what's not to love? That's what Patrick is saying to Christine.

Antoinette's laughing at me and Carmella because we're dancing real crazy. It feels so good to move your body all around. Christine and Rosemarie are doing the jitterbug, which is fun to watch. That's how I learned to dance—by watching my older sisters and brothers. I also watch the dancers on *American Bandstand* with Dick Clark. That show is great!

My older sisters are partial to the song "Run Around Sue" because they think Sue has the right idea—break all the boys' hearts. They think Sue is real smart.

Christine puts on another record—"Dedicated to the One I Love" by the Shirelles, a girls group we're fans of. It's a slow dance, and since there is no way our brothers will slow dance with us, we sisters dance together.

Mom comes into the living room and sits in her favorite chair to watch us dance. Christine puts on another record—it's called "The Twist," and it's by Chubby Checker. We saw him on *American Bandstand* last week doing this new dance and singing. Now we're all dancing, even the boys. John's really good at the twist. George is too stiff, and in fact none of us can dance like John. Not only is he really good at the twist; he can do the Bristol Stomp too.

Now Mom says that *she* can do the Bristol Stomp. "Put that record on again," she tells Chris, "and I'll show you."

Chris puts on the record by the Dovells and Mom gets up and starts doing the Bristol Stomp. Laughing, moving her legs and feet back and forth, coming down on her feet really hard, she looks like a little girl. Christine and Rosemarie laugh and ask Mom, "Who taught you how to stomp?" Now we all laugh and circle around Mom to join in her dancing. The record is on loud, and we feel the beat. This is crazy-time for all of us, and we're loving every minute of it.

John is yelling out from across the living room, "Mom—when did you learn to stomp like that?" She's not talking, though—she's putting all her energy into dancing. Christine goes over to the record player to play it again.

That's when we hear the doorbell ringing and someone calling into the house. It's the police. A cop is yelling through the front porch window screen. Mom goes out to see what the problem could be. The cop tells Mom someone called the police to complain about the noise.

"Could you please turn your record player to low or off?" the cop asks. "We don't want any more complaints tonight." Mom tells the cop that we are finished with the music for the evening. He wishes us good night and walks down the steps.

Mom turns toward us and says, "Now that's a nice policeman."

It's time to have our watermelon, Mom tells us. It will cool us off. We all go into the kitchen to enjoy our dessert.

Fernando

Whenever you smell Mom's pound cake baking you know it's Saturday morning. Saturday is the only day of the week she will bake her yummy cakes. The aroma of the butter, flour, and anise seeds baking makes your stomach scream, "I'm hungry!" We all run down the stairs to get the hot, sweet cakes.

One Saturday morning, Chris is the first one at the bottom of the stairs. She's looking at someone on the sofa, and asking, "Who are you?" Now all of us are down there, curious about who Chris is talking to. There's this really cute guy sitting on our plastic-covered sofa. (We have plastic covers on our sofa and chairs so they don't get dirty—it's an Italian 1960s thing—plastic on all the seats.)

The cute guy is smiling at us and introducing himself. Fernando. Fernando has a real big smile that shows off his beautiful white teeth. He has nice dark brown skin and dark brown hair—lots of it. He tells us he is from South America, his father is wealthy, and they have many servants. In fact, they have so many people to wait on him hand and foot that he never has to do any chores.

Chris laughs. So does Pat, who asks Fernando if he's in the wrong neighborhood or what, because no one here is rich, and we certainly don't have any servants. I can tell Pat thinks this guy is a snob, and already doesn't like him. Now Chris and Pat are asking him a lot of questions. They pile question upon question, hardly waiting for replies. But Fernando stays with them on every question. It's really funny watching this go on, but on the other hand, I do want some cake while it's hot. So off I go into the kitchen to get a slice of cake and a glass of cold milk. I'm too busy to talk, and I really don't have any questions for this guy. First things first—I need to eat, and then I'll join in on the fun.

But before you know it, one by one everyone is coming into the kitchen, even Fernando. He sits down at the table with the older siblings, and now he's telling Pat that they are the same age. They're all laughing and eating, and this guy Fernando seems to fit in with us. He's the same color as us—but he's rich. And then I think—who cares if he's rich? He seems really nice.

My brother John is questioning Fernando on why he's here in America. Plus there's another really important question: "Why are you here in our house?" It gets very quiet in the kitchen as we all stop eating to hear the answer to that one. What does he want with us anyway?

Mom speaks up. She tells us, "Fernando is here for the summer months. He will live with us until the end of August. He will share the back bedroom with the boys. He'll sleep on the cot. Just like your brothers, he is not allowed in the girls' rooms. And he will only use the bathroom in the basement, because the bathroom in the basement is only for the boys. He will stay here with us and follow all my rules, just like any of you. So … does anyone have any questions?"

John has a question: Does this Fernando get to wash dishes like we do, in weekly turns? Also, does he get to take out the garbage? Then Patrick wants to know if Fernando has to find a job. Chris, laughing, asks, "Will he do the dishes for me when it's my week? Because my fingernails break when they're in the water for too long." We're all getting loud and silly, but Fernando doesn't think it's funny.

He is again telling us he's rich, and, at that, George is stuttering, trying to say to Fernando, "We don't care if you are rich. Because, in this house, you are one of us." Poor Fernando—he doesn't know what to do. Who does he have to fight to survive in this house? Probably all of us.

"You're living in our house now—not yours," George is telling Fernando. "You will be treated just like us. We don't care if you're rich—that doesn't mean anything to us." I am thinking the same thing.

Mom steps in because the atmosphere is getting hostile. If Mom doesn't step in and get things under control, Fernando and three of my brothers will come to blows. So Mom, with the help of John, gets the boys to settle down. Mom stresses to them that Fernando will be one of us—no different. John is right behind her, telling us not to worry. If Fernando gets out of hand, he will get Pat to kick his ass. Now, we're all laughing again. Even Fernando thinks it's funny.

We think Fernando will be fine, but we all want to know—where in the world did he come from? Where did Mom find him? Why is he leaving by the end of August? Mom tells us that at lunch she will explain everything, but, right now, we should let her brain settle down. We are too loud for her, and have too many questions.

So after we finish Mom's yummy cakes, off we go to do our Saturday chores. We inform Fernando that he will get to pick out a piece of paper from the hat, and that will tell him what his chore is for today. We do this every Saturday, whether we like it or not. We let Fernando go first … he picks a piece of paper out of the hat … and his chore is … to clean the dining room. This is the hardest room to clean. You have to wash the entire dining-room set—the table, the server, and all the chairs. When you are finished with the furniture, it's on to the hardwood floors—you sweep them first and then you get on your hands and knees and wash the floors with the scrubbing brush and Fels-Naptha soap. Fernando thinks this will be an easy job, but we who know the truth laugh behind his back.

So how did Fernando get the worst job on his first day? My beautiful brother John—he wrote "dining room" on all the little pieces of paper! Then, after Fernando had first pick, another set of chore papers was quietly substituted. Poor Fernando—he's going to be the butt of our jokes for the next three months. This is going to be lots of fun—but not so much for the rich kid. We poor kids will teach him a lesson. John is going on and on, joking about us being Fernando's obedient servants. We all love hearing John's plans for either breaking him or killing him. But John warns us: Do not tell Mom what we are up to. She will kill us if we hurt her new baby boy!

Now I'm wondering—her new baby boy? He's about seven years older than me, and I'm already eleven. Besides, we don't need 13 kids in our family—twelve is quite enough, thank you. Let's get rid of him now, I tell John. Let's kill him today!

Pat, George, and John tell me, "Josephine, we were just kidding. We can torture him, but we can't kill him. So let's have some fun with the rich kid, and in three months' time he'll be gone. And don't worry—Mom won't love him more than she does us." Of course, they say, Mom will protect him from us if we get out of hand. So we shouldn't let her hear or see us plotting against him. We all make a pact to be sneaky when it comes to Fernando.

Christine is flirting with him—she's in the dining room, helping him clean. She doesn't like to clean but she's on her knees scrubbing away. What's up with my crazy sister? Is she in love with the rich kid?

Now we get a break from cleaning—it's lunchtime. Mom will tell us how she found this South American mystery man. When we all settle down in our seats at the table, she begins.

Mom asks us if we know Consuela, that lady on Chester Avenue. John knows her the best, because her son and John are best friends. Consuela loves John; she calls him "her monkey," because John is always climbing on roofs, and jumping on the backs of trolley cars and transit buses. Everyone knows him in the neighborhood, but Consuela loves him a lot. I bet she would take him as her son—but she'd better never ask. My mom would kill her if she took John away from us.

Mom goes on with her story. Consuela is from South America. She knows this rich guy who has a son who goes to the University of Pennsylvania, right here in Philadelphia. Carmella yells out that that must be Fernando. Right, Mom says. This rich man wants to teach his son a lesson—a hard lesson. Now we're all staring at Fernando, and he's uneasy with all the eyes on him. He's squirming in his chair like a little boy.

So, Mom continues, this rich boy almost failed this year at the university. It seems he had lots of girlfriends, and went out to party every night. Rosemarie is giving Fernando dirty looks, and then she says to him, "You really are stupid—your father sends you to one of the best universities, and you goof off and almost flunk out. You're a moron." Christine yells out, "But he's a good-looking moron!" which Rosemarie does not appreciate.

Mom tells us to settle down so she can finish. So we concentrate on eating our lunch. Mom's made us steak sandwiches with cheese and fried onions on long Italian rolls. They smell and taste so good, and Antoinette is saying to Chris, "Who cares where he came from?—Let's eat!" Antoinette asks Mom, "Could you finish the story at dinnertime, please? I just really want to eat my lunch and go outside and jump rope." Anna agrees—she wants to go with Antoinette after lunch and play outside.

But I want to stay with the older siblings and find out about this rich kid. I turn to Patrick and ask him if I can stay with him. He tells me to keep my mouth shut and just listen. I obey as Anna and Antoinette go outside to play, and Mom continues with the story.

Fernando's dad is teaching him a lesson by not allowing him to stay in his apartment in downtown Philly, and not allowing him to go home for the summer. His punishment is to stay with us for the summer! He will be treated as Mom treats us. "Oh, come on, Mom," Rosemarie says, "he knows he's not one of us. Come September, he'll be back in his apartment, and back at Penn. Meanwhile, he'll have a clean house and three good meals a day. So what is he really learning?" I can tell Roe doesn't care for him, and wishes he wasn't here in our house.

But Mom isn't backing down. Fernando is staying here, she says. "I can use the money his father is paying to keep him here. Now—that's the end of the debate—and not another word on this."

As it turned out, we all had lots of fun with Fernando. For three months I had a fifth brother. He turned out to be a nice guy. More than just good-looking, he was sweet and caring. He spent most of that summer talking and playing cards with us. He never showed any disrespect toward my mom, or us. It's true that at times he would let us know, yet again, that he was rich and had many servants. After hearing that statement too many times, we would say, "So what? What good is it? You're here, not there."

But we did all get along, and he did do his Saturday chores. After a while we let him in on the secret of how he got to clean the dining room on that first Saturday. He laughed and told us he would never get the dining room to clean again. And he never did.

At the end of the summer Fernando went back to the university. We missed him at first, but by Christmas our house belonged to us. We were happy being "just" us twelve again, not having to share our mom with someone else. My feeling was that I did miss Fernando, but he had been here long enough.

We never did see or hear from Fernando again. I would, once in a while, think of him, and wish only the best for my fifth brother.

Dad – at his vegetable stand, circa – 1948

Mom – 27 years old, circa – 1933

Uncle Nick – Josephine – Aunt Myra, circa – 2005

Dad & his father (my grandfather) at Coney Island, circa – 1910

Dad at 12 years old, circa 1914

Ralph, Trudy, Grace & Christine, circa – 1947

Dad & Ralph – Ralph home from the army visits Dad at his store, circa – 1954

Josephine, Antoinette, Anna & Carmella at the Philly Zoo, circa 1959

Josephine and Carmella playing cards, circa 1960

Mom – at age 53 years old, circa 1960

Josephine ten years old – 1959

George sixteen years old – 1961

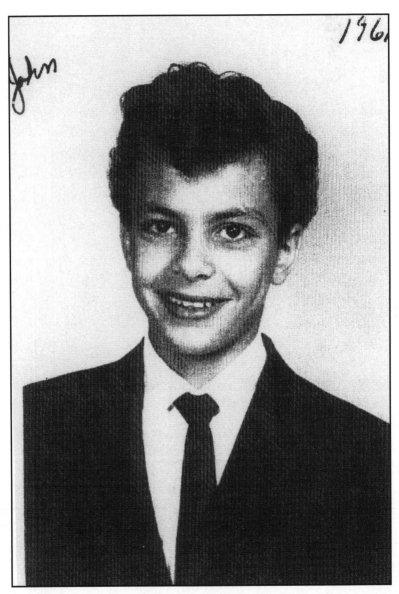

John fifteen years old – 1961

Josephine and Carmella, circa 1961

Mom and Josephine, circa 1970 – Carmella's wedding

Christine and Mom, circa 1959

Christine and Lee - Circa 1959

Mom – Alone, circa – 1972

Family Dinner - circa 1972

Rosemarie and John before he turned 16 and quit smoking, circa – 1962

John and his son Johnny, circa 1972

Josephine, Antoinette, George and my God Daughter, Mona

Antoinette and Anna, circa – 1964

Josephine on drugs and Mom, circa – 1972

The Pasquarello Family
cordially invites you to attend a surprise
65th Birthday Party for
Romania Pasquarello
on Sunday, the tenth of September
nineteen hundred and seventy-two
at five o'clock
at King's Caterers
2378 Orthodox Street
Philadelphia, Pennsylvania

Mom's 65th Birthday Party, circa – 1972

Mom's 65th Birthday Party, circa – 1972

Nicole – my daughter, circa 1978

Josephine – now is straight, circa – 1981

Pasquarello Party, circa 1974

Christine and Bill (her boyfriend), circa – 1990

Christine and her son Stephen - circa 1990

Grandfather Pescatore and Ralph - circa 1934

*Pasquarello Memorial with Josephine's granddaughters,
Alana and Isabella, circa 2006*

Dad – before he married Mom, Atlantic City, circa – 1932

My dad, Pasquarello Family, 1st generation, circa – 1928

Mixed generations, circa – 2009

Mom and her four boys, circa 1972

Our Little Friends at Christmas

It's December 24th, the night before Christmas. Our house is so busy. We always put the tree up on this night. While we kids start on the tree Mom is in the kitchen cooking and Christine is baking cookies, plus pies—lemon meringue and apple.

The house smells so good with all the different aromas in the air. We are having home-mades on Christmas—pasta made from scratch, not from a box— maybe spaghetti, gnocchi, or ravioli. I can't wait to run my crusty Italian bread across my plate of gravy. I let the soft part of the bread soak up the gravy until it can't hold any more; then I stick the big hunk of bread into my mouth. Our Italian Christmas meal is always the finest part of the holiday, and my taste buds are going crazy just thinking about it.

But first we have to decorate the tree, which is always fun. We put lots of glass balls, tinsel, garland, and candy canes on our tree. It's always a real tree; my brother John is usually the one to come home with it on Christmas Eve. Then we all get moving in sync.

It's so hectic, but there's so much love and joy. We don't get gifts—Mom doesn't have the money. But we do have each other. Our time together and the good food that we share—that's our celebration, and we're fine with that. Actually, we have the best gift anyone could have—our mom.

Antoinette comes down the stairs to help us with the decorations. She's telling me to pass her the red balls with the Santa faces on them—and only

187

them. She's so bossy—she can drive you crazy if you listen to her. So I move to the other side of the tree. That's where my brother John is putting the lights around the top of the tree.

John tells me he needs my help tonight.

I say, "I'll help you with anything if you get me some cigarettes."

John laughs and says, "I will if you do what I need help with…Yes or no—tell me now, Josephine—yes or no?!"

"Yes, I'll do it, John, but I want my cigarettes first."

He tells me to go in his coat pocket and take five cigarettes out of the pack. "Leave the rest in my pocket. And don't take any more than that or I'll tell Mom I saw you smoking." Boy, is he a pain, but I do love him.

Right now I'm actually a little bit mad at him because I'm thinking about how the boys are always getting away with what we girls get disciplined for. I tell him, "Keep your cigarettes—I'll get some from Christine." (In truth, I can't stand Christine's nonfiltered ones. The tobacco can get on your tongue and it's really bitter. I'd rather smoke John's Marlboros—they're much better.)

John is saying, "Come on, I'm only teasing you—take the cigarettes and help me. After we get the tree finished you will help me get something done. I wanted to do this last year but we didn't have enough candies and cookies. This year we have plenty of candy because Christine bought loads from you girls, during your school sale. And she bought some from the Strawbridge and Clothier candy department too." (They have the best chocolate-covered pretzels!)

I don't know what the heck John is planning; all I know is that I am going upstairs to smoke a cigarette. Mom is busy in the kitchen; she won't even know I'm gone. As long as Antoinette doesn't rat on me, that is. Antoinette has the biggest tell-all mouth of all of us. We call her the rat and a few other choice names. She runs to Mommy when we do that. Not that Antoinette doesn't smoke or act bad sometimes. She like to tattle, and, seriously, she gets on my nerves when she does that. So I don't always let her know what I'm doing, even if it's something fun. It's safer to keep her nose out of my business.

After my smoke, I come downstairs, go over to John, and ask, "What is it that you want me to help you with?"

He says, "You know that family down the block with the five kids?—well, not five yet—she's got the fifth on the way."

"Yes, I know them—the Hamiltons." John looks at me and he's getting real serious. He's telling me that Mr. Hamilton came over to the Penn Fruit parking lot to get a Christmas tree for his kids. (John works there during the holiday season.) Mr. Hamilton didn't have enough money, so my brother gave him a tree. "The man only had a dollar," John says, "so I gave him the biggest tree we had. My boss doesn't know I gave the tree away; if he finds out, I won't have a job there next year. But I felt so bad for Mr. Hamilton's family. His kids need a tree for Christmas, from Santa."

"Well, what do you want me to do? How can I help the Hamiltons?"

"I want you to collect the chocolates and cookies and make special bags for the kids. I bought some Christmas bags. They're small, but you can fill them with goodies, and put some gum in there too." John tells me he's also bought some candy, and he shows me the dining room table, which is now covered with goodies—hard candies, chocolate Santas and reindeer, and chewing gum. "Just pack it in real good," he tells me.

John and I are filling the bags in the dining room. We count each piece of candy and each cookie that we put in the bags, so that the kids will all get the same amount. It's a kid thing—John and I know that we kids would have counted every piece in the bag.

Mom and Christine walk into the dining room and want to know what we two are doing. John tells them about Mr. Hamilton and his family. Christine tells John to go in the basement—there's a shopping bag at the front of the basement, below the windows. In the bag, she says, are little stuffed teddy bears, five of them. "Bring them up here," she says. "I was going to put them on the Christmas tree, but let's give them to the Hamiltons."

John comes back with the bag. Christine pulls out the bears and they're so cute—white bears with red bells around their necks. She says she will wrap them up as little gifts, and put bows and ribbons on the packages. Then John and I can add them to the gift bags that we are giving to the kids. Mom watches us and smiles, not saying a word, not objecting to our using whatever goodies we want for the gift bags. John, Christine, and I are laughing, knowing how Mr. Hamilton will love this. Well, anyway, we hope he and his family will be happy.

Christine tells John and me that we have to bring all of this down to their house soon. It's getting late and they might go to bed early. She also gives us a fresh-baked apple pie to bring over to the Hamiltons.

189

Off John and I go to drop off the gifts and help another family have a nice Christmas. I'm nervous because I want this to go well. In fact, I am crying because I want so very much for the Hamilton kids to have a great Christmas, and to believe in Santa. We in our family know how it feels to feel empty, and I don't want that for the Hamilton kids.

"But what do we do?" I ask John. "Knock on the door or just drop the things off on the porch and run?"

We talk about what to do as we walk down the block. John says we will knock, leave the things, and run. When we get a little bit away, we can hide between two cars and no one will see us. It's really dark out here and there aren't many streetlights down at this end of the block.

We follow John's plan. He and I quietly walk onto the front porch, hoping that none of the wooden planks will creak. We place the gifts on the porch floor, then John rings the bell and knocks once on the front door. Then we make our getaway. John's faster than I am going down the front steps—he can jump every three steps, while I jump every two. Once we're on the street we run as fast as we can.

My heart is pounding really quickly, and I am laughing because this is so exciting and fun. I follow John into the space between two parked cars and sit on the cold street. We see that the Hamiltons' front porch light has been turned on. Then we hear the front door open. Mr. Hamilton looks to his left, then his right. "Is anyone out here?" he asks. Then he looks down on the porch floor, and sees our big surprise.

We can see the smile on Mr. Hamilton's face. John and I laugh with happiness for the Hamilton kids. "We did good tonight," John says.

I tell John he's a good brother. "You're not a jerk all the time," I say. "That's what I like about you. You are fun and loving to everyone. I am proud you're my brother. Now, can I go to mass with you and your friends tonight?"

No. John laughs at me as he tells me to go to church with Anna and Antoinette. "You can't hang out with me and my friends—we're too old for you. You're just a kid."

We watch as Mr. Hamilton picks everything up off the porch floor. It takes him three trips in and out of the house to gather all the gifts. On the final trip Mrs. Hamilton comes out with him to help. As they go back into the house, Mrs. Hamilton turns and says, "Good night and merry Christmas! Thank you!"

Off we run to our house. We still have to finish up with our tree and do some last-minute Christmas preparations. Then we have to get ready to go to mass. Then it's off to church and then back home to watch my favorite movie, "Scrooge."

• • •

We had a great Christmas. And I ate just like a pig —I ate anything and everything I could get my hands on. We drank red wine with dinner, and with dessert we all drank anisette. This was how we celebrated our Italian Christmas—with lots of food, lots of heart, and lots of giving. How could it get any better than that?

The Wooden Box

My grandmother kept a glossy wooden box under her bed with the instructions that my mom and my grandfather were never to open it. She told them that the box contained her mementos and her life secrets. She informed them that she refused to share the contents with anyone because they were her precious possessions.

My mother was forbidden to touch the box. She wasn't even allowed in her mother's bedroom without her mother being there. But sometimes my mom would go in and snoop around the bed, looking under it to see if the box was still there. She wanted so badly to get up the courage to look inside that shiny box—to see all the treasures my grandmother had hidden inside it. But of course she didn't want to get caught. The problem was that when you lifted the lid of the box, a bell would ring loudly. She heard that bell every night when her mother would open the lid. This was my grandmother's ritual— every night she looked at her items. This was her sleeping pill—she would fall asleep holding some of her papers. She would hold them close to her heart and drift off. Then in the morning my mom would hear the bell again, signaling that my grandmom had closed the lid for the day.

My grandmother had a hot Italian temper and would easily snap at my mom, making her feel like a bad little girl. So she would hesitate to do anything that would set my grandmother off. My mom had a great curiosity to understand her parents as well as herself. She felt that if she could see and touch the items in the box, no matter how large or small they were, she could learn more about her parents' lives in Italy and now here in America. My mom had no siblings or any other family members to guide her, or to fill her in on the secret family knowledge that every child wants to find out about. So she hoped that her parents would indulge her curiosity one day. She needed to know the origins of their love for one another. She wanted to understand their feelings for her and her older sister, Rita, who had died at birth. My mom needed to understand her own being—how did she fit into this family?

One day, when my mom had a half day at school, she was in the apartment by herself. Her parents were at work and wouldn't be home for hours. Then her courage came up from her soul. She would go into her parents' bedroom and pull out that box from under the bed. Today was the day she would open it. She would pull the lid up and hear the sound of that bell. But today, nobody else would hear it, so she knew in her heart this was the time to take advantage of the situation. Opportunity had arrived; it was now or maybe never.

When my mother took that box in her hands, she felt such energy coming from it! Her entire body felt weightless, as if she was above the box looking down and through the wood. She placed the box on the side of the bed that my grandmother slept on. She sat next to it and pulled the lid up. The bell sounded loudly, and this was the first time she enjoyed the sound, because now she was in control of the box. She was ready to see what was going to unfold in front of her eyes. She wanted to see all the beauty of her parents' lives and the love they had for each other.

She looks in the box. She sees a few silver coins and a lot of papers. Some are in Italian and others in English. But she is only nine years old and doesn't read all that well. She doesn't understand what the words are saying. She's pulling everything out of the box. She has papers and more papers all over the bed.

Then she hears the front door open and her dad calls out to her. She is frightened when she hears his voice. She's trying to figure out what to do, but before she comes up with a plan her dad is in the bedroom looking at her in total shock. The box is open, the papers are all over the bed, and lots of papers have fallen to the floor.

When her father's eyes meet hers she starts to cry and tries to explain what she was doing. He tells her to be quiet and listen to what he has to say. "If your mother was here, she would spank you," he says. "I don't know if she would forgive you."

My mom tries to explain herself. "Dad, I want to see who my parents are and how we three are a family. Please, help me understand. Tell me about all these papers. Then, I promise I will never go in this box again ... I promise to God."

My grandfather agrees to tell her all about the papers, to explain what everything means to him and to her in terms of family. He starts with the paper from when he came to America. Then he finds the papers for my mom and grandmom's voyage to America. But when he picks up the next piece of paper, he starts to cry.

"What's that paper in your hand?" my mom asks. She is hugging her father and kissing his cheek. He says this is the paper from the cemetery in Italy. My mom questions him—"What's a cemetery?"

He replies, "That's where they bury the dead."

He goes on. "This piece of paper tells us where your sister Rita is buried. If we ever go back to Italy this piece of paper will tell us what her plot number is and in what section of the cemetery she is laid to rest...Your mom doesn't look at these papers *ever*! She can't face the loss of Rita even after 16 years. Even after all this time, her heart can't mend. That's why your mom doesn't let you go out to play with the neighbors' kids. She's afraid she will lose you too, and your mom couldn't take that. Without you, she would die empty and lonely."

"Don't ever tell your mom what we just did," her father warns. "She wouldn't forgive me if she knew that I told you about Rita. Look at me, Ro, and swear to the Almighty God to never tell your mother."

My mom promises. "I won't ever tell Mom about us going through her box, and that we talked about Rita. But Dad," she says, "I want to talk about Rita. She was my older sister. I love her! If she had lived I would have a sister to play with. Someone to talk with me ... I miss my sister but I will never tell Mom. I will keep this my secret forever."

My mom never told her mother about that day. No mention was ever made about how she'd explored that wooden box and its contents with her dad as her guide.

At the age of nine years my mom could keep a secret. At such a young age she knew when to speak and when not to. This ability would become a big part of her future life.

Cards with the Boys

It's a typical Sunday and the entire family will be here today. Mom's making "home-mades"—meaning her own pasta made from scratch—and she has two gallons of red wine. And we—that is, my brothers, brothers-in-law, and I—will be playing five-card stud. The other sisters—plus the sisters-in-law, along with Mom—will be in the kitchen, talking and laughing, like always.

I get to play cards with the guys if Ralph says I can. He usually does give in to me, although it can be tricky. Ralph thinks I am funny because, at only twelve years old, I like to gamble. How I enjoy cards! While playing, the guys let me smoke cigarettes and drink the Chianti we call "dago red." What else could a twelve-year-old girl ask for? I am at my happiest surrounded by all this fun, excitement, and love.

I do win a lot. My brothers tell me I have good luck. My brother-in-law Carmen wants to take me to the racetrack at Atlantic City and have me pick out winning horses. But my sister Grace has told him she'll kill him if he ever takes me to the track. I've told Carmen—take me, and we won't tell Grace, but he says that he's not ready to die. We do continue to think it's a great idea, though, even if it's never going to happen.

When everyone gets to the house we're all happy to see each other, and there's a lot of hugging, kissing, and laughing going on. All the little nieces and nephews are here too. They're so cute; I play with them a lot. My sisters and I chase them all over the house as they scream and laugh at us aunts. We

197

stop only when one of the older sisters tells us that's enough running around—you are giving us a headache.

It's time to eat Mom's home-mades and meatballs with gravy (our word for tomato sauce), and to drink a glass of wine. We are all around two tables—there are at least 15 of us—talking. Then Trudy starts in with, "So … how are you four girls doing in school?" She's so interested because she used to get 100-percents on her report cards—and she always let us know about it.

But my thinking is—who cares if you were smart? Did you have any fun, or get into any trouble? If so, then you and I could understand each other.

I hope Trudy doesn't ask about my report card. When she starts with the questions, I usually run. She is such a nosey-body, and I particularly don't like the question, "Are you going to school every day?" She asks that because she knows I tend to skip school when I get bored. I try my best to be like the other kids in my classroom. I try my best to be good for Trudy and my mom. But it's hard for me to do everything that they want.

Today, though, I will enjoy hanging out with the Big Boys! I can't wait! Let the card game begin!

After we eat the home-mades and meatballs everyone tells Mom this meal was the best—the best in the world! Mom smiles from ear to ear. Now the boys will have a glass or two of wine. They bring their glasses with them into the dining room, and tell me to clear off the table to get it ready to play. This is girls' work, they tell me. My God—my brothers think they are Italian princes!

My first question is, "How many of us are in the game?"

That's when they start. "You are not playing with us! Go play Monopoly with your sisters. Or go watch your nieces and nephews, so they don't get hurt. This is for us boys. We don't want any girls in here. You don't see any of your sisters at this table, do you?"

"Who cares?" I say. "I am here. You should be happy." My voice is starting to get loud, because if they think I am clearing the table just for them, they are wrong. I'm going to be in on this too!

I say to Ralph, "Let me play just for a little while. I won't be in long; I don't have much money. Oh please, Ralph—I love to play cards—let me in the game!"

Ralph laughs and tells my brothers George and John to leave their sister alone. I love when Ralph stands up for me against George and John. They won't say a word to him. They just give me nasty looks—expressions letting me know they will kill me when Ralph leaves. But I don't care—I am in the game!

My brother-in-law Carmen has cigars; he's passing them around the table. But no one gives me one, so I ask, "Where's my cigar?" They laugh and tell me I will get sick.

"Let me have a puff off your cigar, John?" I try. John looks at me, then hands it over. He tells me to suck on it real hard and swallow the smoke. I do just what he says. Then I am gagging really badly—I can't breathe.

My brothers laugh and say, "You still want a cigar, tough girl?" I hand back the cigar to John, and tell him to keep it. I decide I don't like cigars.

Patrick deals the cards ten cents ante as we begin to play five-card stud. Soon, John's doing great; he has won more than half the pots. He's all smiles. Although I am not winning, it's fun playing cards with my brothers.

I only have about 25 cents to play with. This might be my last hand in this card game. It's Ralph's turn to deal. It's two cards down and one up. Everyone is in this hand. My brother Patrick has a pair of something. I can tell because he's just put 10 cents in the pot, and he only bets when he thinks he's got the pot.

Because sometimes I am stupid, I stay in. Even if I think I am going to lose, I won't back down from my four brothers. Sometimes I get mad at myself for this way of thinking, but it's just my way. It's fun to gamble, so I stay in.

Ralph deals out the fourth card. Oh brother!—John has a pair of kings showing, diamonds and hearts. He's laughing at Carmen because Carmen's hand stinks. Carmen folds and so does Ralph.

We go around the table one more time before we get our last card. My hand is excellent. Face-up I have a ten of clubs and a jack of clubs. Ralph and Carmen tease, telling everyone, "Be careful of Josephine!"

"You know she always comes from nowhere and wins," Carmen says as he puffs on his cigar." I can't stand the smoke, but I am not folding. I am in this hand to the finish. I don't care if I am dizzy from all the smoke surrounding me.

Ralph deals Pat a six of hearts. Pat folds.

Ralph deals George an ace of diamonds. George folds.

Now it's John's turn. Ralph deals him a king of spades. John is looking at me and smiling. He tells me to push the pot over to him. Ralph tells him to back off, because Josephine hasn't gotten her last card.

John says, "Go ahead—give the loser her fifth card. Let's get this hand over with."

I am thinking, *on the table I have a ten of clubs and a jack of clubs. And in my hand I have an ace of clubs and a king of clubs. So John doesn't have four kings. But if I don't get a queen of clubs, then I lose … Oh God, let me get the queen of clubs …*

Ralph deals out my last card. And there it is—a queen of clubs. Nobody else knows that that's exactly what I need. John says, "Okay. Twenty cents in the pot—is that alright with you?" My response is that I don't have 20 cents for the pot. I only have 5 cents.

Carmen says to me, "Here—I'll put 15 cents in for you. That way we get to see your hand." My thinking at this point is that I know John has three kings and I have all clubs. But I don't know if that beats John out or not. And I don't know if he has a pair in his hand, which would be a full house. But I don't care. I'm in with the help from Carmen.

John throws his cards face up on the table. And he has a full house—three kings and two queens in his hand. He's just as happy as can be now.

Ralph and Carmen are saying, "We should do a side bet—that Josephine's going to kick Johnnie's ass tonight." This upsets John. He knows they are only teasing, but he doesn't like it. He just wants that pot in the middle of our dining room table.

John says, "So Josephine, let's see your cards—put your money where your mouth is." He's getting really red in the face as he commands, "Come on—let me see your cards now."

Ralph decides, "We won't do any side bets tonight." Then he tells me to let everyone see my cards. So I lay them out one by one. First comes the ace of clubs, and everyone is laughing except John. Here comes the second card— king of clubs. Third card—ten of clubs … fourth—jack of clubs … and fifth— queen of clubs!

Ralph is cracking up so much the dining room table is shaking. I am looking at Ralph and asking, "Did I beat John?"

Ralph says to all of us, "Is she kidding? She has a royal straight flush!" Then, to me, he says, "You won, little sister! The pot belongs to you!" Everyone is laughing, especially me.

But John is mad. His face is red. He's yelling that girls shouldn't be allowed in the card game, that girls are stupid, and that he won't let me play anymore.

Ralph tells John to calm down. "What did she win? Two dollars, if that."
John replies, "But I lost all my money!"

Ralph tells him, "Look, sometimes you win, and sometimes you lose. Tonight you lost."

John rushes by me and says, "You're not playing with us anymore." He takes off into the living room as I grab all the coins and put them into a little glass. The boys are still laughing about how I won as I start rearranging the tabletop so we can all have pastries and coffee. After that, everyone will gather up their kids and go home.

Before coffee, Anna and Antoinette come running from the front porch. "John just punched the window and it's cracked!" they report. We all go look at the big window on the enclosed porch to see what John did.

"Why did you do that?" Mom asks.

"Because she won the card game."

Mom says, "Okay John, I don't need you to break anything in my house. You will have to pay for a new window."

John is trying not to kill me, and deep down inside I am loving it. I beat him! It's great to have older brothers if you can beat them at something. Mom treats them better than us girls, and so they think they are better. But we sisters know the truth.

We all come back into the dining room for creampuffs, cannoli, and coffee. We are a big crowd, but it's wonderful being together. For now, we are a typical Italian family. Love, eat, and fight—that's what we do!

Mom's Pleasure ... Her Enjoyment

Whatever it was—preparing a meal, washing the floors, or resolving her children's problems—Mom was forever on the move and always working hard. There was probably a good side to always being busy, because if she had had time to think, she might have fallen apart.

But in the evening, it was different. After a long day spent on her chores, Mom liked to watch one of her favorite shows on television. When dinner was over she would sit in her living room chair and put her feet up on the ottoman. And we'd all be there with her.

It might be the Mitch Miller show. We'd all be singing along with Mitch, following the little white ball that danced above the words of the song. That show was great fun. Some of Mom's other shows were Perry Como and Dean Martin—the Italian boys were always at the top of her list. When Dean Martin would sing in Italian Mom was in her glory—she didn't miss a word, singing along. It was wonderful to see her joy in doing that. There was also "Laugh-In," Tony Orlando and Dawn, and Sonny and Cher. But her true, true favorite was Tom Jones. When he was about to come on TV my sisters and I would get excited—we knew she'd be so happy. We'd yell, "Mom! He's on! You'd better get in here! You don't want to miss any of it!"

Mom would come running through the kitchen and dining room to get to her chair. You could see the happiness in her eyes as the "This is Tom Jones" variety show took her somewhere else for an hour on Friday nights. She'd be laughing just about the entire time.

Tom always opened his show with one of his beautiful songs. He had such a great voice. But our favorite thing was when he would dance. He had a lot of hip-moving action, and we girls would tease Mom, asking her if she liked the way he moved. And then at the end—well, that show ended in a unique way—girls and women in the audience would throw their panties at Tom! My mom would sit straight up in her chair, and as panties landed all over the stage and Tom laughed at it all, Mom would be laughing too. Tears of laughter would be rolling down her cheeks; she could barely speak at that point.

At the end of the show, as Tom swayed his hips to his closing song, perhaps "What's New, Pussycat?" my sister Antoinette would ask, "Is that a banana in his pocket?" At that, my mom would just about fall out of her chair.

Then, after all the excitement, when the show ended Mom would always say to us, "I'm not going to watch his show any more." It was just all too much! But by the next week, her declaration was forgotten. We would again be telling her Tom's show was about to be on, she would again come running to see him, and soon we'd all be singing along with him. It was great to be part of Mom's happiness.

We four sisters were getting older now. Mom could speak to us more freely. When there were sexual jokes on TV, she felt she could now laugh, because we four were changing from children into young ladies.

The times were changing too. It was the era of the sexual revolution, which involved not just the burning of bras but women wanting more in life than what had been their traditional role. As for me, that traditional role, involving giving birth and staying home to raise a family, was one I wanted no part of. It was the hardest job on this earth, I felt, and after watching all my mom went through trying to do it on her own, I was frightened. I wondered how I would handle it if God gave me the burdens Mom had. Would I leave the family? Or jump off a bridge?

My mom never left us or thought about jumping, and I don't know how she stayed so strong. I know now that she went to church every morning. I found that out at my sister Christine's funeral. It's funny what you hear at funerals, what people are willing to tell you when you're grieving. I believe it's to console you at your worst time, to give you a little pleasure when you're down and out.

It's odd that I didn't know my Mom had had time to go to church every day. Maybe that's how she got her strength to carry on for another day, by praying to her God. Maybe she would ask her God to carry her through one more day, because that would get her one day closer to being with her husband.

My mom was in an exclusive group. What other person could say they accomplished the task of raising twelve children on their own, with iron principles and unconditional love? She could and did do anything to keep us together as a family. *Her family*. It was the job God had given her, and she worked so hard to perform it superbly. It was only fair that she got a little respite in the evenings to relax and enjoy herself.

The Stepdads That Weren't

After Dad died, would you believe that two men were interested in marrying my mom? I still laugh at the thought of her being someone other than Mrs. Pasquarello. In the end, there was no way she was going to give up her married name for anyone or any reason. These two men didn't have a clue about how to handle Mom (nor did anyone on this earth).

Mom didn't date. She didn't have the desire or the time. Her day went quickly and was so busy that, lots of times, she would bathe in the middle of the night when the house was quiet. You could hear the bath water running and her voice softly singing. This half hour belonged to her. Mom would feel joyful and relaxed knowing that another day was done. Then she would go to bed and sleep as soundly as a baby. Tomorrow would be full again, and she would be ready for whatever was coming her way.

One thing coming her way was Mr. O'Rourke, a man who lived two doors down from us. When we first moved to this street, we would sometimes see Mr. and Mrs. O'Rourke sitting on their porch. He was retired, and she was a housewife with no children. They always looked lonely. Now, I was 12, and we had lived on the block for six years. In all that time, although I would wave to them when I passed their house, and they'd wave back, they'd never spoken to me, and I'd never heard them speak to each other.

One sunny day, I ran into the kitchen to get a glass of water when my mom asked me to take a seat. "I have a funny story to tell you," she said.

"Not now, Mom." I was busy jumping rope with my sisters and friends. But Mom pulled out a chair from the table, gesturing that I should sit down, so I did just that.

She proceeded to tell me that the old man, Mr. O'Rourke, had asked her to marry him. I laughed and said, "Mom, he has a wife."

"Not anymore," she replied. "Mrs. O'Rourke died last week and was buried two days ago."

"I didn't know she died!" I was shocked. "What did she die from?"

Mom said that he hadn't mentioned anything about how she'd died, only that he needed a wife to cook, clean, and do the chores. At this point, Mom was laughing so hard that her face was red, and tears were flowing from her eyes. "I told him to hire a maid because I will not wash his dirty underwear," Mom said.

"Oh, my God—Mom—you didn't say that to him!"

"Yes I did. I even told him he's crazy."

Now I was laughing too, and I joked: "Please marry him. He has a house, a boat, and a car. Mom, we'll be really, really rich. Come on, he's an old guy; he won't live real long. Just think—when he dies all that stuff will belong to us."

Mom shook her head—no. "I don't want that dirty old man."

My sisters Antoinette and Christine had been listening from another room. They stepped into the kitchen to add their two cents. Antoinette begged Mom to marry him: "He's half-dead now, so we won't have to put up with him for long. And he has no kids, so we won't have step-siblings to deal with."

We were all having a good time as Christine chimed in: "Mom, where's your ring?"

"What ring?" Mom asked.

"The big, diamond engagement ring he gave you."

With that, Mom's expression changed to a serious one. "I don't need a ring from him, and I don't need a man in my life other than your father. I have the only ring I will ever want or need—the wedding ring your father gave me 28 years ago. That's the ring I would like to be buried with when I die."

With that, Antoinette, Christine, and I walked out of the kitchen. Mom yelled after us, "I don't need any man because I can do anything a man can do, and sometimes even better!" Then she added, "Whatever you do, don't tell your brothers about Mr. O'Rourke. The boys won't be happy to know he came into our house when I was the only one home."

Antoinette yelled back, "Who cares what the boys think? It's what us girls want now, Mom. Just marry Mr. O'Rourke!"

Beyond all the joking, our feelings were mixed. It's not that we wanted a dad. In fact, not one of us would have called him Dad. We would have said, "Mr. O'Rourke, please pass the bacon." We just thought it would be easier if Mom had a man to help her. But my mom didn't see it that way. In her eyes, Mr. O'Rourke would be a pain. Actually, deep down, we all agreed. We didn't really want a man in the house to tell us what to do, and we wouldn't have listened anyway. So it was good that Mom wasn't going to marry him.

Before the end of the summer, Mr. O'Rourke moved away. Mom said he probably found a wife. He needed one, she said, or he would die soon from loneliness. I let Mom know my opinion: He would have died sooner if he had moved in with us, quicker than from loneliness. He could never have put up with all of us, especially Antoinette. She would have driven him nuts with her big mouth. Antoinette, who was sitting at the table, seemed to be proving me right when she added, "So, goodbye Mr. O'Rourke—we didn't want you anyway!"

Why would any man in his right mind want to marry a lady with twelve kids? With Mr. O'Rourke, the reason may have been loneliness, but with Mr. D'Amico it was sex. And that wasn't with my mom, according to my sister Anna, who told me she thought he would have the youngest four girls for himself. "No way," I objected. "He wants to marry Mom because she'll cook all Italian dishes for him. He knows she was born in Italy, and speaks Italian, and so does he." Anna told me I was stupid. He didn't love Mom or us.

Actually, it wasn't that I believed he loved us or our mom, but I did think he'd be happy with us. Mr. D'Amico had never been married and had no family here in America. He owned his own company, a locksmith business, which is how Mom met him. When our front door lock wouldn't turn with the key, she called him to the house to repair it.

I was 17, and it was four in the afternoon on a hot spring day. I was running upstairs to get out of my school uniform, a wool dress and long-sleeved shirt. Once in my bedroom, I was starting to undress when Mom called up to me: "Josephine, come down. I want to talk with you." I stopped undressing and ran downstairs to the kitchen in my underwear. Mom said to sit down and pointed to the chair next to her at the table. "Why are you in your underwear?" she asked.

"Because you wouldn't let me get dressed," I answered. I was in a bra and panties, but that wasn't so unusual because my sisters and I were always running around in our underwear.

Mom had a strange look on her face, and was playing with her fingers, so I knew something was wrong. "Mom, what's the problem?" I asked. "Why are you upset?"

"You know that locksmith, Mr. D'Amico?" she said. I told her I'd never spoken to him, but I'd seen him in the neighborhood.

"Why, Mom?" Mom looked nervous. "Come on, Mom, just tell me."

"He says he wants to marry me."

Oh, no, not that again. What does this man want from my mom? There were only five of us girls at home. Patrick was married, and George and John were both in the service. So maybe Anna was right when she said this man is a weirdo who thinks he will have six females in one house to himself? Yeah, good luck to you, I thought. Us girls will kill you first. Then we will tell our brothers, and they will kill you a second time.

Mom was telling me that he needs a wife and a family. "He's too old to have kids and wouldn't want babies around, so this would be perfect for him," she said. "But I will talk it over with your brothers and sisters. They might think it's a good idea."

"Mom, who did you tell so far?" I asked.

"Well, you, Antoinette, Anna, and Carmella."

"What do they think?"

"Your sisters said no. They think he's a creep, and they don't want him living in our house."

"Are you serious about this? You always sleep on everything because you need time to think about it." Mom looked bewildered and stressed. Poor Mom—this was a problem she didn't need—another proposal! Mom was already 57 years old. She didn't want sex anymore ... or did she? That's what we girls were talking about. She had us; what did she need from him?

We girls were getting older now. We could take care of Mom. Besides, we were her babies. I believe we were jealous—if she married him what would happen to us? Would she love him more? Oh no, we were going to make sure that didn't happen. That man wasn't getting in our house.

On Sunday, the entire family, about 17 of us, gathered in the kitchen. Those who knew—the young ones—told everyone else about Mr. D'Amico. Then all hell broke loose. Mom tried her best to keep everything under control, but she was having no luck. We were a high-energy family, and we were all talking at the same time. We younger girls had planted the seed to get it started, and it was growing fast.

Ralph and Patrick asked Mom, "What does this old man want?" Before Mom could answer, Christine was telling them she thought he was a pervert and not to be trusted in our home. Christine had a big voice, and Mom would often listen to her. My younger sisters and I loved her for getting our thoughts on the situation across. In the end, we decided to take a vote on whether or not to let Mr. D'Amico into our family.

Before we could, our older sisters, Trudy and Grace, had a question: "Why would you girls like Mr. D'Amico in the house?"

"We don't!" exploded Antoinette. "We don't want the little grease ball here!" Mom got upset and told us not to use the term "grease ball" in her house. "Okay, Mom, we won't call him names. But come on, he's a worm, and you know it." That was Antoinette again, and, to tell the truth, we younger girls were glad that she was expressing what we all thought.

Mom said she felt we were all attacking her, and it was making her uncomfortable. Ralph went over and hugged her. He said, "Let's just you and I sit down and drink a cup of coffee, and we will decide what we should do." Ralph, the oldest, often took on the role of the man of the family. Mom was willing to talk with Ralph, and she relaxed a little. The rest of us were shooed out of the kitchen, so brothers, sisters, and in-laws went into the dining room, where we could hear what Ralph and Mom were saying.

Ralph was telling Mom to think about how everything would change if she married Mr. D'Amico. He talked about how we had gotten this far on our own without Dad here. "We have survived the loss of our protector," he said. "Do you believe this man can fill his shoes? Or is Mr. D'Amico just a stand-in? Mom, are you lonely for someone? For me to help, you must tell me your thoughts and feelings."

With that, Mom broke down … She was crying and talking fast, sometimes in Italian. Ralph said, "Slow down, and don't speak in Italian. I can't understand you."

Mom blew her nose. Then it was quiet in the kitchen for a few moments. Mom got herself together and explained to Ralph that she didn't love or for that matter even like Mr. D'Amico. It was just the she was getting older and starting to slow down. When Mr. D'Amico asked her to marry him, she thought that if anything were to happen to her, at least the girls would have him to protect them.

Ralph had a good answer. "Mom, if I was the one sitting in your chair, you know what you would say to me. Just think it over, and you will know what to do." Soon, Mom and Ralph were laughing.

She called us to come back into the kitchen to give us her decision. "I have made my decision about Mr. D'Amico." I was breathing hard, and my hands were wet with perspiration. I'm sure everyone in that room was just as nervous.

Mom looked at Christine and then at us youngest four girls and said, "I am not marrying Mr. D'Amico or any other man." It was like the weight of the world was off her shoulders. And off ours too! We started laughing and dancing the twist. I was so happy I was crying. I didn't have to worry about walking a straight line for that man or any other man. What a relief! Life would go on as usual. We could be happy as a family unit again. We wouldn't let any outsider bust up our family or our home. It was a secure feeling to know that we wouldn't have any more unwanted surprises.

• • •

It's two weeks after my mom's proposal, and life continues. We are in school. Chris is working at the insurance company, her job of ten years. The family is moving on. This is the way we live our lives. This is our normal.

I am sick today, so I am home with Mom. She's coming in the house with her shopping cart. I get off the sofa to help her, and she looks at me. She asks me to come into the kitchen and have a cup of tea. She needs to tell me something. So I follow her, and she points to the table and says take a seat. Whenever she does this, you start to worry because you never know what she will spring on you. "What's going on now, Mom? What news do you have for me?"

Mom starts to laugh and says I won't believe her. She tells me the meat cutter at the food market is a friend of Mr. D'Amico. When she says that name again, I feel like throwing up. I sit there just staring at her, thinking—please—

no—not him again. She's telling me that Mr. D'Amico died two days ago of a heart attack. His friend from the market asked Mom if she would attend his funeral because he had few friends and no family. Mom told him she would be at the church for his funeral mass the next day. I start to laugh and tell her we could have been rich today. If you had married him, I say, it would have been just two weeks of him. My mom sees the humor in this and we laugh.

The next morning, she attends Mr. D'Amico's funeral mass and says a prayer that he is at peace.

After that, the idea of a stepdad was a terrible thought that we never had to worry about again. My sisters and brothers and I were delighted a stepdad never came into our lives. Looking back, I feel there was no chance my mom would ever have married either man. She loved my dad with her entire being and would never have allowed anyone to overshadow that.

Like a Flash

My brother John was the eighth child of my parents and the youngest boy in our family. He had so much fun inside of him. And because of all that fun, he took it to the other side. He was the daredevil in the family. If you and John were playing something like poker or Monopoly, all you did was argue because he was always making up new rules. Or you might be laughing the whole time because you couldn't figure out his brain pattern. He always seemed to be taking crazy chances, although I never witnessed him being totally wiped out in the process. And if he was, John wouldn't care about that. He'd get right up and start all over again. To him it would be fun.

I had a special kinship with John. I secretly wanted to be the female version of John. He and I had our dad's wild, kinky, dark brown hair. So in my eight-year-old mind, we were connected—through our hair and through our brown eyes and our brown skin as well.

I knew that if I hung out with John—and that would only be when John allowed me to—I would be walking into a danger zone. It was exciting, but also frightening. Sometimes I wanted to emulate his behavior but was afraid to try, fearing I could never do the things he did. For instance, he would ride on the back bumper of the SEPTA trolley or bus. They ran outside our house, so you would sometimes see John on the back of one, waving to us kids playing on the sidewalk. We didn't have to rat on him, because when he entered the house you could smell the gasoline all over him. His gold corduroy coat became stained with it.

That gold corduroy coat … I remember it well. I had a yellow one just like John's; I'd gotten it when Trudy took us to downtown Philly to get new winter coats. Trudy and her boyfriend Patrick drove us youngest six kids to buy coats in John Wanamaker's, the exclusive department store downtown.

We were all excited as we tried on coats. We kids didn't get a new one every year, so this was a wonderful event for us. John came walking over to Trudy and Patrick to show them the coat he liked. It was a beautiful bright gold corduroy with a black knitted collar. He looked so cute in that coat! He told all of us that "this coat is for me."

So Trudy said, "Okay, John—that's for you."

That's when I began thinking, "I'm getting a coat just like John's." But in the girls' section, there wasn't one. So Trudy found a yellow one in the boys' department. I tried it on and thought, "I look just like John!" I told Trudy that I wanted this beautiful yellow coat.

It certainly was bright—I remember Trudy saying, "Josephine, you look like the sun in that coat." Everyone laughed, but I didn't care. I was getting a coat just like John's. I was beyond happy. Secretly, I was now cool, just like John.

That was such a great day for us youngest six. We got new coats and afterwards Trudy and Patrick took us to South Philly for salad and pizza. I didn't want that day to end.

• • •

Actually, John should never have chosen that gold coat because it became a trademark for him. Everyone associated that coat with John. When he would come home from riding on the back bumper of the SEPTA bus and take off his coat, Christine would go over to it and take a sniff. She would start choking from the fumes, and then she'd go over to John and slam her hand across his face, yelling that one day a vehicle was going to hit the back of that bus and he would end up a cripple. John would try to explain to Christine that he would never get hurt. He knew how to jump on and off at just the right time, or so he said. I just loved listening to him and his logic.

We were all afraid he would get hurt but he continued that activity for a couple of years. He was the only kid in our neighborhood who did that. It only ended when Mom told him that she wasn't going to buy him a new winter coat. He had ruined the last one with the splatters of gasoline.

That was when John was about 13 years old and had started liking the girls. He had to look good and be wearing a clean coat. But his craving for adventure still came first. So he let go of the bus-bumper habit and soon took on something new that amused him greatly—climbing up the downspouts to get onto the roof. He was just like a cat burglar. Because he was so small and thin he could run atop the houses on 58th Street, a skill that came in handy when the cops were chasing him. On a foot chase, they could never catch him. He was known in the neighborhood as a monkey. That was an appropriate name for such a mischievous kid.

One sunny summer day John comes into the front bedroom. He tells Carmella and me, "Come outside on the second-level roof and I'll teach you how to climb the downspout to the big roof." You don't have to ask me twice—I am so excited that John is going to teach me this new skill. It never enters my mind that I might fall, or maybe even kill myself.

Out we go through the bedroom window. John is in the lead, then comes Carmella, and then me. We're all laughing and talking. Carmella and I are happy as can be to be with our older brother.

John teaches us how to brace our bodies with our feet against the wall. He tells us to watch his feet climbing up and his hands moving up at the same time. He's looking down at us and telling Carmella to follow him. Then he says I can climb up after her onto the big roof.

I can't wait to get up there to see what's on our big roof. Maybe some dead birds are up there, John tells us. But then we hear our mom's voice: "Get down from there!" I look toward the window and see that Mom is hanging halfway out, trying to grab me.

Mom is telling John, "You could hurt the girls! That downspout won't hold the three of you. Now—never bring your sisters with you again. *You* may be a little nuts, but my girls aren't, and I don't want them hurt! Get in here now before I climb out there to get you." So we two girls climb back in through the bedroom window.

Leave it to Mom to ruin my fun. But also to save us from harm. We probably would have pulled the downspout off the wall. And God only knows what would have happened after that … although, in my heart, I would still have followed him anywhere. He was, after all, my loving big brother John. And anyone with a fun-seeking big brother like him would always want to be close and connected. Because if I wasn't, then I might miss out on something incredible he might be involved in …

Like being chased by the cops. The cops were always at our front door looking for John for one thing or another. He would stand at the alleyway on 58th Street and Kingsessing Avenue while the cops would be down at the other end on 58th and Greenway. He'd be calling down to the cops, "Come and get me!" He'd be laughing and taunting them to catch him, but they couldn't—on foot or in their police cars. John was way too fast for any of the cops.

Sometimes the cops would try to catch John when he was standing with his friends at the hoagie shop on Chester Avenue. The police didn't like to see groups of boys just hanging around socializing, even if they weren't doing anything wrong. So when the cops approached, John would climb up the downspout and stay on the second-story roof until they were gone. Never once did they see him up there; they always thought he'd gotten away. I was always happy to see John evade the cops; I knew that if they got him they'd beat the hell out of him. John was just having fun, but he didn't know when to quit.

One summer the cops from the 12th District were always after John, looking for him for one thing or another. I remember one particular hot day. We kids are outside playing when we see John come running down 58th Street. He's yelling, "Get out of my way!" as he goes flying up the front steps into the house. Mom is running down the front steps because there are three cop cars in front of our house. That means six cops are here.

The cops run up our steps yelling for John to come outside. "Because if you don't come out, John, we will come in to get you! We will count to three and you'd better be out here."

"Three" comes and goes and John doesn't appear. Mom is a few steps from the top and is telling the cops, "No one is going into my house." The cop closest to Mom pulls his gun from its holster. Now Mom is getting really loud with that cop and telling him, "You better put that gun away!" She's starting to cry because she doesn't know if she can handle a crazy man with a gun, whether he has a police uniform on or not. And we all know how Mom feels about cops. (Her theory about cops went like this: "What they arrest us for is

218

exactly what they get away with." So her opinion on their behavior wasn't the greatest. Now that's not to say that all cops were bad, but back in the 1950s and '60s, they could be wild. And the cops in the neighborhood knew we had no man in the house.)

The cop with the gun goes running into the house with his gun out and with Mom right behind him. We sisters are all outside and too scared to even move. As for me, when trauma is happening in front of my eyes, and especially when it involves a family member, I just shut down. Things seem to be happening in slow motion and I can see everyone's expression—my sisters, and even the cops, are in shock.

I am saying silently, "Please, God, help my mom and John." I am sweating so much that the perspiration is running down my back and legs. I seem to be standing in a puddle of sweat. My stomach hurts so bad, I think about throwing up.

We hear the cop inside calling out John's name, but that's all we hear. Even the cops standing outside with us are frozen in their spots. One says to another, "What's he doing? He better not hurt that kid."

Here comes my mom and that cop. She's telling him, "You had no right to take your gun out and run through my house." She lets him know she's happy he didn't catch John because he only wanted to hurt him. "And for what?" she asks. "For standing on the street corner? What are those boys doing? Are they really bothering anyone? They're just being teenagers."

And she has more to say. "Leave my son alone. Get off my steps and don't come back here again. You're just a madman with a gun. You shouldn't be a cop." She tells him that next time he comes looking for John, he'd better have a warrant.

Some of our neighbors are standing on the sidewalk in front of our house. A couple of the women are yelling at the cops for their stupid behavior; they have sons the same age as John. They tell the cops, "You shouldn't be acting this way with Mrs. Pasquarello and her son. What did he do—rob a bank or kill someone? Really, this is unacceptable to be treating the Pasquarello family like this." The cops are embarrassed. A young cop tells my mom he is sorry for what just happened.

So they all got back into their cars and drove down 58th Street. We didn't see John all day, but we knew he was fine. He was like a flash—here now and gone in a second. When he did come home, for dinner that night, he came in the back door. He had avoided the front of the house completely, just in case the cops would be out front in their cars, waiting for him to come home. His maneuver was to climb up to the roof of the house on the very end of the block, then cross over multiple roofs until he came to our house in the middle of the block. Then he climbed down the downspout and came in through the back door, avoiding any sighting by the police. It was simple. For John, that is. For the family, it was nerve-racking. We didn't want our fun-loving brother to get hurt.

. . .

Tonight Mom is making pizza for George and John, who have just graduated from eighth grade. Mom is so proud of her boys. They will go to West Catholic Boys High School in September. So to celebrate she is making pizza for all the eighth-grade boys. She started making the sauce after lunch today, and now the aroma throughout the house is delicious. My brothers help with the pizza dough. Mom ordered over 20 rolls of dough for the party and will be busy making pizza all night. There will be 40 pizzas.

She doesn't mind doing this for her younger boys. She'll bake every pizza with love, expressing her happiness for George and John and their accomplishments as they move forward to high school.

You should see all the boys from our school who are here! It started around 6 p.m. and it's still going strong at sunset and into the evening.

Mom continues baking her pizza like she's running a restaurant. Our front door never stops opening until after 10 p.m. The neighborhood boys just keep coming into the kitchen, asking if there is any more pizza. The Irish boys love my mom and her cooking. They probably haven't had homemade pizza before, so this is a real treat for them. It's also a treat for my brothers because they've never had all of their friends over like this.

The next day our house—from the kitchen through the dining room and the living room—was a mess. Both George and John worked on cleaning things up, with the help of us last four girls, of course. We girls had also had a great time—watching all those boys come and go. It was a good life after all!

. . .

On weekends, John worked at a bakery, along with brothers Patrick and George. John went on to graduate from West Catholic Boys High School. He looked for guidance from our brother-in-law Patrick, who was married to Trudy. John and Patrick both loved beautiful, "cherry"- looking cars. John would help Patrick clean and wax his car at our house. They'd be out there for hours, stopping only to come in for a bite to eat.

I enjoyed sitting on the front steps and talking with them about the car. I knew I was bothering them—but I didn't care. They couldn't shut me up. Even when they would stop answering my silly questions, I continued. It was fun!

It was nice to watch my brother John with Trudy's husband. They had a special bond; they acted like a son and father. I wasn't at all jealous but I did wish I had a relationship with a dad. That is, and always will be, an empty spot for me. John was certainly lucky to have Patrick at his side.

Patrick was handsome, dark with curly hair. He had nice features and beautiful white teeth. More important, Patrick helped John turn into a good man. He got him to stop acting crazy and start acting mature. It probably helped that all of a sudden John went from having a small physique to being six feet tall. He finally got big muscles and gained weight. He wasn't the John from two years earlier; he was looking more and more like a man. He was real sweet to me—which is not to say that he would not pull the occasional prank.

What kid do you know that quit smoking at the age of 16? Usually, that's the age that kids *start* smoking. Not John. He quit at 16 and never touched cigarettes again.

John met his girlfriend Ginny "down the shore." And he was in love— that's all he would talk about. Boy oh boy—did that become annoying to us girls! We would tell him to leave us alone—we didn't want to hear about her anymore. He would tell us we were uncouth, unlike her. "Big deal," we would say. We would laugh and tell him, "If she's with you, she's the one who's un- couth—not us!"

· · ·

John served in the U.S. Army from 1965 to 1970. I remember John leaving our family; we all were nervous, wondering if he might never come back to us. But then the thought came to me that there wasn't anything that could stop John, not even the Vietnamese. I secretly hoped and prayed that this was true.

During his tour of duty in Vietnam he was a helicopter pilot and instructor. So he went from having the cops chase him to having the Vietnamese chase him. But they couldn't calm his spirit down. I don't think there was anything or anyone who could tame him.

He received the Air Medal with 22 oak leaf clusters. Mom was so happy to have her baby boy come home from the war. That's all she talked about—John was on his way to Philly! She almost passed out when he walked through our door. She shook as she held him in her arms, and it was a sight to see, with him so tall and her so short as they held tightly to each other. It was an emotional time for the whole family, and indeed, we are Italians "emotionally," so we were all laughing, crying, and talking nonstop to our brother John. He was back home and we were all so proud of him—with or without the medal. We were so glad to have him back in our arms.

Of course, after a few days back home with us girls, John was himself again, pranks and all.

. . .

John married his girlfriend Ginny. In 1973 he received a bachelor of science degree in aerospace engineering from Penn State University. In that same year he joined Sikorsky Aircraft as a flight test engineer, and he later became a test pilot.

John died on May 19, 1978. He was in a Black Hawk Army utility transport. It went down in the Housatonic River while on a test flight. John was the co-pilot, and there was also a flight engineer. All three died. John left his wife, Virginia; two children; eight sisters; and three brothers.

It was a devastating loss for our family. The one who had always had us in his heart was gone. He was the one who would do anything and everything to make us laugh. Now, who would do that? Who would help us to see life as it comes and not allow whatever happens to defeat our spirits? Who would get us to see the other side of our existence?

We were shattered. But we were determined to get back up and live our lives, thankful for everything we received each day. And we would remember John's smile.

John had been thinking of giving up flying because he started to feel uneasy. He thought it was time to have a regular job, so he could be around to raise his sons. He knew firsthand what it was like not to have your dad to help you become a good person and a standup guy. But his fate on this earth was already determined.

• • •

A little while after John's funeral, I returned to Arizona, where I had been living at the time, and I received something in the mail. It was from Ralph, who, as the oldest of the brothers and sisters, felt he should memorialize John with a poem. I opened up my copy, and was touched to read Ralph's verses. I still am, today. Here is what he wrote:

John Our Brother
By Ralph Pasquarello, 1978

I sit and wonder why
God plucked him from the sky.
I...confused and full of pain...
I'll never be the same.

He was so full of life...

of dreams and goals he set.
God must need him badly to allow
him the fate he met.

He'll teach the angels to fly.
And to show them how it's done,
he has a way about him
to make it seem like fun.

So, if you look to the sky,
a captor you may see.

It may not be of this earth, you know…
John, it may be.

. . .

As kids we used to play with a Ouija board. Christine had brought that board into our family, and we played with it for years. It was fun to ask questions about our future. Most of the time we had lots of laughs as a family when playing.

Sometimes I would ask the board how old I would be when I died, and it always went to the numbers 3 and then 2—or 32. If John was around he would tease me, telling me that I would be dead at 32. This would upset me, but I would never allow John to see me fragile. When John passed away at the age of 31—but in his 32nd year—it shocked me into realizing that maybe the Ouija board had the wrong person. Maybe it had been indicating John's destiny, not mine? The board always told me I would have two children when I died. When John died he had two sons. I had one daughter but I had two pregnancies. And I was only 29 years old.

It's odd that the Ouija board had John and me confused. It was like the board didn't know we two were different people. Maybe it got confused by those two golden-colored coats. The Ouija board's predictions were correct—only for the wrong person. Its predictions were not for me—they were for my brother John.

. . .

Here's how the Ouija board operates (source: *The American Heritage Dictionary*, 4th Edition). It's a board with alphabet and other symbols on it, and a planchette that is thought, when touched with the fingers, to move in such a way as to spell out spiritualistic and telepathic messages on the board.

Planchette—a small triangular board supported by two casters and a vertical pencil that, when lightly touched by the fingertips, is said to spell out subconscious or supernatural messages.

Subconscious—The part of the mind below the level of conscious perception.

The Lost Boy

John had a friend who lived around the corner from us. His name was Rob, and they were very close up to the age of 16. Rob's parents were older than the other parents in the neighborhood—except for my mom, who was about the same age as his, although that was the only thing they had in common.

Until that beautiful, sunny and warm Mother's Day when our lives were about to change and God would again let us know He controls the universe, including all of us. And that He alone would make all the decisions on matters such as life and death. But God—do we really have to go through this again? All the misery ... do we really have to watch Rob's mom in such pain? Come on, God, lighten up on us ... can't we live with a little happiness? There were no answers, and all I could think of was how much pain Rob's parents were going through right now.

We hear the priest saying the "Our Father" at Rob's funeral. He is asking God to take good care of Rob and to keep him in His arms forever. Now let us pray for Rob's soul, the priest says.

John is whispering in my ear, "If God could take good care of Rob, then he'd be here with us." John is really mad at life and at God right now. You can tell he wants to punch someone or something. He is telling me to stop crying or he is going to send me home from church. He's telling me that what the priest is saying up at the altar is all bullshit. Besides that, John says, "Who cares what God is thinking? Why don't you ask me what I am feeling right now?"

Now, John is crying. He's telling Pat that he, John, should have saved Rob from drowning in Darby Creek on Mother's Day. "But he was too big and much stronger than me. I couldn't pull him out of the creek—the current was way too strong for us boys. If only I could change that day—I'd give everything for Rob to be here next to me."

Poor John feels so guilty about Rob drowning that day. All the parents in the area would tell the boys not to go swimming in the creek. The current was always fast-moving, and sometimes the water level was deep. You never knew what was happening in that creek. The boys, though, thought they knew better. And my mom would sometimes admit that "boys will be boys." But now John's heart was broken, and he told Mom he wished he and all the boys had listened to their parents.

John and Rob were in the same classroom at West Catholic Boys High School. They were together all day, and on the weekends they got into whatever young teenage boys do. They had a close bond that none of the other boys could break. John had someone to do all his daredevil stunts with, and the two of them were fun to watch and listen to. They were the kind of friends that meshed perfectly—one was not without the other one—and sometimes you would think that there were two Johns—or was it that there were two Robs?

Until that sad day in May. The paddy wagon is coming down Cecil Street. It stops in the middle of the block. The cop who's driving gets out to open the back doors to let the boys out. There are three boys jumping down into the street, and the last one out is my brother John. He is in shock and confused. He is standing there talking to the two cops who drove the boys home from the creek.

The cop who was driving tells John to stay here by the wagon. He tells John that he is going to Rob's house to tell his parents that Rob just drowned in the creek. John tells the cops to let him go with them to talk to Rob's parents because they know John and Rob were inseparable. John will be able to give them details about exactly what happened in the creek.

They're on Rob's front porch and the cop is knocking on the door. Mrs. Harris answers the door and starts to smile at John. She's saying to the cop, "What did John and Rob get into?"... Then, "Where is Rob? ... Did something happen to him?" Now she is starting to look at the cop and then at John with something frantic in her eyes.

The cop asks her if Mr. Harris is at home. She calls out to her husband to come to the door right away. "Something has happened to our Robbie!"

When Mr. Harris gets to the door, poor Mrs. Harris faints right there. Mr. Harris catches her in his arms. He places her on the sofa and she comes to in a few seconds. She's crying now and asking the cop what happened. "Please tell us now! Please!"

The cop tells her and Mr. Harris that he has bad news for them. Mr. Harris sits next to his wife and is holding her hand. She reaches out to John to hold her other hand. She looks at the cop and says to him, "My Robbie is gone." With that, the cop shakes his head yes. He can't talk, because they are all crying.

He starts to tell them that Rob jumped into the creek from a tree. This was something that Rob had always done, along with John and two other boys. The boys would yell out "Tarzan!" when jumping from the tree, and it was great fun. But this time, Rob didn't come back up. So the three boys went down to see where he was. They saw him kicking around in the muddy water. At first they thought he was kidding around, but when he wouldn't come closer to them they realized something was wrong.

All three boys swam over to Rob to help him but he was fighting them off, and the current was moving quickly. They couldn't grab him to pull him up out of the water. The more they tried, the farther he was moving away from them. Then all of a sudden they couldn't see him any longer. The three boys went underwater to look for him, but soon had to come up for air. When they went back down again, and again, they couldn't find him. Up they came again, but no one else was around.

"The water was muddy," John was saying. "We couldn't see much of anything." The creek water was always cloudy when it was moving quickly.

The boys were panicked about not being able to help their friend. John went down one more time to see if he could see Rob. But when he came up he told his friends that Rob was gone.

Then a man and his son came over to talk to John and his friends. The man told the boys he and his son had been watching them from the other side of the creek. John explained what had happened and the man told John not go down into the water again. He'd go to the public phone and call the police for help—they'd come right back to help them.

About 15 minutes later the paddy wagon came, and then two police cars. The cops tell the boys no one can go in the creek. They have some cops at the other end of the creek to see if Rob comes down that way. We need to find your friend, they say, but we don't want to lose another one of you. Just sit here and let us do our job. John and his friends are trembling with fear for Rob. John keeps asking, how did this ever happen to him, and how can we tell his parents? The three of them are terrified, and John is saying he will never swim in the creek again.

They found Rob's body later that day; he wasn't that far from where the boys last saw him. His body was tangled in the underwater weed growth; they had to cut him free to get him out of the water.

After this terrible accident, John was changed; he settled down quite a bit. He still had his edge, and would still walk a thin line. But he realized that anything could happen to you. You could be gone in a moment. This is when my 16-year-old brother became a young man.

Mrs. Harris

We four younger sisters are outside on the front steps, playing jacks. I love playing jacks because I have long, thin fingers with long fingernails. So I can pick up the jacks and not touch any of the ones still left on the step. I win a lot at this game.

Now Carmella is telling us three younger ones that Mrs. Harris is coming to our house again. We all say hello to Mrs. Harris, and she smiles at us as she walks up the steps to our front door. She rings the doorbell and Mom opens the door to let her come inside.

Mrs. Harris is always in that black dress, the same kind my mom wore for about two years after Dad died. I don't like when the ladies wear their black dresses all the time. It's like a big sign that reads SADNESS. I feel uncomfortable around that—who wants to look at sadness all the time?

Mrs. Harris has been at our house every day since Rob died. She comes around after lunchtime and stays in our kitchen with Mom all afternoon, which is unusual because Mom doesn't allow the neighbors in our house. But Mrs. Harris is an exception because Mom feels Mrs. Harris's broken heart. Mom wants to help her get through the loss of her only child.

They sit at the kitchen table talking and talking. Sometimes Mrs. Harris cries and Mom hugs her. It's so loud—Mrs. Harris's moans of pain—that I just want to run and never come back. But Mom tells us girls to always be kind to

Mrs. Harris, because what she has to endure is unbearable. And she will have to carry this hurt for the rest of her life.

That will all change one August day when I come running into the house to get a drink of cold water. We sisters have been jumping rope outside on the sidewalk. It's about 95 degrees outside—but the hotter it is the better I like it. I am a warm child—keep me in the hot weather and I will thrive. Besides, I like the color the sun makes my skin.

I notice that Mrs. Harris isn't at the kitchen table with Mom. I figure she's here because I saw her ringing the doorbell about an hour ago, and I never saw her leave. So I question Mom: "Where's Mrs. Harris? In the bathroom?" My mother turns swiftly toward me and grabs the glass of water out of my hands, even before I can get one swallow to cool me off. Come on, Mom— give me the glass of water—I am so thirsty.

But Mom sits down on her favorite chair at the head of the kitchen table, and says, "Come over here, Josephine. I want to tell you what Mrs. Harris said to me. And why she went home so soon."

I look at my mom and think, how can I get out of this sit-down about Mrs. Harris? I tell Mom I can't sit with her now—I'm playing with my sisters and our friends. It's going to be my turn to jump rope and I don't want to miss it. She starts to laugh at me and says, "Do you want this water or not?"

"Okay, Mom, but make this story quick—I wanna go play." Mom is sitting straight up, looking at me with a strange look. "Go ahead, Mom," I say, "tell me about Mrs. Harris and you, and what she did … Are you upset, Mom?"

"Well, Josephine, you know how I tried to help Mrs. Harris with her loss?" I nod. She says, "It just broke my heart that she had only one child, and that she lost him so early on." I don't know where this is going, but I can tell it isn't good, because my mom is already sad about it.

Then, Mom lets the bomb drop. "Mrs. Harris said to me today that 'it should have been one of your boys who drowned that day in the creek.'"

Mom tells me that when she heard those words come out of Mrs. Harris's mouth, she could have fallen to the floor. Now Mom is crying, truly upset. She's saying, "How could anyone say something like that to a mother about her child? Mrs. Harris should know better than that—she just lost her son! What was she thinking—because I have four sons I wouldn't miss one of them? I don't want her in my home ever again!"

Oh boy—Mom is really mad at Mrs. Harris. "But wait a minute," I say. I am only 13 years old, but I feel Mom is being a little crazy right now. "You should let Mrs. Harris come back again—she needs your help. Besides that, she likes having us kids around her every day. Mom—she really is a nice lady. Think about it."

My mom is looking at me like she doesn't know who I am. And I'm looking at her with the same question in my eyes. Because I know my mom has a large heart for anyone in need. She knows the pain of life, and that you need lots of help and love at a devastating time in your life.

Mom says, "If Mrs. Harris comes back and apologizes to me, I will forgive her. But if she doesn't, then I don't want her here. I don't want that feeling of uneasiness in my home. Not against any one of my children. I love each and every one of my twelve children as she loved her son. I would never choose any one of my kids to die to save someone else's. A mother could never do this!" Mom did add that although she was upset with Mrs. Harris, she only wished the best for her and her family.

As I was walking out of the kitchen I turned to look at my mom, and I was thinking, Mrs. Harris really didn't mean to say that.

But she never did apologize to my mother, and we never did see her again in our home. We all felt that Mrs. Harris had lost our family, as well as her son.

Movie Star

My younger sister Antoinette and I are sitting outside on our front steps. The sun is starting to set and the air is cool. We two sisters are talking and laughing, which is not uncommon with us. Our topic is BOYS!—how we can't stand them but how we like them a lot. Ant is telling me how easy it is to wrap them around her little finger. She tells me how bossy she is with boys, and how much they love it and give in to her all the time. I'm thinking—what's new?

You can see the devil in her eyes as she smiles back at me. I say, "Please be kind to them. You are known for scaring the boys, but you're almost 15 years old now, so you should grow up and be nice, even if it kills you."

Then Antoinette looks down the street and says, "Oh no, not him." She's pulling at my right arm, tugging at it real hard. I yell that she should let go of my arm—she's hurting me.

"Get off of me, Antoinette!" Ant looks right past me. She looks like she's about to cry. I ask, "What's wrong with you?"

She's not moving her head, but her eyes are following something in the street. She whispers to me, "Don't look now. I'm afraid he will know we're talking about him. I don't want anything to do with him—he is such a jerk."

Naturally—what do I do?—I turn my head to look. To my surprise I see "Movie Star," one of our Italian district cops. We call him Movie Star because he always has a pair of sunglasses on. He looks just like us—dark eyes, hair, and skin. He's cute.

Movie Star has double-parked his car in front of our house. He's watching us and waving to Antoinette to come down to him. He tells her he has something for her.

Antoinette moves closer to me and says, "I am not going anywhere near that weirdo. He scares me—he wants to have sex with me. Whenever I see his police car I turn around and go the other way. What else can I do?"

My thought is that I'm the big sister, so I should take control of this situation. I don't like this cop—for that matter I really don't care for any cop. So this is going to be fun for me as I challenge his authority. I walk down to the car and introduce myself to Movie Star. "Hello," I say, and he smiles at me. I question him about what he wants with Antoinette. He tells me he likes her and just wants to talk to her.

"What is it you want to talk about—the weather? Well, it's cool and breezy today. Now, get lost. Leave Antoinette alone because she's not even 15 years old, and you're about 23 years old, right?"

I turn to go back up the steps to where Antoinette is sitting. I hear Movie Star's engine running and he's laying rubber going up 58th Street. We're laughing at him, and happy he took off. But within a few minutes, here he comes again. Back for more, I guess.

He pulls in front of our house, and demands that Ant come to his car. His voice is strong and loud. He yells at me not to come down to his car again. Antoinette and I are laughing—she's saying to me, "He doesn't know us. He can sit in his car all night—I don't care." I am thinking that this guy doesn't understand my sister. Once you're on her bad side, you'd better watch out. She won't care if there are 10 of you—she's stubborn as an ox. Good luck to you getting her to comply with what you want.

Now I yell to him, "Leave us alone before we call the cops!"… BIG MISTAKE … In an instant, Movie Star is out of his car. Then he's running up the cement steps, then grabbing both my arms. He pulls me up off the steps and onto my feet.

He yells in my face: "Don't you know that I AM A COP!?"

I tell him to act like a policeman and leave us alone. "You know, you scare her. But you enjoy it."

He pulls out his handcuffs and tells me to put out my hands, which I refuse to do. So he turns me around so fast that I almost fall down the steps. But he catches me by the shoulders, cuffs me, and then takes me down the steps to his car.

I'm not saying a word now because I'm thinking this guy is totally nuts. His ego is just too big for his pants, and he did not like being deflated by us. After all, he is Movie Star. I am also wondering, how in the world do I get out of this mess? Is he going to arrest me? And for what?

I tell him to calm down and take the handcuffs off my wrists. He turns around toward me and gets right into my face. He's yelling at me for not listening to him and doing what he told me to do. He's yelling at the top of his lungs that I should shut up. He's saying that if I say one more word I will be sorry. And I'd better not talk to him like that again—or else!

Oh boy, this cop is nuts! I've got to get away from him—but how? He now takes my left wrist and handcuffs me to the passenger back door. He's telling me he is going to arrest me for disorderly conduct. Not thinking, just responding to his craziness, I yell to him to take the handcuffs off of me. But before he can reply, we both notice that the traffic on 58th Street has come to a standstill. Someone keeps blowing their horn. And two women lean out of a car to ask, "What has she done?"

The neighbors are coming out of their houses to see what the all the commotion is about. It's getting out of hand on the street. The lady two doors down is asking, "Mr. Police Officer, what did Josephine do?" Movie Star tells her to mind her own business and go back into her house.

Now he is in the car radioing for assistance. He tells the dispatcher that he needs help, that he's the only cop and things are getting out of control. I too am worried about things getting out of control on this racially diverse street.

I look at Antoinette and see the fear on her face—it's the same fear that must be showing on mine. I tell her to go into our house and get George—but she should do it so our mother doesn't hear her. She should get Anna to keep Mom in the kitchen so she doesn't see what's going on, because if my mother sees what's happening, she might just kill me on the spot. "Not a word to Mom!" I plead. Antoinette goes flying up the steps and through the front door.

I see the guy whose house is two doors away from ours; he's standing on the sidewalk asking me if there is anything he can do for me. As he asks, he moves into the gutter, and is standing in front of me. Before I can answer, Movie

Star tells him to get back on the sidewalk. My neighbor tells him to remove the handcuffs from my wrists. But that doesn't happen.

Now we have four police cars on our street—two from the 12th District and two from the 18th. Things are getting out of hand, and the police aren't controlling this scene.

It gets worse. I hear someone yell, "Mrs. Pasquarello, they have Josephine handcuffed to the police car!" Now my stomach is jumping. I look up to the top of the steps and see my mom charging down and I think I'd rather be arrested than have my mom get me for this one.

The neighbors have been drifting into the street, and I hear Movie Star telling them to get back on the sidewalk. Other police officers are blocking people from going into the street. But my mom makes it over to me. I am shaking from the thought of what she'll do to me.

Before I can say a word I hear my brother George talking to the cop. He's close in age to Movie Star, so maybe he can smooth things over. But George is saying to him, "Let her go. So she and Antoinette made fun of you—so what?!"

My mom talks to another cop from the 12th District. She asks, "What is wrong here that you have time for all of this? He doesn't have anything better to do on the streets of southwest Philly than arrest my daughter?"

Now my mom is walking back toward me, and I can see she is upset with me. At this point, I decide it would be nice to be inside the police car; it would be better than having my mom clobber me. I try to get into the car but I can't because I'm handcuffed to the outside of the door.

Desperate, I say, "Mom, first listen to what he was doing." I pour it on really thick about how this cop frightened poor little innocent Antoinette and about how I had to come to her aid. From the sidewalk Antoinette is acknowledging that what I'm saying is absolutely true. (You always need backup when convincing Mom that you're not lying.)

Movie Star approaches my mother and tells her to get on the sidewalk. Now George is taking Mom's arm to help her walk away. But before he can, Movie Star gives George a push on his shoulder, to get him to move quickly. So George and Movie Star are having words, and things are getting scarily hostile. I wish they would just take me to the police station, because I don't like this situation at all. We've got cops and cop cars all over 58th Street between Kingsessing and Greenway Avenue. I'm getting nervous that someone might get hurt—if not me then someone else. This was never supposed to happen. I'm wishing everyone would just calm down.

Here comes another police car; this time it's the police captain from the 12th District. The captain walks over to me to question me on what's happened. My mom walks over to us, along with George and Antoinette. We tell the captain word for word what was exchanged among the three of us. The captain calls Movie Star over to question him in front of us. But Movie Star's version of the truth does not match ours. He blames me and Antoinette entirely for this problem.

The police captain asks Movie Star, "Are you interested in Antoinette or not?" He actually replies that he thinks that she is pretty, and now Antoinette and I are laughing at this bozo-head. The captain tells him to drive back to the police station and to wait for him there. "But first," he says, "uncuff Josephine from your car."

The police captain tells everyone to calm down—he has the situation under control. This was a misunderstanding, he explains, and everyone involved is fine. "Please, go back in your homes and allow us to do our job out here, maintaining safety on the streets of southwest Philly."

He turns to Mom and tells her he will take her and me to the police station to fill out some papers there. He will drive us in his police car and have an officer drive us back home.
George asks Mom if she is okay with that. "Are you going with Josephine, or should I go with her?" Mom says she'll go; she wants George to help settle the neighbors down. She says she'll be back as soon as possible, and she tells George to keep Antoinette at his side.

The police captain instructs Movie Star that he is to go straight to the police station and we will all settle this over there. Mom and I get into the back of the captain's car. He drives down Woodland Avenue toward 63rd Street, where the 12th District police station is located. Mom and the captain are talking the entire time about the incident. She informs him that she knows what her daughter did today was totally uncalled for, and that she will handle both me and my sister when we get home.

But then she goes on. "On the other hand," she says, "your police officer's behavior was ridiculous. Did he have any training? I feel that if he did he may need more time to understand people. As for Josephine, she was only protecting her younger sister, which happens to be the way I raised them. The older one always takes responsibility for the younger one."

And she has more to say. "Your police officer could have started a war. Does he realize the turn of events that could have occurred because of his actions? He is the one who is supposed to defuse situations, but today he provoked one. For what reason? Because he is a policeman and people are supposed to be afraid of him? I guess, as my daughters learned today, no one is always right."

At the station we sign the papers and the captain tells one of his officers to drive us home. But before we leave, the captain calls Movie Star into his office to apologize to us. He orders him remove his sunglasses, which he does, not that he makes eye contact with us as he says he's sorry. The captain asks him, "Why did you cause all this commotion? Why take it so far?"

His reply: "Josephine was a smart mouth and needed to be taught a lesson."

Now my mom wants to get at him! But before she can do anything, the captain tells him, "Do you know you are an ass? Get back in your car and onto the street, and keep the neighborhood safe!"

My mom expresses her thanks to the captain, as do I. As we are driven home, I tell Mom I agree with the captain's description of Movie Star's character. Mom says that she thinks the captain is a gentleman. If we had more police officers like him, she says, our neighborhood would indeed be nice and safe.

• • •

Mom waited until we got home to correct me on my actions. She told me that if something like this happened again, my sister and I should get up immediately and walk into the house. We must never lower ourselves to anyone else's way of thinking or being. She asked us if we realized the trouble we'd caused. Then she said she'd actually thought about having me stay at the 12th District police station overnight, to teach me a lesson. The reason she hadn't was that she knew that what I had been trying to do—protect my sister—was a good thing. Whew! I thought—some people are saved by the bell—I had been saved by Antoinette!

When she heard Mom and me talking, Antoinette came into the living room. She wanted to know what had happened at the police station. Mom filled her in on everything, and told her how the police captain was a good man. But she was sorry to say that that officer (Movie Star) should be ashamed of himself, especially since he was one of our kind.

As for cops in general, she repeated something she'd said many times before, that cops were not one of her favorite kinds of people. "Of course," she admitted, "their job isn't easy in any way." She ended the conversation with this request: "Girls—do me a favor and stay away from them."

Later, Antoinette and I sat together on the sofa talking about how crazy it had gotten. We laughed as Ant offered the opinion that tonight Movie Star was driving around in his police car and crying because he didn't get his way with her and because two little Italian girls took him down. And then decided that we would no longer call him Movie Star. His new name would be The Italian Asshole. For us, that was the end of him!

That night, as my mom went upstairs to get her evening bath, she turned to us and said, "Remember, he is one of our kind. But he is not one of us."

We didn't see him for maybe six months after that day; he stayed far away from the front steps of the Pasquarellos.

The Second Stair from the Top

The day after my father's death, my oldest brother, Ralph, came home from his army service. He lined all of us up on the stairs. We each had our own stair to sit on; I was the second stair from the top, looking down at Ralph. As he talked to us, we stayed real still, not saying a word, just sitting there and listening to our brother tell us what we would do. He said we would all help Mom and we would listen to him. Then he put his finger to his lips and said we would never talk about this ever. So for 15 years I never did. I had dreams about my dad, but never spoke of the dreams or his death.

That was the beginning of my entire family's carrying around a big, dark secret. As far as we children knew, our dad had killed himself, and we weren't going to tell anyone because suicide was considered a shameful act. During my childhood and into adulthood, no one ever spoke a word about it until the night my youngest sister, Anna, woke me from a good sleep demanding, "Wake up and tell me what you know about Daddy's death." I could not believe she was saying this to me. Mom was in the bedroom next door, separated by a paper-thin wall. She had an uncanny way of always knowing what we were up to, and if she heard me talking to her "baby" about this taboo subject, she would be very angry at me. I worried, too, that Mom hearing us talking about our dad's death might cause her to fall apart. Perhaps she thought it best for us not to know what really happened. Where would our knowing take us?

Would we see that this father we loved wasn't the superior being our mom made him out to be and just an ordinary person?

I asked Anna to keep it down and asked her what she knew about Dad dying. She looked at me with such hurt and anger in her eyes. Eighteen-year-old Anna had been just three when he died. In those 15 years, she had never been told about this worst time of our lives.

I guess I should go back to the day my dad was said to have eaten rat poison and to have stabbed himself in the chest. Suicide is a really strange word when you are only six and hearing about it for the first time. I really didn't understand what it meant. All I knew was that my dad was dead and that we were all terribly sad and scared. It was then that I became a little girl with a huge amount of fear. Afraid that my life would crumble again, I started to have panic attacks.

I would wonder, why would my dad leave twelve children and a wife? I thought he loved me and the family; had he suddenly stopped? Or at 53, could he not handle having that many children around making so much noise?

Dad had a rough life. He was just 18 when his father died in 1921, only 22 when his mother died four years later. This was before the age of penicillin, and both his parents had died terrible deaths from syphilis. Dad and Aunt Rosie were left to raise their seven younger siblings. At the same time, in order to support the family, Dad worked the streets of South Philly, selling produce. At 31, when his younger siblings started to marry, Dad married Mom.

Now, Anna was upset with me for never telling her what I knew about our father. The little she knew had been supplied by our older sister Roe. "Tell me what she told you," I said, "and we will go from there."

Anna replied, "Dad ate rat poison and stabbed himself in the chest." Now we were both crying.

It was time to tell Anna what I had known for 15 years but never talked about. How could I do this without losing control of my emotions? How could I release all that I had held inside of me for so long? I had so many feelings to deal with in that instant that I didn't know if I could handle it. But for Anna's sake, I tried my best.

Starting from the beginning, and whispering so Mom wouldn't hear us, I told Anna all I remembered as a six-year-old. I related how Mommy had told me, Rosemarie, and Carmella to go to Dad's store to tell him it was time to come home for dinner. It was dark outside when we knocked on the front door, and I could hear Queenie, the German shepherd watchdog, barking in the backyard. We kept knocking, and Dad finally opened the door. He asked what we were doing out this time of night, laughing at us like he always did. We told him that Mom sent us to tell him it was time for dinner, and he said that he wouldn't be coming home with us tonight. "Here is something for each of you," he added, placing an Indian head nickel into each of our palms.

I remember thinking, "Great—a nickel for candy!"

Dad instructed us to go right home to our mother, eat our dinner, and go to bed. We kissed him goodbye and left. Once we were home, Mom asked where Dad was, and we reported that he wasn't coming home for dinner. This was strange because Dad had dinner with us every night. Mom looked at us with an odd expression and then told us to eat our dinner.

The next day, we heard the shocking news. Our dad was in the hospital, poisoned and with a stab wound close to his heart. The doctors told Mom that they could do nothing. Although the knife wound was not fatal, the poison was already in his system. All they could do was wait for him to die. Five days later, our dad died, sitting in a rocking chair in the hallway of the hospital.

I was home when the news reached us, sitting on a chair in the front room watching all these people with Mommy, everyone speaking softly, some crying, some looking at us with sadness. Someone said, "Here comes Trudy." Trudy, our oldest sister—already 18 at the time— ran through the house, heading for Mom. All of a sudden, she was on Mom's lap, screaming and crying, and holding onto Mom with all her might. Mom and Trudy rocked back and forth. Mom had Trudy's head in both her hands and was saying something to her while Trudy was shaking her head yes to whatever was being said. It appeared that both of them had come to an understanding as they continued to rock back and forth. No one said a word as we watched the two of them in their despair. We little ones didn't know what we should do, so we took the lead from our older siblings. That's what you do in a large family—just follow the older ones because you figure they know more than you do. That day, Mom didn't move off the sofa, and I stayed with my older siblings so they would take care of me. It seemed to me that if Mom had tried to get up, she would have fainted.

Dad and Trudy were not just father and daughter; they were great friends. Mom later told me that two weeks before his death, Dad had gone to see Trudy at her job. They'd sat on a park bench and talked. But about what, Mom never said. I was afraid to ask her questions about that meeting—she might clam up and never tell me any of her stories about Dad again. So I never asked.

After Dad died, we moved from our house. Mom couldn't handle all the memories of Dad in that place. We moved to start over without him. But that didn't erase him from our memories. Dad always stayed with us; we could feel him still loving us, watching over us and protecting us from evil.

As Anna and I lay in my bed talking, with my mom in the next room, I wanted to go to Mom and ask what really happened to my dad. I am not a little girl anymore, I felt like saying— I'm 21 years old—just tell me! But I knew I couldn't hurt her. She had been through so much. The younger children didn't know the truth, but the older siblings must have known. Still, we never heard anyone ever talk about his death when my mom was alive. No one wanted to hurt her any more than she was already hurt.

Today, my feelings about life are definitely—JUST TELL ME! Keeping everything hidden is not healthy. Life is going to give you events that are unpleasant, but you must carry through with life. Had we talked about our dad's death, it would have been easier. But of course times were different then.

I believe Anna understood why I never said a word to her about Daddy. I would have been betraying the family secret, a secret that Anna believed she was never in on. A plus side to this is that maybe she never felt the shame of suicide as I and the older ones did. It was a shame that made us feel, at times, totally worthless. Maybe Anna, having been spared what we understood as the harsh truth, was the luckiest of us all.

When someone close, such as a parent, commits suicide, an abundance of shame comes along with that. I thought everyone knew what my dad did to himself, and if they didn't, I had to keep it to myself. Whenever the thought of his death would surface, I would push it back down, and I guess that's what we all did. Strange how it's always there, all this agony, yet no one talks about it.

I once wrote a poem about what I could not speak aloud. It went like this:

I still cry
How could you leave me to stand alone
To hurt
To cry

And wonder why
You could have stayed to hold my hand
It's so hard for me to understand
To live
To die
And wonder why
I'd like to know why you left me here
Why oh why
My father died
By the hands of suicide

By Josephine Pasquarello
3-18-2000

As a young adult, when I learned about liquor and drugs, off I went. That helped kill the pain at first, but the pain shot up again and again. Then one day, after my conversation with Anna, I got stoned with some friends. We were high from wine, pot, and "orange sunshine" (LSD), and I was so high that I couldn't even move a limb. Out of my mouth came, "My dad killed himself." I couldn't believe I had the nerve to say that. It was like I was watching myself stoned, running the words through my lips.

That day was actually the beginning of my road to recovery. I knew there was no stopping me now. I looked to see how my friends were responding to what I had said, and expressions of shock were on their faces. What the hell did I just say, and what the hell did they just hear me say? Then came the questions—how, when, where, and why? On one level, I felt a sense of relief at having finally talked about the suicide—or what I understood as such. Maybe now I would be able to settle some of the questions running through my head for the past 15 years.

Then I began to feel guilty at having betrayed our family secret. Oh, why did I say anything at all? No one else in the family was talking about it to their friends or anyone else. But how much longer could they old onto that madness in their heads? I couldn't stand the feeling of shame any longer. Part of me didn't care what anyone thought of me, my family, or my dad. I no longer wanted to hide all the shame but to scream at the top of my lungs, "That's right, my dad killed himself when I was six years old! Fuck you if you don't like it!" Another part of me wanted to be gentle and ask for forgiveness. That's what shame does to you. You don't know what to expect from yourself. I would play the scene over and over again in my head and ask myself, "Dad, why?" It took years of the same question before I finally said, "It doesn't really matter why. I just miss you, and I will always love you."

I can't say that I never felt anger toward him; it's just that I was never given the chance to explore those feelings and express them. That's mainly because my mom never ever said a bad word about Dad. She loved him with her soul and I felt I had to follow her lead. If she loved him, and she was the one left here to take care of us, then we ought to feel the same way she did.

For a while, early on, I was always getting stoned. I told myself it would help me, but seriously, that was all bullshit. I liked getting high from smoking hash and pot and taking LSD so I could escape it all. And I loved snorting meth. I was high every weekend and many days in between. Was that because I thought my dad committed suicide, or was that because I liked drugs?

Whichever it was, I didn't take responsibility for anything I did. I would work a little to make some money and then say the heck with that—let's get stoned. I was a true idiot during the time I call my years of drugs. Now that I look back on that time, I see that I wasted many of my beautiful days. That's what I should have shame about, not my dad's death.

At present I am on the road to accepting my father's death and learning how to handle the painful emotions from having been abandoned as a child. I am looking forward to figuring it all out. I am going to go deep into myself and hopefully come out with a great knowledge of it all. While I will never completely get over my father's leaving, I understand more and more as I talk about that time in my life to anyone who wants to listen, first with their hearts and second with their heads. I've come to see that sometimes people check out for reasons none of us will ever understand. I guess that's one of life's mysteries. I like the word "mystery" much more than the word "secret." It has a better feel to me and it's not dark.

If my sister Anna hadn't questioned me on the death of our dad, I don't know if I would have started on the road to recovery at the age of 21. I do know that I still hurt and that there is still a large hole in my being because of this loss. I will never get over it, and I will continue to miss my dad for the rest of my life. But Anna's questioning did turn something around for me. I had been feeling such pain for so long, with no idea when or how that would change. After my sister confronted me, I could finally, as a young adult, begin to look at my father's death with loving feelings, instead of shame, which was beautiful to me. I had walked in the valley of suicide for 15 years. I had been weighed down by the secrecy I was sworn to that day we were lined up on the stairs. Now, I could start to release that weight from my being and rejoice in the beauty life has to offer.

Still, at times, the most important question in my life is: Why, Dad?

Two Guardian Angels

It's around dinnertime as I wake up from a sound sleep. But there's no dinner—I am in this guy's little pickup truck driving through Florence, South Carolina. Lana and I spent the night before in a holding cell in North Carolina—a cop got us for walking on the interstate—we were arrested and given a fine. Lana's brother-in-law sent us the money to get out of jail, and we couldn't get out of there fast enough.

It's 1971, I'm 22 years old, and we've been on this road trip hitching to Florida for two days. We left Philly to go south for some warm weather. It's snowing and cold up north. So far the trip is not going smoothly. But we've decided to keep going south to Florida and maybe things will get better.

So after the cops released us from jail we got back on the interstate. As soon as we got on the highway again with our thumbs out this old guy pulled over onto the side of the road. He told us he's going to Savannah, Georgia. If he dropped us off there, that would get us closer to Florida. We could continue hitching farther south.

Whenever we are offered a ride we both have to agree about the feel of the situation. We must both say yes to the ride. This time, without any fear or hesitation, Lana and I jumped into this old guy's pickup. I guess we felt that after our night in jail, things couldn't get worse. Oh, were we naive!

I usually don't sleep in strangers' vehicles because I like to keep my eyes and ears open. But this time I was so tired from being up since the previous day. I didn't sleep when they had us in jail. Some of the girls there were nice, but a few of them were odd, to say the least. One was there because she had killed her husband; she was thrilled to tell me, with a big smile on her face, that she had shot him dead, and I never saw any remorse. I sure wanted to stay away from her! I knew that this jail was not the place for me. I wanted out—freedom became a very real concept for me.

Our driver stops at a gasoline station but doesn't buy gas. He gets on the public phone and stays on it for about ten minutes. I ask Lana as we get out of the car, "What's up with this guy? Who is he talking to?" She tells me he's a nice old man. He wanted to stop to call his daughter to see how she and the granddaughter are doing. Then Lana tells me he gave her some pills. I look at her and see that her eyes are dilated. I ask, "What kind of pills did he give you, uppers?" Yes, she says.

Now I'm upset with her and the situation we're in. "This guy is an ass," I tell Lana. "Who the heck is this guy? Aren't you thinking at all, Lana?"

She's getting really pissed off at me. "Don't talk to me like I'm stupid! I know what I'm doing! He's a grandfather—a cool guy."

I want to shake her to put some sense in her head. But she's yelling at me. "Don't you ever trust anyone? There's something wrong with you, Josephine. Ask him for some uppers—you'll feel better and not be a bitch."

The man gets back into the truck and starts the engine. We get back in, with Lana sitting in the middle next to the guy, and me near the door. I ask, "Where are we going?" He tells me he will take us close to his house, and will drop us off near the interstate. I continue to have a bad feeling and soon I ask him to let us out—now. He starts to drive faster, going down dirt roads. This is not going to end well for me and Lana. Inside, I am getting frantic.

It's dark down these roads with no streetlights—there's just the light from the moon. Lana is now pleading with the guy to stop the truck. He tells her to shut up and not to open her mouth again. Lana grabs my left arm and squeezes really tight. She says to me, "Let's jump out!"

But he's holding her left leg so she can't move, and now all three of us are screaming.

"Stop and let us go!" I yell. The old guy is screaming that if I jump out he still has a hold of her. I could jump out of the truck but no way am I leaving Lana in there with him.

We're passing through an industrial area now. There aren't many cars on the road. I know in my being that if he gets us to where he wants us, we are probably dead. Our challenge now is to stay alive.

We pull up to a traffic light. It's red. On the right is a gasoline station, but it's closed. On the other three corners it's all open fields. We have nowhere to go. But in my head, I am saying, "Fuck this! Kill me—but you will have to get me first!" My plan: to jump out—with Lana. It will mean a tug of war.

I grab Lana's right arm and leg. The two of us push the guy away while he pulls Lana really hard toward him. She pulls his hair and grabs his eyeglasses. He's driving all over the road.

I am scratching his hand—the one that's on Lana's leg. He loses himself for a few seconds, and that's when we jump out of the truck. Our survival instinct has kicked in but now we are freaking out. What are we supposed to do next?

On the other side of the road there comes a bus. I hear my father say to me, "Jump in front of the bus! You got to get this bus to stop and help you. This could save your lives."

I listen to my father's advice. Crossing the road, I charge straight over to the bus. I am thinking, "If you won't stop, then run me over." Lana is right behind me telling me to get the bus to stop for us. I have never felt this much fear in my entire life. I would rather die by bus than let this old hillbilly creep get me and Lana.

We hear the bus tires screeching so the bus can stop before it hits me. The bus driver and I are a few inches away from each other, and he has fear all over his face. I am screaming at him for help; I know that I look like a madwoman. The bus driver won't open his door and I am banging on the front window. Now I think he's more frightened than I am. He drives the bus around the shoulder of the road so he can get away from me as quickly as possible. He drives away down the road.

Now we hear voices calling our names. We hear that slow southern drawl, look at each other, and start to run. We see the little pickup truck; there are two guys in it now. And near them is a station wagon with four guys. They are calling our names and telling us to stop running—because they are going to get us one way or another.

We run toward the gas station with the two vehicles behind us. They have shotguns out the windows and are yelling that they will shoot us if they have to. *God, please help us, please help get us away from these beasts!*

Lana and I are running toward the gas station. The only cars around are the ones that are after us. When we get to the gas station we run to hide amidst the piles of trash. Everything is happening so fast, and we are literally shaking in our shoes. We hold on to each other, not knowing what to do next. The guys are having fun taunting us, enjoying our increasing fear.

The two cars are headed toward the back of the gas station but still in the street when we see headlights coming toward us from the opposite direction. Lana says, "Let's run out and stop that car!" I hesitate for a second—what if this new car is filled with more rednecks? But Lana's already out in the middle of the intersection. She's jumping up and down, waving her arms and yelling. So I go right behind her and do the same thing. The two cars stop and wait to see what's going to happen.

"We've got to get this car to stop!" Lana says. "If it tries to go around us, I'll jump in front."

The car is flying toward us down the road. Will they see us soon enough? We're yelling at the top of our lungs: "Please stop! Help us! We need your help!"

The car stops. It's a Mustang; inside are two teenage boys. They're laughing and asking us, "What are you doing out here?"

Lana tells them that the guys in the two cars across the intersection have guns. "We need you to get us out of here—FAST!" I ask the boys if they know the guys in the other cars.

The driver says, "I don't know anyone out here. Get in the car and I'll get you girls out of here." Now the station wagon is coming across toward us in slow motion. The men in the back seat are sticking their guns out the windows.

At first, Lana and I aren't sure if these two boys are here to help us, or to help those guys. (I believe we were starting to lose our sensibility.) This is a nightmare, and we just want to wake up.

Lana's screaming for the boys to let us into their car. The passenger opens his door and we both dive into the back seat. You can hear the men yelling at our young driver, telling him that he better let their wives out of his car. I look out the window to see the little pickup right in front of this kid's Mustang, and the station wagon is about five feet from our driver's door. I'm thinking that we aren't going to get out of this alive.

But our driver tells us to calm down—he will get us all out of here. He keeps repeating to himself, "We're getting out of here, we're getting out of here."

Lana's telling the driver to look at us and then look at those men. "Do we look like we're married to them?" she asks. Now all four in the wagon have guns on us. Our driver turns to us and says, "Hold on—we got to get away now." As he pulls away he looks at us, panic-stricken in the back seat. He laughs and tells us, "I know you're not their wives. They're big, fat slobs. You are girls from a big city. I knew you weren't married to them." The other boy up front laughs and agrees.

The two cars are following us but they can't keep up with the Mustang. At times we are driving on the road and at times on the fields. We ask the boys, "Where are we?"

They tell us, "You're down in the meadow. You don't want to be down here. Not too much good goes on down here."

I ask, "Why are you down here, then?"

"We came out to drag race and to see if anyone was here. The cops never come down to this area. So we can drive crazy and won't get a ticket."

Then we hear the station wagon moving on us. The men are still yelling, "Let our wives out of your car! We will shoot if you don't!" Our driver is laughing and telling us everyone down here has guns. So we shouldn't worry—we will be fine.

"They can't catch us in that old piece of crap," they say.

And they are proved right—we lose the old creeps, and finally we are driving through an area with houses and streetlights. I have never been so happy to see streetlights!

We didn't realize at first how very much these two young men helped us, until we pulled up in front of the Salvation Army, where our rescuers wisely took us so we could get a safe night's sleep. I don't think I ever uttered the words "Thank you" so many times in a row.

Whoever raised those young men should be proud of what fine men they turned out to be. They put their lives on the line that night, and did it for people they didn't even know.

• • •

You would think we would have learned about the dangers of hitchhiking that night. But we were young and stupid. The next day found us back on the interstate, hitching our way to Florida.

253

Fortunately, someone or something was watching over us. We did make it to Florida safely. It was sunny and warm there. We did have a great time, although at the end of that trip I was certainly happy to return home safe and sound.

I still had a few more years of traveling on the road. But one trip down south for me was enough. I wasn't going down there again. Now was the time for Europe—to see how the roads were over there. I couldn't wait to meet the Europeans … to taste their food … to see their beautiful cities and history-filled countries. This was going to be my next great adventure.

Bad Mouth / Good Snow

Here we go again. My mom is chasing me. If she gets her hands on me I am dead meat. But I can outrun her and make it up the stairs. Usually she won't come up the stairs after me. She's under five feet tall and on the heavy side, so she doesn't like to climb the stairs. However, this time she's right behind me—yelling something in Italian. Whatever it is she's saying, it's the same phrase over and over again. It might just be, "I will kill you if I get my hands on you!" So I run for my life.

I am truly nervous this time because it seems like she will catch me. How do I get out of this mess I have created? And how exactly did this start? ...

We four younger girls are at the breakfast table. We're all talking and laughing about how nice it's going to be—one more week of school, then summertime in our city with, hopefully, lots of fun.

Mom is at the stove making pancakes, which we'll have with lots of butter and maple syrup. They are the best thing first thing in the morning! All that sweetness and butter to start the day, along with a large, cold glass of milk. With the exception of Mom's Italian cake, this is the best breakfast for me. As we're eating and chatting away, my sisters are asking me, "Just how stupid *are* you to have to go to summer school for religion?" This part of the conversation is not so pleasant for me. It's about the fact that I am about to finish up my junior year in high school, but in order for me to start my senior year, I have to attend a summer course in religion. This is not because I have failed religion, or any of my other subjects at West Catholic. It's because the nuns want to punish me for my bad behavior.

The IHM (Immaculate Heart of Mary) nuns are known for their rules and their discipline. They can be quite a pain. And, my being an uncontrollable teenager, I have paid no attention to their rules. Actually, I often pay no attention to them in any way.

I had so much hurt and anger in me, much of it due to my having lost my dad at the age of six. As a family we didn't talk about suicide or losing our dad. So I just kept it all down inside of me. There was no way I was going to listen to a bunch of frustrated ladies tell me how to live my life. That's how I put it at the breakfast table that day.

But running my mouth off like that was not such a good idea; it didn't go over big with my mom. She looked at me and said, "Don't speak like that at my table."

"But Mom, you know why they are messing with me! Come on—you know I had after-school detention more than half the year. Those nuns want me to talk their talk and walk their walk."

They had me in detention class for 45 minutes each day doing long division problems. Despite my not liking mathematics, I got really good at division. But to fail me for religion—come on—give me a break! I had been in Catholic school for eleven years now. I should know something about the Catholic faith.

Sister Helen is the one doing this to me. She's been after me all year—every time she sees me she gives me dirty looks. She yells at me all the time. "Pasquarello—take off the earrings!" Then, sweetly, she says, "You have detention for this today." No matter what I do—I am wrong—and the price each time is detention. Lots of girls wear earrings and I never see them in detention.

My sisters are continuing to tell me I must be really stupid to fail religion. They laugh, asking me if I will miss having the summer off from school.

In my usual sweet way of responding I tell them to "fuck off." That's when the room goes silent, but not for long. My mom has heard what came out of my mouth. And everyone realizes it. Now, my sisters are all happy and excited. Before I can react to them I feel the back of my head being pulled. I jump up as fast as I can, to run. My sisters are yelling to Mom: "Get her!"

I make a mad dash for the stairs. I'm hoping she won't chase me but if she does I might be able to outrun her and hide. But to my surprise, she's right at my heels, climbing each stair almost as quickly as I am. She's saying something in Italian, which makes me quite nervous. I know this time she's going to catch me. This catch is really important to her.

I could tell her, "Mom, I just got overexcited with what they were saying about me. I reacted with my big mouth." But that won't save me. I am going to have to pay for my attitude and mouth. I should let her catch me now and get it over with.

Maybe, if I pray to God for His help I will make it out of here alive ... No, even God can't save me now. I will pay for this big-time. I can't stand myself right now. What is wrong with me? Why do I disobey everyone? For what reason? As I run into my bedroom I jump on the bed and hide under the blanket. My mom rips the blanket away and onto the floor she flings it.

She backhands me across the mouth. I feel blood on my lower lip. I am thinking I need to get away from her, or else calm her down. But I don't know if I'm capable of either one.

I have never seen her like this—she is really mad at me. She has never hurt me before. I see rage coming out of her eyes. She's looking at me in disgust that I am her child. How could I have disappointed her like this? I tell her that I am sorry for using that language at her table. "I won't talk like that again in your home," I say. "I love you, Mom, with all of my heart."

I don't know why I disrespected her like that. I wasn't aiming at her—I was just frustrated with my sisters. I wasn't thinking—that's all.

My mother is telling me to go downstairs and apologize to the others, which I do right away. I am in the kitchen telling them, "My language was uncalled for, and I will try not to curse at you again."

They laugh, and tell me to grow up. Just go to summer school, they say, so you can graduate next spring.

That's exactly what I did. I graduated from West Catholic in the class of 1967. I was 18 years old.

I couldn't wait to get out of there, away from the nuns. But I knew I would miss my friends. These were girls I'd been with since first grade, so I'd known most of them for twelve years. I realized that once you're out of high school, your life will change, whether you want it to or not. I did think it would be easier with no nuns to listen to, no one watching over me with eyes in the back of their heads.

Did I fool myself? In the world of work there would always be rules and regulations to follow. When I realized that, boy oh boy, did I feel trapped!

For "senior week" after graduating, a bunch of us girls went to Wildwood, New Jersey. We spent our days on the beach, and at night we partied, with lots of liquor. I didn't like alcohol, but I did do a little drinking. That's what we girls in Pennsylvania did for senior week. It was a week away from our families, and to us that meant lots of freedom and lots of fun. I did enjoy soaking up the sun and playing in the ocean.

Senior week was when I knew I didn't want to go back home. So I went to my friend Patricia's house, in Darby (near Philadelphia). I stayed with her family for three months, enjoying every minute of my freedom. I got a job at Dunkin' Donuts on the Cobbs Creek Parkway. That job kept me nice and busy, and I liked interacting with the customers. But then, Patricia's mom started to put restrictions on me, and I began to feel like an animal in a cage. After about two weeks of answering to her about every little detail of my existence, I went out one night and never returned.

I went back to Philly, to my family. For a while everything was fine and I was getting along, working doing chores around the house. Then, my sister Carmella was renting a condo "down the shore," as we from Pennsylvania and New Jersey say. She asked if I and one of my girlfriends would like to stay down there for the entire summer. I couldn't get there fast enough! Off I went with my friend Terri; it would be from May until September.

We had so much fun going to the beach and getting stoned on pot. We worked only when we were in need of food. Other than that we were beach bums. When we were living that beach lifestyle again in 1969, Terri took off to go to the Woodstock Music Festival, and I went to Wildwood to hang out with my sister Anna and her friends. When I was there I ran into Lana, a girl whom I had hung out with when we were younger. We became good friends— because we both liked drugs.

Nineteen sixty-nine was the summer I found drugs and hitchhiking. Looking back, I see myself in that era being high and standing on the highway with my thumb out, trying to hitch a ride. Where? Anywhere! In the 1960s that's what was called being a "free spirit." It was exciting to see where you would, or could, end up. It was fun to meet new people in different parts of the country.

In 1971, when I was 22, a friend and I thought we should go over to Europe. I couldn't wait to get to Italy. Being Catholic, I was eager to see the Vatican, and view the works of Michelangelo. Plus Italy was my mother's homeland.

The Vatican was truly a place of beauty. You didn't even have to believe in the religion to appreciate it. Walking around, you felt all the spirits, from hundreds of years ago, roaming around with you. So many souls had passed through there.

We went through Italy, France, and Germany, hitchhiking a lot of the way. Then we took a train to Poland. At the first stop we were told by a Polish soldier that we had no papers to get into the country. We had paid the Polish conductor for a visa, but all he did was keep our money. The soldier kept us at a Polish army base for 13 hours. We had to buy food at their cafeteria or we wouldn't have gotten to eat at all. The soldiers there would pull their guns out and say, "Bang bang Nixon." And then they would laugh at us.

We didn't speak Polish and they didn't speak English. That was probably a good thing for both sides because we didn't like each other.

When the train back to Germany came down the tracks to the depot, four soldiers escorted us to the compartment we were to stay in. Saying their goodbyes to us, they pulled their guns out again. As we sat in our compartment we heard them outside with their loud laughter, saying their goodbyes to us and to Nixon. We couldn't wait to get out of Poland and to friendlier ground.

We spent a few days in Germany before returning to Philly. What a wonderful travel opportunity for two young women to have! The natural beauty of the countries we hitchhiked through was something I will always remember, and I know I will be back there again.

We were in Europe for almost four weeks, and spent only a few hundred dollars. We stayed in hostels and ate well—I even gained five pounds on that trip. We never had a bad thing happen to us, unless you count the Polish soldiers being less than hospitable. But everyone who gave us a ride was so kind to us, and so helpful.

That trip was definitely worth it in a lot of ways. I remember standing on the autobahn outside of Munich in February with the snow coming down and the wind blowing—it was so cold! Yet there was a feeling of peace with all the beauty nature had given to that country. I remember being out there with the cars flying by—not that there were many in such bad weather. But I knew one kind soul would stop for us. And he did.

This was when I understood my mother and her way of looking at life. *Stay firm in your beliefs and all will work out the way it is supposed to, even with no control on our part. Take whatever it is and master the outcome. This will make you a good person and a believer in yourself no matter what the circumstance.*

Why hadn't I felt this before? Well ... better late than never. Out there on that long stretch of road I could feel myself growing, maybe even growing up. I was finally finding my place in the world.

It was a beautiful feeling standing out there on the autobahn with the wind blowing and the stillness of the world. I could hardly see through the falling snow—it was as if a snowball was surrounding me, protecting me. This was my moment to go deep into myself. It was good to feel like no one else was there—no one to hear or see me. I saw only the reflection of myself. Some of what I saw is what I enjoyed about myself. I also saw what I disliked and knew I needed to change. It was fine to be out there in the freezing weather. Somehow the snow, and that wide open landscape, made me feel that my life was going to be good. I would have to work on myself and allow what was to come to me, to come. I would accept that fate.

There would be no more protecting myself from life—I had to open my arms to the universe. I had to accept that my dad had died when I was six years old. Not me— *I* hadn't died—I had to live my life. It was time to take on all the consequences of my actions and not run away.

Mom's Death and Funeral

The morning of the day Mom died, I woke up not wanting to go to work. It was cold and cloudy out, and there was snow on the sidewalks. I wished winter was over. They call the 21st of March the first day of spring, but in Philly it's surely still winter.

I debated whether to go to work or go over to Mom's house. I could hang out over there, I thought; it's my sister Anna's 22nd birthday, and some of the siblings will be over there to celebrate. So the entire morning I fought with myself about going over to Mom's. Part of me was saying go see Mom, and the other part of me was saying go to work. I didn't like this responsible streak in me.

I get ready to go to work. I am in my waitress uniform and putting on my snow boots for the quarter-mile walk to the first bus stop. (I have to take three public transportation vehicles to get over to the Main Line.) I walk to the bus stop, and then, when I'm aboard the first bus, I'm thinking, "I could have lunch with the family today." But then I tell myself, "You'd better get off this bus and get on the el. You'd better get to work."

I am on the platform waiting for the elevated train. It is so cold and windy today! And the atmosphere out here is gloomy and ugly. The train arrives; I get on and find a seat at the window. It's always cold on the el, and it certainly is today.

In a while, we are at Front Street, and I look out to my left; six blocks over is my mom's house. If I got off now, I could walk over there. Oh, I wish I was there! Still, I continue on to 69th and Market Street and catch the bus that goes to Lancaster Avenue. It takes me almost two hours to get to work on this day, because the streets still have so much snow it's hard for the buses to move through them.

At work, I set up the dining room for our lunch customers. We always set up the salad bar area; this place has great salad and Italian bread, and that's what I eat every day when I work here. My manager, Walt, comes into the dining room and yells for me, but I can't hear what he's saying. I yell back, "Walt— I'm busy—can I talk to you later?"

"No," he says, "I need you now." I go into the kitchen and see him talking on the phone that's attached to the kitchen wall, the one that's used only to arrange deliveries. Walt's face is stony and serious, which is strange because that's not Walt's personality; he's generally upbeat and laughing.

I'm thinking, "Uh-oh—what did I do?"

Walt looks at me and says, "Do you want to take this call here?"

I am now totally bewildered because we employees are not allowed on this phone. Only the manager takes calls from this phone. I say, "Yes, I'll take the call, but who is it?"

Walt says, "I don't know who it is." I start to laugh, thinking he's pulling some kind of joke.

I take the receiver from Walt's hand and put it to my ear. I say hello to the person on the other end. I hear breathing, and the person clears her throat. She says, "Jo—it's me, Roe." My sister Rosemarie is calling me at work—that's odd.

I ask her, "Why are you calling me at work?" She starts to cry and says, "Mom just died."

Something awful surges through my body. I grow weak fast. But I tell myself, "Don't you faint," because I have to hear what happened to my mother.

Now the tears are rolling down my cheeks and I can hardly speak. Roe's talking to me, but I can't hear a word. I do absorb that she's telling me to come to Mom's house. Everyone is there, and those who are not are on their way now.

I hang up the phone and tell Walt I have to go to my mom's. He grabs my shoulders and tells me to get my coat—he will drive me to North Philly. We are on the expressway and all of a sudden the sun is shining. But we sit in silence for the entire drive—there is no way I can talk now. I just sit in the front seat next to Walt and silently ask God, "Who do you think you are?" I tell God I hate him for taking my mom.

It takes us about an hour to get to 7th Avenue and Erie. I tell Walt to slow down—there are about 60 row houses on our block and ours is about a quarter in from the corner. There's my mom's house, at 3852 North 6th Street.

I turn to Walt and thank him for bringing me home. He looks at me with sorrow in his eyes. He tells me he is sorry for my loss. Again, I thank him; then I jump out of the car and run up the front steps to get to the door. Reaching it, I see that someone is opening it from inside. I see my sister Trudy standing there with her arms open to hold me close. We're both crying, holding onto each other in disbelief. Trudy is saying in my ear, "Mom's not here with us any longer." I don't like hearing her say that to me. I tell Trudy I have to see my three sisters from my group. Where are Anna, Antoinette, and Carmella?

Here comes Carmella, into the living room. Looking at me in a new, weird way, she walks toward me and hugs me really hard. She tells me that Antoinette shut down and lost it, so Dr. Desioto had to give her a sedative. Now Anna is coming down from upstairs and telling us that Antoinette isn't sleeping. She's lying down in Georgie's room but can't close her eyes. Anna says, "Josephine, come upstairs with me. You talk to Antoinette and tell her to fall asleep. She needs to get some rest." Anna tells me that Antoinette is talking but not making any sense.

Upstairs the three of us go to see our sister. It's strange—the four of us haven't been all together in a bedroom in years. Antoinette is lying in bed on her stomach. She turns over and her eyes are huge. You can see right into them. I can see the nervousness in her eyes; Antoinette is thinking she can't make it without Mom.

I ask her, "How are you? ... Are you alright?" But poor Antoinette can't talk to us—she's frozen. "Come on, Ant," I say. "We all think we can't make it without Mom by our side. It's not just you—we all need her. But Ant, you must get some rest. We sisters won't leave you. Now, get some sleep. I'll stay with you—don't be afraid." Antoinette closes her eyes and she does finally sleep for a few hours.

When she wakes up, Antoinette has her wits back. Now, like the rest of us, she feels that Mom's death is unfair to us, but that death is a part of life. Now, like the rest of us, she feels that we must all move forward and handle this as a family. Well, these things are what you tell yourself, even if they aren't exactly what you feel.

My oldest brother, Ralph, tells us we should all meet in the living room. We'll discuss how the funeral and further details should be handled. So we twelve, and the spouses, all cram into this little room. We, who all adored Mom, are now listening to Ralph explain the details of her funeral. Ralph gives instructions, although anyone else who wants to give input is welcome to.

Then, the conversation turns into a dark one about how Mom died today. Rosemarie is telling us the story. At the house earlier in the day, three of my siblings were with Mom in the kitchen when she told them she had a headache and was going to lie down. Anna and Antoinette went with Mom upstairs to her bedroom. When Mom got into bed she started to foam from the mouth. She told Antoinette her chest hurt … she turned blue … she wanted to throw up.

Antoinette called down to George to call an ambulance—Mom was really sick. George called for an ambulance, then called Roe to come over to the house. Mom was talking to the ceiling and telling her own mom and dad she loved them. When the ambulance got there, they carried her out of the house, and as they took her out the front door, Mom was calling out to her dad, her mom, and my dad.

And then she called out each of our names. "Ralph, Trudy, Grace, Christine, Patrick, Rosemarie, George, John, Carmella, Josephine, Antoinette, Anna."

My mother's last words were to the sky. "I love you, Brownie," she said. She knew she was dying. She died before she got to the hospital.

We are all now crying softly. We are crying for Mom and for the eight of us who weren't here for our mother's last minutes on this earth. We all wish we had been here so we could have held her hand, just as she had held our hands through life. I think we all agreed: Our mother most definitely was a gem on this earth. No other shined as brilliantly as she did.

The next three days we stuck together at the house. At the end of each day we all would go home, exhausted from our raw emotions and from planning our mother's funeral.

• • •

Before anyone came to the funeral home for the wake, the funeral director called to ask who would be coming to look at Mom, to make sure they had her looking like herself. Antoinette and I said we would go over. So we walked around the corner to the end of the block. The funeral home appeared to be a small building, and I wondered how all of us were going to fit into it. Antoinette looked at me and laughed. "No way are we all going to get inside this place," she said. "And it's so cold out today—we can't have the family waiting outside in the cold."

I told her it was a little too late to think about that. We were having Mom's wake that night, no matter what. "Don't say anything to anyone when we get back to the house," I advised. Antoinette agreed with me—we would keep our big mouths shut. (I thought—that's really going to be hard for Antoinette!)

Approaching the entrance to the building, we are so nervous. I ask Antoinette for a cigarette, and we decide to smoke one together. While we were smoking Antoinette told me that after Mom died Ralph told her to get in his car and he would drive her to Mom's house. When they got in the car Ralph broke down. She said that Ralph held his hands up to his face and sobbed uncontrollably. Ralph's breakdown was such a huge surprise to Antoinette because she always thought of Ralph as the unemotional big brother. After the cigarette we look at each other and hold hands. We walk into the foyer and freeze there. Antoinette gives me a little push toward the room straight ahead, where our mother is.

The funeral director, Mr. Sasso, comes to greet us. "You must be the Pasquarello girls," he says, "here to look over your mom." With that, Antoinette tells me she's going outside to smoke a cigarette. I grab her by the back of her coat.

"You have to come in the room with me to see how Mom looks," I say.

But my sister says, "You go in there. Then come out and tell me how she looks."

I start to walk into the room and I see the bottom part of the coffin. My knees get weak and I can't seem to move. I hear Antoinette talking to me—somehow she's still with me—but I can't make out what she's saying. I can only see the coffin, the entire coffin. So I must be walking ... but I can't feel my feet moving. Then Antoinette puts her arms around my waist to hold me up. I would like to run out of that funeral home. But I can't. I must look at my mom. This is so strange—I have to look at my mom dead. In some stupid box

… Oh, Jesus, my mother is lying inside of a box! I don't want to remember her like this.

Actually, the coffin is beautiful. It's cherry wood, with cream-color satin lining. Now I hear Antoinette saying, "They polished her fingernails." Now we are both laughing because they put blush, lipstick, and hairspray on her.

I tell Antoinette, "She looks really pretty with all of that make-up."

Antoinette's telling me, "When we come back I'm going to brush her hair to the left side of her forehead, just the way she always had it. Don't worry, Jo, I won't touch the make-up." (The fact is, Mom only ever wore lipstick.)

They have her dressed in a beautiful sky-blue dress that she had worn to her surprise 65th birthday party. We know everyone in the family will be pleased when they see her, and we tell Mr. Sasso we like the way our mother looks—beautiful and peaceful. We thank him for taking good care of her.

• • •

Our mother's wake went well, with many people attending—so very many family members, friends, and neighbors. Her wake would have pleased her. We felt the same way about the day we buried her with our dad. She was placed on top of his coffin. That way, he could carry the weight of her through eternity. Now that's true love.

Conversation in the Basement

"Because I could not stop for Death—He kindly stopped for me—"
—Emily Dickinson

This is one of the saddest days of my life, if not the very saddest. It's March 21, 1974, and my mother has passed away. It's an awful and empty day for my family. Our queen, the one who has presided over our existence, is forever gone.

Mom always said she would live until the youngest was 21 years old. Twenty-one was when she felt you were an adult and could stand on your own two feet and carry on with life. True to Mom's word, she died on her baby's 22nd birthday. She waited until the last minute she could to stay with us. But no longer could she wait for her beloved husband to put his arms around her and whisper, "We are together forever in eternity." To hear my dad say to her, "You did a beautiful job of raising our children—I am so proud to have you with me, in my arms forever"—that would be the ultimate for my mother.

Wait, Dad—what are you doing? You are taking her from all of us so she can be with you. But what about us? What about me? Dad—you have no right! You left us! You killed yourself! So what gives you the right to come back and take her away? Away forever!! I am so mad at my father, and at God too. Who do they think they are? To take her love and caring from me … from our family! Don't they get what they are doing?

Many times I told myself that my mom should push me off the Walt Whitman Bridge. I was uncontrollable, and life for her would have been easier if I wasn't around. I actually don't understand how she handled me for as long as she did. She never gave up on me or on her other eleven children. She always gave us direction, understanding, and love. And she was always honest in telling you how she felt about you. You could then look in the mirror and really see who you were—not what you thought you wanted to be. That's how truthful Mom was.

Except in one area—the truth about my dad and his death. She never did sit me down and give me all the information about my father. I guess she didn't want to tarnish the image she created for him after his death. What was that all about?

I walked around with a lot of hurt, never knowing why my dad had left us. Or—even more important—why he had left me. There were so many unanswered questions, starting with, how did he really die?

Now all of this will go with Mom to her grave. How will I ever know the truth about my family?

I wanted to hear it from her. I wanted her to sit me down at the kitchen table, as she had so many other times. I wanted the two of us to have a heart-to-heart conversation about the entire truth. I wanted her to speak to me as an adult. I wanted and wanted and wanted from her, but now that need will never be satisfied.

We need her to stay here with us. Yet we have no control. And we all do know that she planned this. Her moment of truth—the focus of her entire being—was to be with my dad. That's what she lived for—for her end of life. Her destiny—her eternity—was going to begin now, with her love by her side.

Oh boy—now she would laugh, smile, talk with him, and feel all of him. That was her fulfillment—he was for her. She had ached for his touch, his smile, and his sound, and now she had reached happiness in being with him. She was at peace.

But what do I do without her? What do we do as a family? How do we carry on with life? Look at us—not one of us twelve children of Romania Pasquarello knows what to do or understands all this confusion. We are a bunch of zombies.

The older siblings are trying to hold it together for us youngest four girls. Even though we are all in our twenties, we are still the babies of this family.

268

We are the ones raised more or less without our dad, and we are the ones most distressed at this time. Not that the other eight siblings are not in a lot of pain. Look into their eyes and you can see it. We will never be the same family from this day forward.

We feel we must all stay extremely close to one another. We must all try to keep in touch—if only to hear one another's voice. But—most important—we must keep it together for the next three days. That's what we have all agreed to do—to take care of saying our goodbyes to our mother, and to keep her burial proper and religious. We will create a loving farewell to Romania Rita Pasquarello, because that's exactly what she would want. We must bury her the right way—and then we can fall apart.

The day after Mom's death we gather at her house. All of us siblings and the spouses are there, and we have a lot of planning to do. But I am totally overwhelmed with everything and everyone. So, I think, it's time for me to go downstairs into the basement to talk to Mom—just as she did when she needed to talk to Dad. I am following in her footsteps.

When no one is in the dining room I make a dash to get downstairs. I move quickly, desperate for this private conversation with Mom. When I reach the last basement step I look to my left, where the washing machine is. That's when I see, on the floor near the washer, a pile of her clothes. I pick up the dress she wore, the day before. I hold the dress against me, hugging it and inhaling the odor. It's her deodorant, "Sutton," which has a clean, fresh smell. That was her scent. And now, for a second, I am holding her in my arms, and I feel so good!

I am telling her I will miss her with all of my heart. Then I say, "You called me last night." I go on to explain, "In my sleep I heard the phone ringing, and when I answered, you were on the other end. You told me you were fine and not to worry about you. I saw your face when you were talking to me. You were smiling and happy. That's when I knew I have to let go of you. But it's harder to do that with you than with Dad… I know you are with him and he will take good care of you…"

Then I tell her, "I am sorry for not being the daughter you wanted me to be. I wish I had been better. I hope you will forgive me, Mom. I love you! And I am sorry! Goodbye!"

We all have to say goodbye to Mom. For me, this was the only way I knew how. After 19 years of watching and hearing Mom in the basement with my dad, I knew she'd be down there waiting for any of us to join her in conversation. And there will be many more conversations to follow.

I go back upstairs and look around at all my siblings. They're sitting around totally still, looking like they are afraid to move. It's as if they think if they move a muscle their world will shatter. But it already has. There is not a worse thing that could have happened to us.

I should tell them to take turns and go down into the basement for a conversation with Mom. On the other hand, maybe they'll think I'm a little strange in the way I'm handling this. So I keep my idea to myself. Maybe I *am* a little strange, but I feel better knowing that my mother is at peace, and that I have made my peace with her.

Now, I must move on and deal with all of this one day at a time. During this period of mourning I want to walk through my mother's death slowly, while embracing her life. That is the way I will show my respect, and my love.

Josephine

A year after I returned from Europe I was on my way to Arizona, the Sunshine State. I had never been there but I'd been told how warm and clean it was there. I thought, why not get on the road and head out west, go to the desert and see all the beautiful cactus plants?

It was January in Philly with lots of snow, ice, and freezing temperatures—downright miserable. What a great time to head out west with all that sunshine and warm temperatures. John, a cook at the Italian restaurant where I worked, told me how he loved Arizona and how, if I ever went there, I wouldn't want to come back east. It was so pleasant there, he said, with the sun always shining, and we could go out there together. So I figured, how could I pass that up? How much fun to be on the road again! I'd never traveled with a guy before, but I would give it a try. I was addicted to being on the run and seeing new people and places. And maybe someone would have some dope to get high?

John was my first male friend to travel with. He was gay, so this was only friendship. We started out early on a Sunday and it took us four days to hitch across the states to Arizona. When it's two girls looking for a ride, people will stop for you quicker than when it's a girl and a guy.

This trip my usual traveling partner, Lana, couldn't make it. She had gotten a job and was taking on more adult responsibilities than I was. I sure did miss her, but I knew she was moving on in life. I was happy for her but I still had the old itch to just go, whenever and wherever.

We got to Tempe, Arizona, late in the evening, so I didn't really get to see the area until I awoke the next morning. When I felt the sun on my face and the warmth on my body, I knew I was marked with good fortune. Even before I got out of bed, I knew I'd be staying there for the winter or longer.

That day, I went and got a job at a little department store. John and I found a trailer to rent on a small piece of land. For me, this was going to be home. I met some new friends and was on my way to starting a new life. Everyone that I met was from somewhere else. So everybody around me was looking for home, and this helped me feel comfortable being there. I was not thinking about returning to Philly. This—Tempe, Arizona—was home.

I would work all week and on the weekends I'd party. On days off I would go into the desert, which was a lot of fun. There was so much beauty out there, and it was exciting to be in a new environment.

I met my first husband, Chuck; he was a neighbor from across the street. He and his friends would ride their Harley motorcycles right through the front door of their house. They'd park their bikes in the living room. This carefree life was fun! But it was short-lived.

I became pregnant and I knew I had to get back to Philly. Here, I was always doing drugs and not taking good care of myself, but now that I was going to be a mother I had to change my drug habits, to stop somehow because this lifestyle was not good for me or my baby.

So we went back to Philadelphia, making our plans to get married and start our family. For our first three months in Philly, we stayed with my mother. During that time I gave birth to our son, after only six and a half months of being pregnant. He didn't survive his birth. The doctor told us his lungs weren't fully developed. He passed away a few hours after birth, and I was heartbroken. I couldn't believe I had allowed drugs to do this to us, and I still haven't forgiven myself for this.

Four months later the world came crashing down on me again. My mother passed away from a stroke and heart attack. She had had such an extremely hard life, and her body gave out when she was 66 years old.

We stayed in Philadelphia for another three months, to mourn the loss of my mom and to be close to my siblings for support. No one knows the pain, unless it's the family. We were all distraught over losing our mom.

Then in June it was back to Arizona for seven years. I had my daughter, Nicole, there in 1977. This was three years after the loss of my first pregnancy, and I was overjoyed at having a healthy baby girl. I had stopped all drugs when I was trying to get pregnant with her. I knew I wanted to be a good mother, just like my own mother had been. I was starting to take life seriously.

I was content living out west in such a beautiful place. I did miss my family back in Philly, but I had Nicole to take care of, and that filled my heart with love and happiness.

However, things were changing with my husband; we were no longer getting along. We had grown apart, and I seemed to want more out of life than he did. I wanted more kids. That, to me, is the purpose of life—to give love to your offspring, to watch your children flower and grow. I was so prepared for that. But my husband still wanted to do drugs. Seven years had passed, but he was still as carefree as the day I met him. He hadn't grown, and it was a shame for us as a family.

So I left Arizona with Nicole and came back to Philly. Once again, I was in need of moral support from my family. I knew there was no hope for our marriage. Now I was preparing for my divorce. It took me about a year to get back on my feet, but I did it. In fact, if I had known I was going to be this happy, I would have left him three years earlier.

My last ten years of working were spent in the restaurant business, and most of that time I worked as a waitress. But waitressing takes a huge toll on your body, and I got tired of it after developing a bad back and aching legs from standing eight or ten or twelve hours a day. I went on to a job in a Jewish deli/restaurant. I was a hostess and cashier in that job, and it was easy and fun. I found an apartment and started a new life with just me and Nicole. This life was good to us; we didn't have much but we did have peace of mind. The many beautiful experiences I had with my daughter were worth every drop of sweat. I believe that a healthy mix of sweat and tears is great for the soul.

Now I knew the joy my mother had from watching her flowers grow. This was the beauty of life, passed down from a mother to her children, and from one generation to the next.

• • •

Of course at times I thought I wouldn't be able to pay one bill or another. Somehow, though, I made it happen. Now I could fully understand the anxiety my mom must have felt every day—and she had it eleven times more than I did! My older siblings did help Mom out. As soon as you got a full-time job you were told to help with the living expenses, and my siblings gave Mom $20 a week in order to live at the house. That small amount of money couldn't do much, but it did help.

Often, when I would struggle as a single mother, thoughts of my own mom would surface. She had been able to balance all the demands of everyday family living. So when at times I felt lost, I would tell myself to pull it together and get it done. Don't question yourself—just do it! If she could be the elegant matriarch of her family, then I could try to follow in her footsteps. Even though I would never get close to my mother's standard, I was thankful for the opportunity to try. She instructed me in my path in life, not by what she said, but through her actions. Not that I got the lessons right at all times—I most certainly didn't.

I am proud to say that I had an Italian woman as my mom. I am honored that God gave me such a wise, fair, honest, and strong mother. Even when she was kicked down, she got up and still carried herself as a lady. No one could take that from her.

I still have images of my mother in my head. In my dreams, what beautiful conversations we still have! I say to my mother, "Mom, you are perfect. I will never be perfect or even come close to you."

My mother laughs at me with a big belly laugh. She can't even speak because her laughter has her fully engaged. After a few seconds she looks at me with her big, brown, piercing eyes. And without blinking her eyelashes she says sweetly to me, "Josephine" —saying my name with her wonderful Italian accent—"you are wrong, my daughter. I am not perfect; I am just Ro, your mother … your mother who only did what she thought was best for her family."

Shame on Us

"*A word is dead when it is said,*
Some say—
I say it just begins to live
That day."
—Emily Dickinson

Life as we knew it as a family was going to change—and not for the better. Who would ever have thought we would not stand strong or stand together? That we would crumble under pressure from the outside? This was something our mother had stressed to us never to allow. But when she died, in 1974, that's exactly what happened.

You could always hear Mom's wise words in your head: "I don't care what your friends are doing out there. You won't carry that into our home. Keep it outside where it belongs." As it turned out, it wasn't so much the influence of our friends that changed our family—it was who we all married. One by one our family changed.

Something that had held us together as a family was that we were all entangled in the web of our secrets. The big one was the death of our dad. To survive that ordeal, we had to never allow anyone from the outside into our immediate circle. That was a nonverbal agreement, as were many in our family.

275

About three months after my mom passed away, I moved to Arizona. I was 25 years old, and suddenly, for the first time ever, I was without the support of my brothers and sisters. It was foolish of me to move, but I did it anyway. I met my first husband in Arizona, and lived there for six years.

When I came back east, I saw immediately that the family wasn't the same. We had all changed. I knew *I* had—I was going through a divorce. But what had happened to the others? They weren't as close as before. They talked about one another in such a negative manner, sometimes downright hostile. Some of them were in a group, but a few others were out there on their own. It was heartbreaking to witness this new ugliness and division. What had happened?

After I had been home for about two weeks, my sister Anna invited four of us over for a visit. Within an hour we five were in the kitchen on the phone with another sister. At first, I thought this conversation would be fun. It started with humor and laughter, but turned nasty. The four on my end of the phone were all criticizing our other sister about her husband and marriage. I listened for a few minutes and then realized I wanted no part of that. So I walked out of the kitchen and sat in the rocking chair in the living room. I was thinking: What were they saying about *my* marriage and its failure?

Anna came into the living room with a big smile on her face. She wanted me to come back into the kitchen and join the fun. But I just sat there, looking into her eyes and wondering who she was. Who were any of them, and where did I fit in? Actually, I realized that for a long time I had only partly fit in. I'd never fully been one with them because I'd always been restless, picking myself up and wandering off whenever the mood struck. That had started when my dad died.

I told Anna I was happy sitting by myself. She asked, "Is there anything wrong?"

My reply, a lie, was "No."

It took me a while to get over my uneasiness with the new situation. But as time went on, and I witnessed more disloyalty and hostility, I started to join in. I wanted to be part of the family again.

Of course I knew from the start that this behavior was wrong. But I joined in like a coward. Then I started to find excuses for why I couldn't attend family functions. I attended only if they were very important to the family; otherwise, I chose to keep my distance. I didn't want the others to realize what I was doing, for fear that they would criticize me. Then I would be the target of their jokes, and who in their right mind wants to be kicked around like that? I wanted to feel secure in my family circle.

But that wasn't to be. The harshness ran through the family like wildfire. Had my mother still been alive, she would have stood there with a fire hose. She always had the apparatus to cool anything down. Now, we weren't fire-proof from the outside world—or from the inside of our own world. The fire was running rampant in our family, and not one of us could control it.

It did burn our feelings for one another. I wished the others no harm, but I had to step back from them. Because now, you always had to take one side or the other in the arguments—sort of like when we were kids—but less playful, more mean-spirited. For me, it was easier to just stay away than to get caught taking—not one of their sides—but my own side. Then I'd end up having to go it alone permanently, and how could I survive being without my family? It was such a large one, and had been such a large part of my life.

I would think, one day I will be without them. But on another level, I never really thought that would come to be. That was until my sister Christine passed away, in 1994. Now, at age 45, I saw that things were going to change for me and my siblings forever. There were now an enormous amount of hurt feelings between many of us. I could no longer handle their careless remarks, and I no longer cared what, if any, good feelings they had about me. Christine had meant so much to me, and when she passed away my heart broke. She was such a good, loving person—not only to me and my daughter, Nicole, but to anyone who was in need of her help. She was generous toward everyone, but my family treated her with such disrespect. It seemed to me that they broke her heart, the heart that had stayed with our mother. Christine had helped Mom raise us last eight siblings. Had the others all forgotten her caring for us?

It was now always you against them, or them against you—that's the way it ran in our family. At one time we had had a long-term commitment toward one another, but that no longer existed. I understood that siblings naturally have conflicts. But this behavior seemed intentional and cruel. I felt like we were dodging bullets—they will get you at one time or another, so you have to run for cover. It's not that you are a coward. I simply felt I needed to protect myself and my daughter from injury.

After Christine died I laid out a plan to keep in touch with three siblings. However, that didn't last long because one of them disliked one of the other two, so there was always conflict. If you were at an affair like a wedding, someone was always in a fight with someone else. A great time to have a disagreement—at a beautiful event like a wedding! I was feeling lost in my family, like I couldn't be true to myself. It just became too much.

And now, the hostility has entered into the next generation. At first, I tried to ignore it. But when my daughter told me again and again what was happening, I couldn't avoid Nicole's situation like I had mine. They were now mistreating my daughter because she was an extension of me. So we are both putting up a cement wall between us and the family. I'm accustomed to them mistreating me, but it would hurt me more to see Nicole hurting from their petty ways. I was tired of trying to keep the peace. It was more important to keep the peace within myself for my own well-being.

So now, for me, it's easier to stay away. Believe me, it's quite lonely not to have your family. But at least you know exactly where you stand. In that knowledge, there is peace of mind.

If my mother were alive today she would be shocked at the results of all her hard work. Mom believed family was everything. Today, I would say that she was partly right and partly wrong. Whatever the end results, we all must go on with our lives, living the way each of us has chosen.

I wish the others much happiness and fulfillment. I hope they all wish the same for me. If this is true, then perhaps my mother was a success in her plan, and all of her hard work did pay off in the end. And if it is not true, then shame on us.

More About Christine

How were we to understand Christine and her mental illness? My mother knew about Chris's problem but it was not something she talked about. We never spoke of my sister's state of mind—just her strange behavior.

She became Mom's confidante; they were always in the kitchen together, talking and whispering to each other. Most of the time you couldn't hear what they were saying, but it certainly seemed like my mother trusted Chris with her innermost thoughts. Christine became a woman at the age of 16 when she went out and got a job to help support the family. She put her own life on hold. No one else in our family was as generous.

On payday Chris would give us all money to go to the drugstore and buy ice cream cones. Or she'd send us to the bakery to buy two big boxes of baked goods. Sometimes she'd take us to the exclusive John Wanamaker's department store, to get dresses. She always had each and every one of us in her thoughts.

When I think back to those times I wonder how Chris pulled it together every day. How did she do this with no medicine through her teens and twenties? I guess she went through the motions until she could no longer function.

She was one tough cookie—that is, until she lost it at the age of 40. Life became too heavy for her then; she no longer had her husband or her son, and she couldn't take on any more stress. She couldn't handle life any longer, so she shut down and lost it.

• • •

When Bill and Chris got together they found each other at the right time. Both were in need of someone who understood the experience of mental illness. They were great together. Each accepted the other's quirkiness, and they supported each other no matter what. Whatever came down the road, they would stand together, and no one could break their bond.

Unfortunately, Bill and Chris didn't get many visitors at their apartment. That really upset Chris. She would tell me, "I know the family doesn't like me and they think I am dirty because I don't clean my apartment. But do they have to treat me and Bill like we are diseased? When they see us they don't kiss us hello." Chris was terribly hurt that the others didn't even acknowledge them. "I love all my siblings," she would say. "Why don't they feel the same about me? Or Bill?"

One Monday morning Chris called me to tell me about what had happened at a family party the day before. I had driven her and Bill to the party that Sunday, and when I drove them home there hadn't been any mention of the fact that no one had talked to them. So I was very surprised to hear about this awful silent treatment toward them.

Chris said that she felt so isolated from the family. She could see that no one wanted her or Bill there. I felt really bad that she was so torn up, and I tried to calm her down. If our mother was alive, I thought, this never would have happened.

Chris told me that she was not going to go to any more family parties. Why go, if no one wanted her there? I went over the list of people who had attended the affair the day before, hoping that maybe she'd forgotten someone who had come to sit with her or said hello. But no, no one had.

I asked Chris what she wanted to do about this. She didn't know; she could only cry, and ask me, "What's wrong with them? Don't they know they hurt me? Do they even care?"

"But Chris, what can you do?" I asked. She was really upset, and could not think of a solution—other than, "That's it—I'm done!" In the future, she said, if they wanted her and Bill to show up, they'd have to show her that. But right now, she planned to stay away. Then she started to cry uncontrollably.

I was really upset too. "How dare they think they have the right to forget all that you did for this family! Shame on them! If they think they can treat you with disrespect—then Chris—I say to hell with them!"

My anger seemed to help her feel better, and soon Chris was laughing. She said she was alright for now. She needed time to think things over, and she'd come up with a conclusion on her own.

Although we called each other at least five times a day for the last three years of her life, we never spoke of this again.

• • •

Christine was perhaps the finest of us twelve. She had more honesty and integrity than any of us. Part of the beauty of Christine was that she would never hurt anyone intentionally. Plus she was always there for you. She helped me a lot by babysitting my daughter, and it was during that time that Chris and I grew close. She and Bill would take my daughter on Saturday evenings so I could go to work. They spoiled my Nicole and enjoyed having her around them. And Nicole loved them both with all of her heart.

Due to her mental illness, Christine had a sad life. But she lived her life, or at least parts of it, with an eye to her own enjoyment and amusement. She always had something going on. She was fun to listen to and watch. In fact, she was our teacher, introducing us to so many things, from Wanamaker's department store to *Mad* Magazine. I still miss her wisdom and love, and I know in my heart she watches over me.

I often think about the way Chris's mind was always moving. She had a sharp intelligence, and she was charismatic too. Because of these qualities she tended to have a flock of people around her. So I suspect that when I die, Chris will introduce me to more different souls than I will know what to do with. But I say to her, "Bring it on! I will love it!"

Dad, Mom, and Me

Mom was a powerful woman, raising us on her own … and on her own terms. But in a sense she was not on her own, because she never walked, talked, or thought without my dad in her head, heart, and soul. He whispered in her ear about what she should do, sometimes pushing her beyond her means. She felt him holding her in his arms at all times. She remained madly in love with him, and lived with dreams of being with him for eternity.

She never forgot his smell, taste, or touch. She told me many times, "You have your father's hair." You could sense her happiness at looking at my dark, curly hair. It stuck out all over my head; it was crazy Italian hair. But my mom didn't care how unruly it could be. She saw the beauty of my hair because it took her back to when she could touch his hair. She could run her hands through my hair and smell the sweet smell of the Prell shampoo he used to use on his. She would always kiss the top of my head. In that way, she could taste his hair again and again.

It is my belief that Dad truly adored her. He knew that if anyone could pull off bringing up twelve children without a man in the house, that person would be Mom. It was obvious that their children's needs were always first in their minds. They accepted that they were second to us.

That's what parents do—they take care of the family. And Mom performed her duties until the moment of her death. We Italians have a strong bond with our offspring. We believe the children always belong to the parents, no matter how old they are.

Here is what I foresee: When I die, they both will be there to take me across. My dad will reach out to hold my hand. He will smile at me with his big, brown, sparkling eyes. I can hear him tell me to come with him and my mother, and that I will always be fine with the two of them. His voice will be strong and reassuring.

I must show him I trust him with my being. After all, he left me when I was six years old. Now, I must prove my trust to him and myself by reaching out to take his hand. I must show that I know he will always protect me in death as he did in my life. Because he never really left me—only in a physical sense. His spirit was always with me. He is here with me now, helping me write our story. Maybe somehow this will help us mend and feel good about ourselves despite what we have lost?

My mother is standing next to my dad, with both of her arms extended out toward me. Now, I must let go of all the lies she imposed on me. Only I can forgive her in this moment. I let her embrace me tenderly as I hold onto her with all of my being. I will tell her, "I forgive you for lying about my dad." I know in my heart she has forgiven me for not understanding why she did all that she had to do. She's telling me she lied to me to make life easier on me— not to cause more pain.

The three of us cry as we let go of all our pain. We are all together now. They both take my hands …We will go into eternity as a complete family. That's all I ever wanted—my dad, mom, and me. How beautiful it would be for me to feel the warmth from the both of them again! That to me would be heaven.

On My Lap, I Hold a Photo

On my lap, I hold a framed photo of a young, beautiful Italian woman. It's a full portrait of her face. Her gorgeous olive skin does not have a single blemish or wrinkle; life has not yet marked her complexion. And there's not a strand of gray hair on this woman; it's all dark brown, with a natural curl around her face. The woman's small nose looks like the nose of a Roman goddess. Her lips are thin and slightly crooked, and she has a big smile. Her large brown eyes sparkle with happiness, and the long, dark, upper eyelashes reach to the bottom of her eyebrows. You get the feeling that she might just wink at you, and that you would feel her happiness if she did. Oh, what youth does, and hopefully will do for her throughout life!

At the age of 27 she has just given birth to the first of what will be twelve children. It's a boy! In an Italian household that's a big deal. This baby will always be known as her first; that's a bond between the two of them no one will ever break.

The young woman in the picture is my mother. She and my father, and my oldest brother, Ralph, are starting their lives together as a family. There isn't anything that can hurt them now or in the future; there will be joy and contentment only! Or so it seems, if you judge by the eyes of the lady in the portrait.

This lady is definitely 100% Italian. She speaks Italian and broken English through her beautiful crooked lips. She's flawless at this young age, not that I knew her then. I wish I had. I would have enjoyed her playful manner, her pleasure in the small things in life, and her silliness during these carefree days. I bet she was silly many times with my dad. She always wanted to keep him happy. She would later tell her eight daughters, "Always be with your man." Do whatever he wants and drop everything for him. Because if you don't, he will find someone else who will. Today this is not fashionable advice, but it was then, and she did do an excellent job of keeping her husband happy. They had 22 beautiful years together, probably the best years of their lives.

After 22 years of married life my mother lost her husband to the Italian mob. After that, she never allowed her twelve children to forget him. She always had a story for you if you were willing to listen—some absolutely heartwarming and some not so good. But they were his and her stories, and that's how she taught us younger kids about him. We would get to know him through her eyes—those big, dark, welcoming eyes, the same set of eyes that would light up when my dad walked into the room.

So this was the person I called Mom. She was so strong and powerful that she took care of us twelve kids all on her own, with unwavering determination and pride. For Mother's Day in 2008, the *Philadelphia Inquirer* published women's reminiscences about their moms, and mine was included. I'll quote it here, because I think it says a lot about the lady whose photo I hold in my lap:

> *My mother, Romania Pasquarello, was an only child born in Pescara, Italy, in 1907. She married my father in the United States and had 12 children. He died when I was 6 years old, and she never remarried. On Sunday, you could smell the meatballs and gravy cooking all day while we were all playing or fighting over a card game. We had lots of fun in that house. I will hold her in my heart forever for being a wonderful role model, and for teaching me her philosophy for life: respect everyone as I would like them to respect me.*

> *Josephine B. Pasquarello*
> *Kennett Square, PA*

On Mother's Day

It's been 40 years since my mother died and today is Mother's Day. I am going to the cemetery to celebrate with my mother. This is a very special day for me. It's time to ponder on the existence of my mother. In the *American Heritage Dictionary* the meaning of the word "ponder" is "to weigh in the mind with thoroughness and care."

Actually, in my mind, thoroughness and care are what define my mother's being. Her love and care for all of her family were thorough and unending. That's why, after all these years since her passing, I still think of her every day. I feel her around me often. I talk with her always, and cherish the conversations. I do miss the sound of her voice and listening to her broken English. How I would love to hear and feel her again, in a physical way.

Mother's Day is an important occasion involving both my mother and my daughter. I am standing by Mom's grave telling her new information about me and my family. I know she wants to hear all the news about them.

As I stand here talking and praying with her, I ask her if she is fine and happy where she is. Although I know she's as happy as can be—she's with my dad, after all, and that's all she truly needs. That's her happy.

I am picking up trash that is on or near our family plot. I go around pulling out the weeds and longer grasses, especially near the stone. With the area clean and the weeds gone, everything's looking spotless.

I always come here with flowers because my mom loved flowers. I put the pansies with the brilliant colors against the tall stone. It all looks beautiful and feels peaceful, and I myself am starting to feel peaceful with this visit.

I seem to have picked up the tradition of keeping the family plot looking like the area is cared for with love. I got that from my mom, who took care of the plot when she visited Dad. My daughter, Nicole, has taken up that element of our culture, as have her two daughters. Alana and Isabella enjoy coming to the cemetery to pray for our family and show respect. We also go to my mother's family plot, and to my father's. We stop at each grave to say hello and to pray for their souls.

Right now, I can feel that Mom is grateful that I came to visit with her. But really it's me who is grateful that I had such a loving mom.

So this is how I spend my Mother's Day—giving Mom the love she gave me every day of my 25 years with her. Yes, she would expect no less from me and my girls. But we do this because we want to with all of our hearts.

Happy Mother's Day, Mom.

Father's Day Thoughts

I really don't know my dad on a personal level. Yes, I know of him through conversations with my mom and my sisters and brothers. Plus there are a few memories I keep very close to my heart. But I never had a chance to know something as small as his favorite color, or as major as his love for my mom—and all his kids.

Some things I know: He enjoyed a cold beer at the bar after work. When home he would have his red wine with a plate of spaghetti. When with his "goombahs," he was always ready for a card game.

But there are so many, many other things I would love to know about him, things that any child would like to know about her parent—especially if, at six years old, she lost him forever. In that case, you have so many questions about who he was.

What made him get up every day? What was his belief about his purpose in life? I know that people who knew him would say, "Mike's reason for living was his wife and children. That's what made him the man he was."

I wanted the two of us to grow as father and daughter. I wanted to know firsthand who this person was. How did he feel about God? Did he even believe there was a God?

At times I would look at my Uncle George and Uncle Nick and imagine how my dad would physically look. I would analyze my two uncles feature by feature and create what I felt would have been my dad. He was tall, dark, and

289

handsome. But what did his voice sound like? My uncles and aunts told me he could sing a good opera aria.

I would have loved to watch my dad grow old—to see his hair turn gray and to witness all the changes that life would bring him.

It would have been wonderful to watch him become a grandparent, with all the kids around him—what a scene that would have been! All that love with him that I have never felt nor ever will! This is one of my great losses in life— my dad's love.

Today, I will say a prayer for Dad. I will tell him how much I've missed his companionship and love. I do this every year for the two of us. For, after all, we are father and daughter.

Reflections

Maybe our dad wasn't as perfect as our mom wanted us to believe? As for me, perfect or not, I still love him.

We went to church every Sunday and on our religious holidays. We were there praying to our Great Almighty God to forgive our sins. What sins? I was only six years old in 1955. So what could I have done? But the nuns would tell us to pray and you will go to heaven. If you sin, you will go to hell. They put a lot of fear in us.

My dad is dead. Is he in heaven or hell? Back in the day, if you committed suicide you were said to go straight to hell. That's what the Church told us. So what is all this praying going to do for my dad? This is way too much pressure on me. I am just going to run however far it takes to get away from it all. That way, I might be happy again. I don't want to know anything about how my dad died. Besides, my mom is not going to tell me anyway. She can keep a secret forever.

They kicked us out of our neighborhood—now we have to move to our new house. I am so nervous but I am not going to tell anyone. It's better to keep quiet, just like Mom. She is so sad to leave our house with all the memories. Mom tells us she's happy to be moving, but she's lying, because she sees Dad all over the house. And it's too much for her to handle. She's trying to be brave for us kids.

Maybe in our new house our lives will be normal again. We could all be happy, just like before. That's what I will pray for. I will ask God to please let us be happy again. I will promise to be good forever. I will tell God I will never sin against Him. I pray to God all the time … but does He hear me?

My mom is doing her very best to keep us all together as a family. She's doing it all on her own. She's shy and quiet, but clever when it comes to dealing with others.

At times a thought would surface: What would happen if we lost Mom? What would all of us kids do? Who would help us? Not anyone from my dad's family. I don't think they like us. I have three uncles and five aunts. They don't help Mom at all. I guess that's the way it will be. But Mom never says anything bad about them. Ever!

In her mind, Mom says, I made these kids, and I will take care of them. I don't need anyone to help. We will all do this together as a loving family. We are there for each other and we will watch over each other.

As for me, I was so mad at God and my dad that I decided to do whatever I wanted. For instance, in third grade I played hooky for a week. When I got older I started to hitchhike all over the states, and in Europe too, with no thought of the harm that might come to me. I was a lost soul looking for my dad's love. Of course I wasn't going to find it on the highway. Dad was gone, and I had to accept that fact of life. I was numb and feeling lost … I just went whichever way the wind was blowing. And I was fine with that—at least I *thought* so.

When our dad died it was a really scary time for my family. It felt like everyone else checked out on us. It was a time when we needed comfort, compassion, and guidance, but no one was there to give those things to us. Maybe others didn't know how to help, or they didn't care.

We feel such shame about our dad's suicide. I am so worried that someone will question me and be able to figure out that we were lying about his death. The way I carried myself reflected my shame; I kept my head down, looking at my feet. My shoulders were round, to keep myself inside my own thoughts. I was, as I still am, high-strung, and I see this as an aftereffect of a young child losing her dad. That's what shame can do to you—weigh you down, and make you feel like you are never good enough. That is—until you make yourself equal … to a friend who has a dad. Some of my friends didn't realize they were sharing their dad with me. When I was at their home, I enjoyed every second of time with their dad. Just one small conversation with a friend's father made such a difference to me. How nice it was to have a dad and a mom—two parents who could help you with your questions about life, and who would love you forever! It seemed like such a feeling of completeness. Even if, for me, it was just a few stolen moments.

My mom grew old and tired before her time. That was due to her nonstop work rule: Don't stop until you drop. There is always cleaning or cooking to be done. Our home was clean and her cooking was always great and healthy. She would make something out of barely anything. And it would taste superb. She was truly an incredible cook.

Mom passed away at the age of 66. She was too young to leave us but she was ready to go. After all, her destination was to be with her husband. Finally!

After Mom's death our family started to fall apart. We were no longer true to one another. Was it because we had all married? Or was it because some in the family didn't care for others? Whatever the reason, we no longer had the sense of a true, loving family. Our battles were now with each other. This one didn't care for that one, and that one didn't care for this one. If Mom had been alive, she would have defused the situation. But now it was up to us, and all we did was add wood to the unruly fire. All I could do, and all the others could do, was watch it burn. And others put more wood into it. As time went on we became distant from and unfamiliar to each other.

It was a shame, but without Mom around, there was no way to pull it all together. Our mother would have been so dissatisfied with each and every one of us. She had worked so hard to keep us twelve children together!

It's been 40 years since my mother passed away. That's an enormous amount of time for bickering. This has caused total erosion among us all. Our family value system of respect and love has long faded away. Even if we each prayed to our God, our belief system wouldn't be enough to connect us as a loving family at this point. There is too much jealousy and hurt going around. We can't see clearly.

It's a complex situation, and I don't believe that anyone knows how to remedy it. We have tried, but it always goes back to hurt feelings. Where in the past, we each had the others there for us, now some of us stand alone. Some are alone due to their own choosing. Others are alone due to the group vote. They had their own thoughts and opinions, and it was seen as stepping outside of the family circle. Being strong and standing up for your own beliefs has caused some to be "excommunicated."

It doesn't make sense that some family members should shun others. We weren't raised to be opinionated about others' beliefs, and I don't understand how exactly this started in our family. Maybe, if I dig deeper, I could relate. Did it start when my dad died? Or when my mom died?

Safe Harbor—Camp Charlie

"Silence is sorrow's best food."—*James Russell Lowell*

Safe Harbor is the name of Abington Memorial Hospital's program for grieving children, teens, and their families. This Pennsylvania hospital runs Safe Harbor for anyone who has lost a loved one to suicide, homicide, or natural causes. The majority of the losses the children are dealing with involve the male figure in the family.

When my husband, Robert, and I found out about the Safe Harbor program, I was so excited to go to the facility to see what was there. We met the program director, Debbie Teasdale. She took us into every room so we could get a feel for the activities going on.

I remember going in and out of the rooms. But what really impressed me was the artwork the children had done, which was hanging on all the walls. I remember one painting in particular. It was of a small child's figure, and painted onto the body were marks that seemed to represent many points of pain. As I stood looking at this painting, I realized that the figure could be me, not only as a child, but even now. I had all those points of pain in my body—even after 60 years. I too felt the emptiness and abandonment of death, and I could relate to this child's artwork as if I had created it myself.

I had so many thoughts and feelings as I looked at the painting. I wanted to cry. I did understand that it was natural and normal for me to want to. At the same time, I felt such a relief within my body and mind. I felt that they were finally united as one. Now was the time to say goodbye to all the hurt.

How fortunate it is that families can now come to a place like Safe Harbor, a place that acknowledges that we are all fragile and may at times need help. It is so valuable to have a place for children, along with their families, to express and even just experience their feelings—through art, talking, and being together with people who understand what they are going through. What a great bonding experience for these children and their families.

I wish I and my family had had such a place when I was six years old. My family could have grieved and bonded in a healthy way, with no shame attached. We could have expressed our sadness and emptiness after the loss of our dad, and it would have had such a positive effect, both then and now. But of course, at the time, my mother never would have accepted the help, even if it had been available.

Robert and I ended up volunteering to help at a week-long summer program run by Safe Harbor, called Camp Charlie. Children participating in Camp Charlie have activities on the hospital grounds aimed at helping them get through their loss, and at just having fun. It was a pleasure to play games and talk with all the kids. It was so rewarding to see them smiling and having a good time together.

For anyone who needs help like this, I believe there are programs like Camp Charlie everywhere. If you can't find one, call your doctor or local hospital. Those in the medical field can help you get the support you need. With help, hard work, and prayers, you can make it through loss.

Epilogue: Long-Awaited Answers

In January of 2009 my Uncle George passed away. He was 92 years old. Except for my dad, my father's side of the family lived long lives. At Uncle George's funeral his oldest son, Ralph, sat next to me. I told him his dad had always been my favorite uncle. I said that my first memory of his dad was when my own had died. "Your dad always had a big smile and was nice to me," I told him.

Cousin Ralph smiled and whispered to me, "Thank you for saying that." He told me that when he was a kid his father would take him to my father's store. And he always enjoyed his visits there. "I have lots of funny stories from those visits," he said. "Do you want to hear some of them?"

I couldn't get the words out of my mouth fast enough. My reply: "Anything you want to say is fine with me." We both laughed, and I felt like a little girl who is about to receive a gift—a really, really big gift, one that she has been waiting for for a very long time.

My ears and eyes were wide open to his words. I was getting so nervous as we sat in church and spoke, although it was really Ralph who did all the talking. He always had a beautiful smile on his face. We laughed as I heard about the old days at my dad's store. All of these were wonderful stories to me.

Then his tone got serious and his face became sad. He grabbed my arm and looked deep into my eyes. He said, "Josephine, you know that your dad was killed by the mob. Your dad didn't commit suicide. He would never have

297

killed himself. He wouldn't leave Aunt Ro and all you kids. Your dad was a good man and he loved his family."

My jaw dropped and I could've slid off the church pew. But Ralph was going on. "I don't know exactly what Uncle Mike was into, but he was always into something. He always made me laugh and I enjoyed my visits with him. To me his was a 'Big Character.'"

By now, my body was raw, and I was sweating from the top of my head to my feet. I couldn't say a word—I was absolutely dumbfounded.

Ralph was looking at me, now without his usual beautiful smile. He took both of my hands into his. Looking at me straight, he whispered, "I am sorry. I thought you knew. Maybe not the entire story, but something?"

I couldn't get any words out, so I shook my head—no.

I was now looking down at the floor because my eyes were going to flow like a river, and I would not be able to control it. I was shaking. The other people in the church didn't seem to notice, but to me it seemed that my arms and legs were moving around like I was having a fit. I guess I was—inside.

When I was able to speak again I told Cousin Ralph that I really never knew what had happened to my dad, because my mom never told me. It had all been a big, dark secret to us kids. But I was happy now that he had told me the truth. The fact was that the only one in the family who had ever said a word about it had been my sister Christine, but I had been fearful that what she told me was her mental illness talking, that her saying Dad was killed was just one of her delusions.

I felt like it was just me and Ralph in this church. I couldn't hear or see anyone else—that was how absorbed I was in what my cousin was telling me. It was as if the world had stopped for me for a few seconds.

I put my arms around Ralph and gave him a hug. I thanked him for telling me the truth. He said that I could call and question him on anything, and that he would always tell me the truth. "I have no problem with that," he said. "You should know the truth about your dad and family."

"I will call you sometime and we can talk," I said.

Smiling at me with his big brown eyes he said, "Call me whenever you like."

Sitting near me in the church was my husband, Robert, and sitting next to Robert was my Uncle Nick. The youngest of the nine children in my father's family, Uncle Nick was the only one of them still alive at the time of his brother George's funeral. I'm sure Uncle Nick had heard my conversation with Ralph, but he never joined in. Of course Uncle Nick had known all along how my dad had died, but he had never breathed a word. Now, just like me, he was caught off-guard. He probably didn't like his nephew talking. But what could Uncle Nick do now? He simply sat there, quiet and still.

After 54 years, our family secret was finally out in the open. It had taken me over half a century to find out the truth. Well, as they say—"Better late than never!"

I never did get in touch with Cousin Ralph. I couldn't bring myself to call him. It's hard when you carry a lie all of your life. It's tough to open up and deal with the truth. I needed time to process the information Ralph had openly given to me.

Ralph passed away a few years later. What a wonderful cousin to have had in my family— a man of truth!

But now, what do I do with the truth? No one in my family will be open to it.

· · ·

In 2014, as I was nearing the end of writing my family's story, I got a chance to meet with the only surviving member of my father's generation, my Aunt Myra. Aunt Myra was Uncle Nick's wife. A little while after Uncle George's funeral, Uncle Nick too had passed away, and now, with all of the siblings gone, Aunt Myra seemed more open to talking about the family's past. She was kind enough to sit with me and fill in a lot of the blanks about how the feds and the mob had treated us. I had had bits and pieces, but now I learned more about how we lost everything—the real estate holdings, the money, and—most important—the head of our family.

While I finally have more answers, I still don't know how deep my father's involvement was with the mob. I may never know. I do know that a year before my father died the feds were harassing him. He had acquired a lot of real estate and was doing quite well with his produce-grocery store. He had little formal education but he did have insight into life that was learned on the streets of South Philly. With a wife and twelve children, Michael Pasquarello managed to grow wealthy.

My father ran card games on the second floor of his store, as well as a bookie setup. The mob would use one of my dad's properties for what were called the mattress wars when they were going on. A gang would fight their rival gang, but they would bring their own mattresses to the place where they fought—the idea was that no one would sleep at home or be near his family for the duration so that no one other than those involved would get hurt. They would use one building and stay together until the war was over, and may the best side win.

One day the feds told my father, "We will seize all of your real estate and money if you don't give us the information we need." Within one year the feds had taken just about all of his real estate and money. They gave him an ultimatum—"Either rat on your associates in the mob or we take everything from you and then throw you in prison. You won't see your twelve children grow up. Your wife won't wait for you forever. Make your decision soon because we are losing patience. We will charge you with racketeering, which will keep you in jail for a long time. You have your hands in a lot of wrong dealings. But we also know you witnessed at least one killing. Give us the information on that."

My father's mob associates wanted him to go to prison and keep his mouth shut. They didn't want to pay the price for their wrongdoings; my father was supposed to be the one to pay for everyone. The mob didn't want to take any chances, so my dad was stuck in the middle. Which side should he take for the betterment of his family? It was a tough decision to make. Should he get killed by the mob or go to prison for a long time? He had to figure out what would be best for his wife and children.

The mob decided to take matters into their own hands. In their eyes, my father was a problem that there was only one way to solve: They had to kill him. So they poured rat poison down his throat and stabbed him in the chest.

Not only was my mother totally shocked at how my father died, she then had to figure out how to hide that information—all the while continuing to care for her family, and keeping it together. Until that awful day her life had been consumed by her children and her house. She didn't know anything outside her world. With no father to help feed and guide us, what was she to do?

As my father lay dying in the hospital, the feds came to try one more time to convince him to talk. But he, being the man that he was, told them to f—-off, "I am dying anyway! What can you do for me or my family now?"

Also, one of his goombahs came to offer him money to help with the family if he kept his mouth shut. He and my father came to an understanding that they would not hurt any of my father's family. They would give us money to move out of the neighborhood. It ended with an agreement and a handshake, all for the sake of other people having a better life.

They did give us the money to move, and we did.

• • •

What did my mother know about the mob or the feds? We were left high and dry by one organization that was legal and another that was not. To me, they are the same. They need you when they need you. When they don't, you're finished.

In the end, the burden of this horrifically sad experience fell on my mother's shoulders. She did an incredible job carrying it. I don't know of any other woman who could have done what she did all on her own. She was my family's angel on earth.

I remember one thing in particular that my mother always said to us: "Keep your head held high—don't be ashamed of who you are." And that's what we always tried to do as we struggled through life without our father. We found out what it was like to be on the other side of the mob, and the law. They both got away with what they did to us, but neither the feds nor the mob could tear us apart. They never took away the allegiance my father and mother had for the family, and, looking back over the years, it seems to me that my mother's love and loyalty triumphed over both of them.